**IGE-KBFG INTERNATIONAL CONFERENCE**

# IGE - KB금융그룹
# 2024 지속가능성 글로벌 서밋

글로벌 대전환과 정책기조 피벗을 넘어서:
지속가능 성장과 금융의 미래

글로벌 대전환과 정책기조 피벗을 넘어서:
지속가능 성장과 금융의 미래
Navigating the New Waves of Global Transformation and Policy Pivot:
Towards a More Resilient and Sustainable Future

초판 1쇄 발행    2025년 8월

| | |
|---|---|
| 펴낸이 | 전광우 |
| 지 원 | 김경진, 김시연 |
| 펴낸곳 | 세계경제연구원 |
| 전 화 | 02-551-3334~8 |
| 주 소 | 서울시 강남구 영동대로 511 무역센터 2505호 |
| E-mail | igenet@igenet.com |

ISBN 979-11-6177-052-9 [03320]

종이책 정가 25,000원

*이 책은 저작권법에 따라 보호받는 저작물이므로 무단 전재와 복제를 금합니다.
*이 책의 전부 혹은 일부를 이용하려면 저작권자와 세계경제연구원의 동의를 받아야 합니다.
*잘못된 책은 구입하신 서점에서 바꾸어 드립니다.

# 글로벌 대전환과 정책기조 피벗을 넘어서: 지속가능 성장과 금융의 미래

## Navigating the New Waves of Global Transformation and Policy Pivot: Towards a More Resilient and Sustainable Future

# 목 차

머리말 · · · · · · · · · · · · · · · · · · · · · · · · · · · · · · · · · · · · · · · · · · · · · · · · · · · · · · · · · · · · · · · 07
프로그램 · · · · · · · · · · · · · · · · · · · · · · · · · · · · · · · · · · · · · · · · · · · · · · · · · · · · · · · · · · · · 09
개회식 · · · · · · · · · · · · · · · · · · · · · · · · · · · · · · · · · · · · · · · · · · · · · · · · · · · · · · · · · · · · · · · 11

    [개회사]    **전광우** 세계경제연구원 이사장
    [축사]    **나경원** 제22대 국회의원/국회 인구기후그리고내일 대표의원
              **주형환** 저출산·고령사회위원회 부위원장(부총리급)
              **김병환** 금융위원회 위원장(FSC)

    [컨퍼런스 기조연설]
              **세이케 아츠시(Seike Atsushi)**
              日고령화대책위원회 위원장, 日적십자사 총재/前 게이오대 총장
    [특별연설]    **정운찬** 동반성장연구소 이사장/前 국무총리, 서울대 총장
    [특별대담]    **조셉 스티글리츠(Joseph Stiglitz)**
              노벨경제학상 수상자/컬럼비아대 석좌교수

**세션 1 | 미 대선 이후의 세계경제 및 지정학적 변화와 전망** · · · · · · · · · · · · · · · · · · · · · · · · 49

    [좌장]    **신성환** 한국은행 금융통화위원회 위원
    [기조발표]    **니콜라스 라디(Nicholas Lardy)** Senior Fellow,
              Peterson Institute for International Economics(PIIE)
    [패널]    **후카가와 유키코(Fukagawa Yukiko)** 와세다대 교수
              **윌리엄 페섹(William Pesek)** Nikkei/Forbes 수석 칼럼니스트
              **이종화** 고려대 교수/前 한국경제학회 회장, ADB 수석이코노미스트
              **최병일** 이화여대 국제대학원 명예교수

**세션 2 | 지속가능성장을 위한 기후금융 및 상생금융의 혁신** ····················· *85*

    [좌장]    **홍종호** 서울대 환경대학원 교수
    [기조발표]  **비노드 토마스(Vinod Thomas)** Senior Fellow,
                  Institute of Southeast Asian Studies, Singapore/
                  前 세계은행 수석 부총재
                **산제이 팻나익(Sanjay Patnaik)**
                  Director of the Center on Regulation and Markets,
                  The Brookings Institution
                **구본재** Deloitte Consulting 부사장/파트너
    [패널]    **이형희** SK SUPEX추구협의회 Communication 위원장
                  **이 진** 금융감독원 금융시장안정국 국장

**세션 3 | 인구위기 극복 전략과 금융의 역할** ······································· *143*

    [좌장]    **이인실** 한반도미래인구연구원 원장/前 통계청장
    [기조발표]  **조앤 윌리엄스(Joan Wiliams)** 캘리포니아주립대 법대 교수
                **찰스 유지 호리오카(Charles Yuji Horioka)** 고베대 석좌교수,
                IARIW 회장/前 日경제학회 회장
    [패널]    **서정호** 한국금융연구원 인구변화대응연구센터장
                **김경록** 미래에셋자산운용 고문
                **정신동** KB경영연구소 소장(전무)

# 머리말

전 세계는 지금 미국 대선을 비롯한 주요 정치 일정을 기점으로 지정학적 긴장, 통화정책의 전환, 기술 혁신의 가속화 등 복합적인 변화의 소용돌이 속에 있습니다. 여기에 기후 위기와 인구구조 변화라는 구조적 도전이 더해지며, 회복력 있고 지속 가능한 성장 전략이 그 어느 때보다 중요한 과제로 부상하고 있습니다.

이러한 시대적 전환기에 세계경제연구원(IGE)과 KB금융그룹은 "글로벌 대전환과 정책기조 피벗을 넘어서: 지속가능 성장과 금융의 미래"를 주제로 국제컨퍼런스를 공동 개최하였습니다. 이번 서밋은 지정학과 거시경제, 기후 및 인구 문제, 기술 혁신 등 다양한 글로벌 이슈에 대응하기 위한 금융의 전략적 역할과 정책적 해법을 심도 있게 논의하는 자리였습니다.

이 책자는 컨퍼런스에서 발표되고 논의된 주요 내용을 정리한 것으로, 급변하는 글로벌 환경 속에서 지속가능한 미래를 모색하는 모든 분들께 의미 있는 통찰과 실천적 지침을 제공할 수 있기를 바랍니다.

끝으로, 본 컨퍼런스를 풍성하게 빛내주신 국내외 연사 여러분과 참석자 여러분께 깊이 감사드리며, 공동 주최 기관인 KB금융그룹의 적극적인 협력과 지원에도 진심으로 감사의 말씀을 전합니다.

감사합니다

세계경제연구원 이사장<br>
전 광 우

# IGE – KB금융그룹
# 2024 지속가능성 글로벌 서밋

글로벌 대전환과 정책기조 피벗을 넘어서: 지속가능 성장과 금융의 미래

날 짜 | 2024년 11월 21일 (목)
장 소 | 콘래드서울 그랜드볼룸

| 시간 | 구분 | | | |
|---|---|---|---|---|
| 09:00 ~ 10:20 | 개회식 | 개회사 | 전광우 세계경제연구원 이사장/ 前 금융위원장, 국민연금공단 이사장 | |
| | | 축사 | 나경원 제22대 국회의원/국회 인구기후그리고내일 대표의원 | |
| | | | 주형환 저출산·고령사회위원회 부위원장(부총리급) | |
| | | | 김병환 금융위원회 위원장(FSC) | |
| | | 컨퍼런스 기조연설 | 세이케 아츠시(Seike Atsushi) 日고령화대책위원회 위원장, 日적십자사 총재/前 게이오대 총장 | |
| | | 특별 연설 | 정운찬 동반성장연구소 이사장/前 국무총리, 서울대 총장 | |
| 10:30 ~ 10:50 | | 특별 대담 | 조셉 스티글리츠(Joseph Stiglitz) 노벨경제학상 수상자/컬럼비아대 석좌교수 | |
| 10:50 ~ 12:30 | Session 1<br>미 대선 이후의<br>세계경제 및 지정학적<br>변화와 전망 | 좌장 | 신성환 한국은행 금융통화위원회 위원 | |
| | | 기조발표 | 니콜라스 라디(Nicholas Lardy) Senior Fellow, Peterson Institute for International Economics(PIIE) | |
| | | | 조동철 KDI 한국개발연구원 원장 | |
| | | 패널 | 후카가와 유키코(Fukagawa Yukiko) 와세다대 교수 | |
| | | | 윌리엄 페섹(William Pesek) Nikkei/Forbes 수석 칼럼니스트 | |
| | | | 이종화 고려대 교수/ 前 한국경제학회 회장, ADB 수석이코노미스트 | |
| | | | 최병일 이화여대 국제대학원 명예교수 | |
| 12:30 ~ 13:40 | 오찬 | | | |
| 13:50 ~ 15:40 | Session 2<br>지속가능성장을 위한<br>기후금융 및<br>상생금융의 혁신 | 좌장 | 홍종호 서울대 환경대학원 교수 | |
| | | 기조발표 | 비노드 토마스(Vinod Thomas) Senior Fellow, Institute of Southeast Asian Studies, Singapore/ 前 세계은행 수석 부총재 | |
| | | | 산제이 팻나익(Sanjay Patnaik) Director of the Center on Regulation and Markets, The Brookings Institution | |
| | | | 구본재 Deloitte Consulting 부사장/파트너 | |
| | | 패널 | 이형희 SK SUPEX추구협의회 Communication 위원장 | |
| | | | 이 진 금융감독원 금융시장안정국 국장 | |
| | | | 김혜성 김앤장 법률사무소 변호사 | |
| 15:50 ~ 17:00 | Session 3<br>인구위기<br>극복 전략과<br>금융의 역할 | 좌장 | 이인실 한반도미래인구연구원 원장/前 통계청장 | |
| | | 기조발표 | 조앤 윌리엄스(Joan Wiliams) 캘리포니아주립대 법대 교수 | |
| | | | 찰스 유지 호리오카(Charles Yuji Horioka) 고베대 석좌교수, IARIW 회장/前 日경제학회 회장 | |
| | | 패널 | 서지호 한국금융연구원 인구변화대응연구센터장 | |
| | | | 김경록 미래에셋자산운용 고문 | |
| | | | 정신동 KB경영연구소 소장(전무) | |

# 개회식

**[개회사]**
전광우 세계경제연구원 이사장

**[축사]**
나경원 제22대 국회의원/국회 인구기후그리고내일 대표의원
주형환 저출산·고령사회위원회 부위원장(부총리급)
김병환 금융위원회 위원장(FSC)

**[컨퍼런스 기조연설]**
세이케 아츠시(Seike Atsushi) 日고령화대책위원회 위원장, 日적십자사 총재/
前 게이오대 총장

**[특별연설]**
정운찬 동반성장연구소 이사장/前 국무총리, 서울대 총장

**[특별대담]**
조셉 스티글리츠(Joseph Stiglitz) 노벨경제학상 수상자/컬럼비아대 석좌교수

# 개회사

**전광우** 세계경제연구원 이사장

---

존경하는 내외 귀빈 여러분,

먼저, IGE-KB금융그룹 국제 컨퍼런스를 개최하게 된 것을 매우 큰 영광으로 생각하오며, 본 행사의 모든 주최 및 후원 기관을 대표하여 여러분을 진심으로 환영합니다. 특히 해외에서 참석해 주신 저명한 연사 여러분께 깊은 감사의 말씀을 전합니다.

오늘 우리는 글로벌 정치적 리더십의 변화, 지정학적 갈등, 거시경제적 불확실성, 그리고 기술 혁신이 맞물리는 중대한 시점에 모였습니다. 더욱이 점차 심화되고 있는 기후 변화와 인구구조 변화의 압박 등은 작금의 현실을 더욱 복잡하게 만들어 회복력 있고 지속가능한 성장을 추구하는 우리의 노력을 한층 더 어렵게 하고 있습니다. 이에 금번 국제 컨퍼런스는 이와 같이 전례 없는 글로벌 대변혁 시대를 성공적으로 항해하기 위한 경영 전략과 정책 결정의 핵심 과제와 기회를 심도 있게 다루고자 합니다. 본 행사는 글로벌 금융의 최근 동향과 향후 전망을 논의하고, 혁신적인 미래를 위한 해결책 중심의 실질적 협력을 촉진하는 중요한 플랫폼이 될 것입니다.

특히, 오늘 컨퍼런스에서는 미국 대선 이후 변화하는 세계 경제 환경, 지속 가능한 발전을 위한 기후 금융 및 포용적 금융 혁신, 그리고 오늘 국제행사의 핵심 주제인 인구 위기에 대응하는 전략과 정책을 집중적으로 논의할 것입니다.

이를 위해 국내외에서 약 30명의 권위있는 다양한 분양의 국제적 오피니언 리더들께서 이 자리에 참석하셨습니다. 시간 관계상 모든 분께 일일이 소개 인사를 드리기 어렵지만, 오늘 특별 강연을 해주실 정운찬 전 국무총리님, 기조연설을 맡아 주실 세이케 아츠시 일본 고령화대책위원회 위원장겸 일본 적십자사 총재님, 나경원 국회의원국회 인구기후그리고내일 대표의원님, 주형환 저출산·고령사회위원회 부위원장님, 김병환 금융위원회 위원장님께 특별히 감사의 말씀을 전하고자 합니다. 또한, 노벨 경제학상 수상자인 조셉 스티글리츠 교수님, 피터슨 연구소의 니콜라스 라디 박사님, 세계은행의 수석 부총재를 역임하신 비노드 토마스 박사님, 와세다 대학교 후카가와 유키코 교수님, 국제적인 칼럼니스트인 윌리엄 페섹님을 비롯한 모든 연사 분들께도 깊은 감사를 드립니다. 이렇게 많은 세계적으로 명망 높은 전문가들과 함께할 수 있어서 매우 큰 영광으로 생각합니다.

아울러 30년 전 세계경제연구원을 설립하신 사공일 박사님, 저희 연구원의 활동을 아낌없이 후원해주신 영원무역그룹의 성기학 회장님, 그리고 이번 행사를 지원해주신 KB금융그룹의 양종희 회장님께 진심으로 감사의 말씀을 전합니다.

본 컨퍼런스가 한국과 세계의 더 나은 미래를 위한 많은 영감을 주는 생산적인 행사가 되기를 바라오며, 참석해 주신 여러분 모두의 건승을 기원합니다.

감사합니다.

# 축사

**나경원** 제22대 국회의원/국회 인구기후그리고내일 대표의원

---

안녕하십니까? 반갑습니다. 나경원입니다. 먼저 오늘 이렇게 의미 있는 행사를 마련해 주신 세계경제연구원 전광우 이사장님 그리고 KB 금융그룹 양종희 회장님께 감사드립니다.

저는 무엇보다 이번 컨퍼런스의 주제가 정말 시의적절하다는 생각을 합니다. 특히 오늘 마지막 세션에는 인구 위기 극복 전략을 논의할 예정인데요. 제가 사실은 국회에 '인구기후그리고내일'이라는 포럼을 만들었습니다. 인구 문제와 기후 문제에 어떻게 대응 하느냐에 따라 결국 대한민국뿐 아니라 전 세계의 지속 가능 성장의 명운이 달려있다고 봅니다. 이를 위해 과학기술을 어떻게 활용하느냐도 굉장히 중요한 문제라고 생각을 해서 요새 국회에서 인구기후그리고내일 포럼을 만들어서 열심히 활동하고 있습니다.

그런데 얼마 전 미국 대선이 끝나고 나서 모두들 굉장히 혼란스러운 상태인 것 같습니다. 하지만 저는 트럼프 대통령의 당선이 바로 대한민국의 위기가 아니라 기회라고 생각을 합니다. 트럼프 대통령이 지금 아메리카 퍼스트를 주장하고 있는데, 미국의 제조업 리쇼어링이라든지 글로벌 공급망 안정화 등을 위해서 한국만큼 좋은 파트너가 없다고 생각하기 때문입니다.

저는 COP 29 총회에 갔다가 엊그제 귀국했는데요. 거기서 미국 대표단을 만나 많은 논의를 했습니다. 미국 대표단과의 양자 대화 결과에 따

르면 미국이 겉으로는 기후 문제에 있어서 예전과 다른 기조로 가는 듯 보이나 한국 기업이 걱정할 상황은 아니라는 얘기를 들었습니다. 오히려 걱정하는 저를 안심시키려는 모습이었습니다. 결과적으로 저는 미국에 있어서 한국은 여전히 좋은 파트너이고, 그래서 트럼프 당선 이후의 변화는 한국에게 위기이자 기회라고 생각을 합니다.

또한 이번 COP 29의 주제가 바로 기후 재원의 문제였습니다. 기후 재원 확보의 문제뿐 아니라 기후 금융에 관한 논의도 활발히 이루어졌는데요. 결국 기후 위기를 극복하는 문제가 이제는 탄소 중립 목표 이행의 문제로 귀결됩니다. 따라서 기후 관련 금융 구조를 어떻게 짜느냐도 역시 굉장히 중요한 문제라고 생각합니다. 미래지향적인 금융 구조가 오늘 컨퍼런스에서 광범위하게 논의되었으면 하는 바램입니다.

저출생 고령화 문제는 대한민국뿐 아니라 결국 한국과 전 세계의 지속 가능한 성장을 담보하는 데 있어서 아주 근본적이고 구조적인 문제라고 봅니다. 또한 그 경제적 파급 효과와 금융 산업의 미래에 미치는 영향이 굉장히 크기 때문에, 저출산 관련 위기를 면밀히 진단하고 전략적이고 정책적인 금융 해법을 만드는 것은 금융산업이 선제적으로 해야 될 일이라고 생각합니다.

또한 이 저출산 위기를 극복하는 데 있어서 금융의 역할이 굉장히 큽니다. 제가 저출산고령화사회위원회 부위원장을 맡고 있을 때 헝가리 저출산 대책을 해법으로 제시한 바 있는데 그 핵심은 주택 금융 대책이었습니다. 결혼할 경우 1%대 초저리 장기대출을 해주는 금융 인센티브로 결혼과 출산을 장려하면서 결국 일종의 저출산을 극복하는 좋은 예가 되었습니다. 1% 장기대출로 주거 안정성을 보장하고 이자 탕감이나 원금 탕감 등의 지원을 병행하는 정책이었습니다. 아주 공격적인 정책이지만 한국의 저출산 문제에도 좋은 해법으로 참고할 수 있을 것이라고 생각 합니다.

　모쪼록 오늘 이 자리에 함께해 주신 정부 고위관계자 여러분과, 글로벌 석학분들, 주요 기업인들, 언론인들을 비롯한 많은 전문가분들께서 머리를 맞대시고 대한민국의 지속가능성장을 위한 아주 실질적인 해법을 논의해 주시기를 기대합니다. 좋은 논의에 대해서는 저의 국회에서도 정책적 지원을 아끼지 않을 것입니다. 다시 한번 오늘 이 자리를 마련해주신 세계경제연구원과 KB금융그룹에 감사드립니다.

# 축사

**주형환** 저출산·고령사회위원회 부위원장(부총리급)

---

먼저, 오늘 '세계경제연구원-KB금융그룹 2024 지속가능성 글로벌 서밋'의 개최를 진심으로 축하드립니다. 뜻깊은 행사를 준비해 주신 전광우 세계경제연구원 이사장님과 행사관계자 여러분께 깊은 감사의 말씀을 드립니다.

아울러, 이 자리를 빛내 주신 나경원 국민의힘 국회의원님, 정운찬 동반성장연구소 이사장님, 김병환 금융위원회 위원장님, 조셉 스티글리츠 컬럼비아대 석좌교수님, 세이케 아츠시 일본 고령화대책위원회 위원장님을 비롯해 함께해 주신 모든 참석자 분들께도 감사의 말씀을 드립니다.

내외 귀빈 여러분,

오늘 저는 대한민국의 지속가능한 성장을 위협하는 여러 도전 요인 중에서도 가장 심각한 문제로 부각되고 있는 '인구위기'에 대해 말씀드리고자 합니다. 현재 한국은 초저출생, 초고령사회, 초인구절벽이라는 소위 3초(超) 현상으로 대변되는 인구위기에 직면해 있습니다.

우선 한국의 출산율은 절대적인 수준이 세계에서 가장 낮을 뿐만 아니라 상대적인 속도 측면에서도 가장 빠르게 악화되고 있습니다. 1960년에 6.0이었던 합계출산율은 불과 20여년 만인 1984년 1명대(1.74)로 하락하였고, 2023년에는 0.72라는 충격적인 수치를 기록했습니다.

고령화 역시 세계적으로 유례없는 속도로 진행되고 있습니다. 내년

이면 한국은 고령화사회로 진입한 지 25년, 고령사회로 진입한 지 7년만에 초고령사회에 도달하게 됩니다. 앞으로 거대 인구집단인 2차 베이비붐 세대의 은퇴가 진행되면서 이러한 흐름은 더욱 빨라질 것으로 예상됩니다. 특히, 80세 이상 인구 비중이 지난 20여년간 5배 가까이 증가하는 등 의료·돌봄 부담이 큰 후기 고령인구의 증가세가 가파른 모습입니다. 이와 같은 초저출생·초고령화 추세가 지속된다면 매년 약 36만 명, 현재 세종시 수준의 인구가 감소하게 되고, 2100년에는 전체 인구가 지금의 절반 이하로 줄어들게 됩니다.

이러한 인구구조 변화는 단순히 통계적 의미를 넘어 경제·사회·안보 전 영역에 걸쳐 광범위한 영향을 가져옵니다. 노동인구 감소에 따른 성장잠재력 약화, 연금·복지지출 급증에 따른 국가재정의 지속가능성 저하, 병역자원 감소, 세대 간 갈등 심화와 같은 다양한 문제가 발생할 것으로 예상되며, 이는 국가 시스템 자체에 중대한 위기를 초래하게 될 것입니다.

정부는 이와 같은 엄중한 상황인식을 바탕으로 금년 6월 '인구 국가비상사태'를 선포하고, '저출생 추세 반전을 위한 대책'을 발표하였습니다. 또한, 매월 인구비상대책회의를 통해 정책 이행상황을 점검하고 새로운 대책도 지속적으로 마련하고 있습니다.

먼저, 당면한 초저출생 문제 해결을 위해서는 정책적 대응과 사회인식 변화의 양대 축을 중심으로 범국가차원에서 총력 대응하고 있습니다. 저희가 저출생의 직접적인 원인을 분석해 보니 우선 결혼 자체가 줄어들거나 늦어지고, 결혼을 하더라도 아이를 덜 낳거나 늦게 낳고, 아예 낳지 않으려는 경향이 커진 것으로 나타났습니다.

이러한 현상의 가장 큰 이유는 아이를 낳고 기르는 부담과 기회비용이 커지고, 가치관이 변화했기 때문입니다. 양육비와 주거비 부담이 과중한 데다 일자리마저 변변치 않고, 일·가정 양립도 제대로 되어 있지 않은 현실은 청년들이 결혼과 출산을 주저하고 기피하게 만들고 있습니다. 이에 따라 정부도 선택과 집중을 통해 국민들이 가장 필요로 하는 일·가정 양립 지원을 중심으로 양육부담 완화, 주거 지원까지 3대 핵심 분야에 정책 역량을 집중하고 있습니다.

보다 근본적으로 보면 저출생은 구조적 문제의 산물입니다. 좋은 일자리가 부족하고, 그나마도 수도권에 집중되어 있는데 소수의 좋은 일자리를 얻기 위해 좋은 학교에 들어가야 하고, 이를 위한 입시경쟁으로 사교육비 부담이 급증하였습니다. 수도권에 인구가 집중되다 보니 집값이 상승하고 물리적·정신적 경쟁압력도 극심해져 결혼과 출산을 더욱 어렵게 만들고 있습니다.

앞으로는 이와 같은 구조적 문제에 대해서도 인구위기 관점에서 긴 호흡을 갖고 꾸준히 대응해 나갈 것입니다. 이러한 정책적인 대응과 더불어 사회적 인식 변화를 위한 노력도 병행하고 있습니다. 가족에 대한 소중함과 공동체와의 유대감을 기반으로 왜 아이를 낳아야 하는지에 대한 질문에 아이가 행복이라고 답할 수 있는 사회가 되도록, 방송·언론계는 물론 경제계, 종교계, 시민사회 등과 함께 범사회적 역량을 결집해 나가겠습니다. 다행히 최근 혼인건수는 5개월 연속, 출생아 수는 2개월 연속 증가하였고, 결혼과 출산에 대한 긍정적인 인식도 확산되는 등 길었던 출산율 하락세의 반등 조짐이 조금씩 나타나고 있습니다.

정부는 앞으로도 이러한 흐름을 더욱 공고히 할 수 있도록 기존에 발표한 대책을 차질 없이, 일관되게 이행하면서 끊임없이 현장과 소통하며 정책을 보완해 나갈 것입니다. 저출생 대책과 함께 당면한 초고령화 대응도 준비하고 있습니다. 현재 우리나라는 초저출생 추세가 이어지는 가운

데 지난 30여 년간 기대수명이 11년 증가하였고 거대 인구집단인 베이비붐 세대가 대거 고령층에 편입되면서 세계적으로도 유례없는 빠른 속도로 고령화가 진행 중입니다.

현재의 속도와 변화 양상을 고려할 때 2차 베이비붐 세대가 은퇴가 진행되는 향후 10년이 고령화 정책 대응의 마지막 골든타임이 될 것입니다.

이러한 정책 대응 과정에서 특히, 다음 세 가지 측면을 고려해야 합니다.

우선, 정책대상인 고령자가 이질적입니다. 고령자는 연령대별로 65세부터 74세까지의 전기고령자와 75세 이상의 후기고령자로 구분할 수 있는데, 전기고령자, 특히 이제 막 고령층에 진입한 베이비붐 세대는 후기고령자에 비해 학력, 소득, 자산 수준이 높고 건강하며, 일할 능력과 의사도 훨씬 큽니다. 둘째, 지역에 따라 고령화 속도와 양상이 상이합니다. 현재 우리나라의 전국 평균 중위연령은 46세인데, 이미 24개 군 지역에서는 중위연령이 60세를 넘었습니다. 또한, 일자리와 생활 기반시설 여건도 지역별로 다릅니다. 마지막으로, AI, IoT, 로봇 같은 기술이 빠르게 발전하면서 이러한 기술을 활용한 스마트 돌봄, 맞춤형 의료 등이 새로운 정책수단으로 부상하고 있습니다.

정부는 이와 같은 고려사항을 토대로 계속고용 및 노후소득 보장, 의료·요양·돌봄, 고령친화적 주거·산업, 사회참여를 핵심으로 하는 고령사회 대응 방안을 준비하고 있으며, 내년 초까지 대책을 마련할 계획입니다.

우선, 고령자가 원하면 일할 수 있도록 계속고용 여건을 조성하고, 다층적 노후소득 보장체계를 강화하겠습니다. 의료·요양·돌봄과 관련해서는 고령자가 선호하는 살던 곳에서 필요한 서비스를 통합적으로 누릴 수 있도록 지역사회 중심으로 정책을 전환해 나가겠습니다. 주거환경과 관련해서는 고령자가 오랫동안 안전하게 자립적으로 생활할 수 있는 여건을 구축하겠습니다.

아울러, 많은 고령자가 활기찬 노후를 보낼 수 있도록 고령자 친화형 문화·체육시설을 확대하고 평생교육이나 사회공헌 활동도 활성화시켜 나가겠습니다.

이러한 초저출생, 초고령화 대응 노력에도 당분간 생산인구 감소 추세는 지속되기 때문에 적응 노력도 함께 추진해야 합니다.

기본적으로 청년 니트(NEET) 70만명, 선진국에 비해 경제활동참가율이 낮은 30·40대 여성, 주된 일자리 퇴직 후에도 근로를 희망하는 장년·고령인력 등 아직 개선의 여지가 있는 다양한 계층에서 적극적인 노동시장 참여를 이끌어 내고, 이민정책 개편 등으로 외국 인력의 활용도 높여 생산인구의 감소를 보완하고자 합니다.

이에 더해 과감한 규제 완화, R&D·교육투자 확충 등을 통해 AI, 바이오, 친환경 등 첨단산업 중심으로 산업구조를 재편하고, 경제 전반의 생산성을 높이는 노력도 함께 추진하겠습니다.

내외 귀빈 여러분,

저출생·고령화 추세는 전 세계적인 현상인 만큼, 개별 국가 차원의 대응을 넘어 서로의 경험과 사례를 공유하고 협력할 때 보다 실질적인 해결책을 찾을 수 있습니다. 특히, 한국과 일본 양국은 인구구조 뿐만 아니라 장시간 근로관행이나 직장 내 성차별과 같은 기업문화에도 공통점이 많습니다.

이에 양국은 정부는 물론 민간, 특히 기업이나 학계도 참여하여 장시간 근로관행, 성차별 개선, 일·가정 양립 지원과 같이 공통으로 관심을 갖는 주제에 대해 우수 사례를 공유하고, 함께 해법을 모색해 나가기로 한 바 있습니다.

이와 유사한 맥락에서 오늘 자리해 주신 국내외 석학들의 발표와 제언도 우리가 직면한 문제에 대한 새로운 관점과 통찰을 제시하며, 해결책을 찾는 데 많은 도움이 될 것으로 기대합니다.

다시 한번 오늘 '세계경제연구원-KB금융그룹 2024 지속가능성 글로벌 서밋'의 개최를 진심으로 축하드립니다.

감사합니다.

# 축사

**김병환** 금융위원회 위원장(FSC)

안녕하십니까? 금융위원회 위원장 김병환입니다.

오늘, 세계경제연구원과 KB금융그룹이 공동으로 주최하는 '2024 지속 가능성 글로벌 서밋'에 함께하게 되어 매우 기쁩니다. 이 뜻 깊은 자리에 초청해주신 전광우 이사장님과 양종희 회장님께 깊은 감사의 말씀을 드립니다. 또한 바쁘신 일정 속에서도 축사를 해주시는 나경원 의원님, 주영환 부위원장님, 그리고 오늘 기조연설을 맡아 주실 세이케 아츠시 고령화대책위원회 위원장님, 정운찬 이사장님께도 감사드립니다.

오늘의 주제는 트럼프 시대의 세계 경제, 지정학적 변화, 기후변화 대응, 인구 위기 극복 등과 같은 중요한 글로벌 이슈들에 대해 지속 가능한 성장을 위한 핵심 과제를 논의하는 자리입니다. 단기적인 변화와 중장기적 구조적 주제가 함께 다뤄지므로, 이 자리는 매우 의미 있는 토론이 될 것이라 기대합니다.

이 행사에 참석하며, 제가 오늘 논의될 주제를 연결할 수 있는 공통된 키워드가 무엇일지 고민해 보니 '협력과 연대'가 떠올랐습니다.

트럼프 2기 행정부 출범 이후에는 보호무역주의 강화와 공급망 분절 등 미국 우선주의가 심화될 가능성이 높습니다. 이러한 상황에서는 특히 우리나라와 같이 대외 개방형, 수출 지향적 경제를 가진 국가에서는 협력과 연대가 더욱 중요하다고 생각합니다. 정부와 기업, 민간과의 협력 뿐만 아니라, 다른 국가들과의 협력을 통해 우리 경제 구조의 집중화를 다

변화하고, 보호무역주의에 대응할 수 있을 것입니다.

또한 기후변화와 인구 위기 역시 국가 간 협력 없이는 해결이 어렵다는 사실을 우리는 이미 목격하고 있습니다. 기후 위기 대응에는 국제적인 연대와 협력이 필수적이며, 국내적으로도 기후 목표를 달성하고 이행하는 과정에서 많은 의견 차이가 있을 수 있습니다. 이럴 때일수록, 우리는 같은 목표를 향해 어떻게 협력하고 고민할지에 대해 심도 깊은 논의와 연대가 필요하다고 생각합니다.

인구 문제는 더욱 광범위한 협력과 연대가 요구되는 문제입니다. 지역, 개인, 정부, 기업 간의 협력뿐만 아니라, 수도권과 지방, 세대 간의 연대 없이는 이 문제를 해결하기 어려울 것입니다.

오늘 이 자리에 모인 국내외 석학과 전문가들이 함께 토론하는 것 자체가 협력과 연대의 출발점이 될 수 있다는 점에서 큰 의미가 있다고 생각합니다.

금융위원회도 이러한 협력에 적극 참여할 것입니다. 저희는 올해 4월, '미래 금융 대응 태스크포스'를 출범시켜 인구, 기후, 디지털 환경 변화에 대한 금융의 대응 방안을 전문가들과 함께 논의하고 있습니다. 그 일환으로, 기후 금융에 관한 목표로 2030년까지 420조 원 규모의 정책 금융을 공급하겠다고 발표하였으며, 이를 이행하기 위해 노력할 것입니다.

오늘 이 자리에서 의미 있는 토론과 정책 제언이 이루어지기를 기대하며, 다시 한번 '협력과 연대'의 중요성을 강조드리고 싶습니다.

오늘 행사 개최를 다시 한번 축하드리며, 여러분의 많은 관심과 참여에 감사드립니다.

# 컨퍼런스 기조연설

## 세이케 아츠시(Seike Atsushi)
日고령화대책위원회 위원장, 日적십자사 총재/前 게이오대 총장

---

먼저, 오늘 이렇게 훌륭한 자리에 기조연설자로 서게 되어 대단히 영광입니다. 초청해주신 세계경제연구원과 KB금융그룹에 진심으로 감사드립니다. 시간관계상 바로 본론으로 들어가겠습니다.

저는 오늘 '평생 활동적인 사회'의 의미에 대해 말씀드리고자 합니다. '평생 활동적인 사회'란 나이에 관계없이 고령층의 의지와 능력을 충분히 활용할 수 있는 사회를 의미합니다. 저는 한국과 일본 모두 '평생 활동적인 사회'를 구축할 필요가 있다고 생각합니다. 그 이유는 매우 분명합니다. 두 나라는 모두 급격히 고령화 사회에 접어들고 있기 때문입니다.

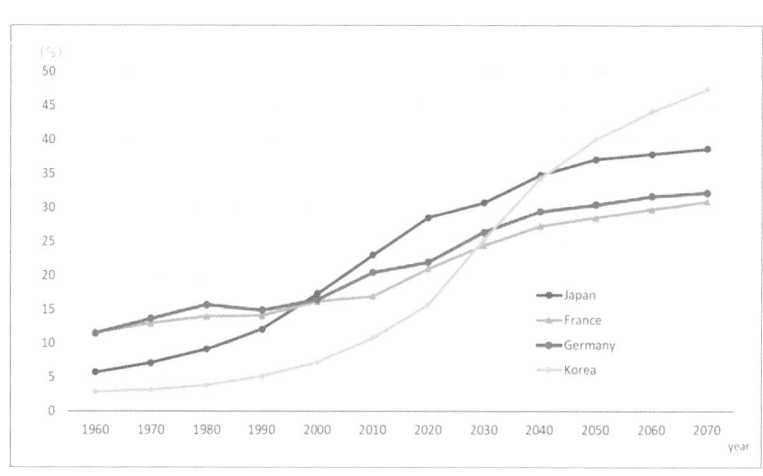

Figure1 Proportion of Population Aged 65 and Over

(Source) National Institute of Population and Social Security Research. *Population Projection of Japan*
Statistics Korea. *Population Projection*

먼저, 일본과 한국에서 65세 이상의 고령 인구 비율 변화를 보여주는 그림 1을 살펴보시기 바랍니다. 일본은 이미 고령 인구 비율이 30%에 근접해 있으며, 이는 세계에서 가장 높은 수준을 기록하고 있습니다. 한국은 약 19%로 아직 일본보다는 낮지만, 2040년대 초반에는 일본을 초과할 것으로 예상됩니다. 이 그림을 보면, 한국과 일본의 고령화 속도가 프랑스나 독일과 같은 유럽 국가들보다 훨씬 가파르다는 것을 알 수 있습니다. 이는 한국과 일본이 고령화 문제를 전 세계적으로 유례없는 속도와 규모로 겪고 있다는 사실을 보여줍니다.

더 나아가, 고령화 사회는 여러 차례의 베이비붐 세대의 물결을 동반합니다. 일본의 경우, 1947년에서 1949년 사이에 태어난 첫 번째 베이비붐 세대와 1971년에서 1974년 사이에 태어난 두 번째 베이비붐 세대가 주요한 인구 증가를 이끌었습니다. 일본의 베이비붐은 한국이나 미국과 달리 짧은 기간에 집중적으로 발생한 점이 특징입니다. 그림 2를 보시면, 2025년과 2040년의 일본 인구 피라미드를 확인할 수 있습니다.

Figure2 The Population Pyramid of Japan in 2025 and 2040

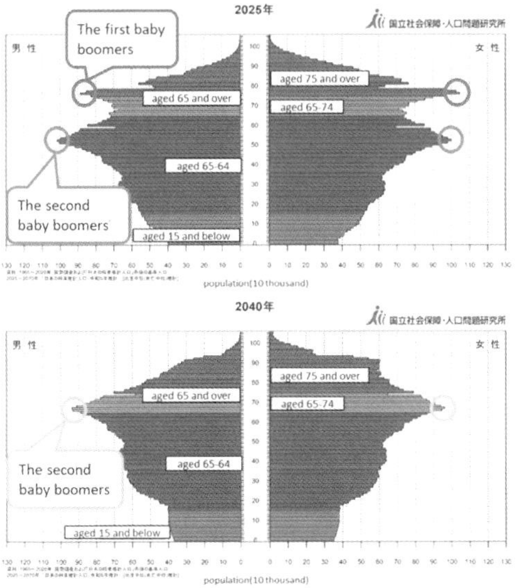

(Source) National Institute of Population and Social Security Research, *Population Projection of Jap*.

2025년까지 첫 번째 베이비붐 세대는 모두 75세에 도달하며, 75세 이상의 고령층은 질병 발생 가능성 증가와 장기 요양의 필요성 증대라는 문제를 동반합니다. 이러한 상황은 일본이 소비세를 5%에서 10%로 점진적으로 인상한 이유 중 하나이기도 합니다. 이후, 2040년에는 두 번째 베이비붐 세대가 65세에 도달하면서 일본의 고령 인구는 급증할 것입니다.

고령화 사회는 많은 어려운 문제들을 초래합니다. 하지만 우선 고령화 그 자체는 경제 발전으로 인한 1인당 소득 증가의 결과임을 말씀드리고자 합니다. 고령화가 가져온 장수 사회는 1인당 소득의 증가 없이는 실현될 수 없었을 것입니다.

또한, 고령화의 또 다른 원인은 출산율 감소입니다. 개발도상국에서 선진국으로 전환하는 과정에서 사회는 '인구학적 전환'을 겪게 되며, 출산과 사망률이 높은 사회에서 출산과 사망률이 낮은 사회로 변화하게 됩니다. 그림 3을 보면, 일본과 한국은 매우 빠른 속도로 인구학적 전환을 경험한 국가들임을 확인할 수 있습니다.

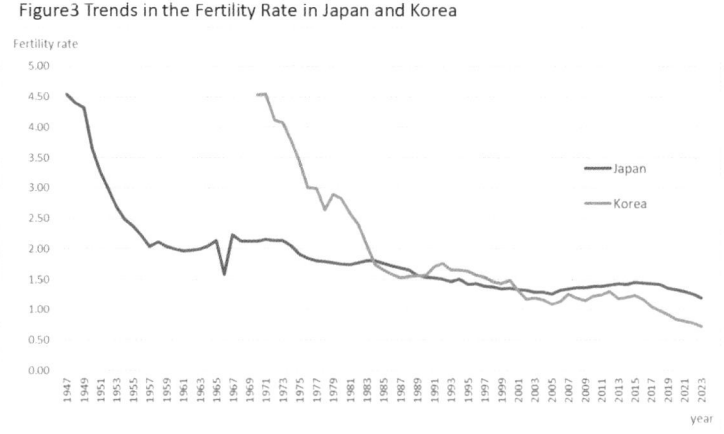

물론, 최근 일본과 한국에서의 출산율 저하는 과도한 측면도 있지만, 그 주된 원인 중 하나는 여성의 자녀 양육 기회비용 증가입니다. 이는 경제 발전으로 여성의 임금이 증가한 결과이며, 아이를 낳고 기르는 데 드는 경제적 부담이 너무 커져 출산율이 지나치게 낮아지게 된 것입니다. 이러한 출산율 저하를 역전시키기 위해서는 여성의 육아 부담을 줄여주는 정책이 필요하며, 이를 위해 육아 서비스 개선과 더불어 남성들이 육아에 참여할 수 있는 근무 환경 변화가 필수적입니다.

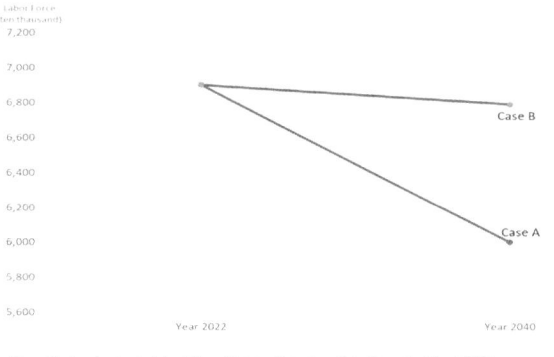

Figure4 The Projection of Labor Force in Japan
Case A (Bule Line): Labor force participation rates will remain unchanged)
Case B(Red Line): Labor force participation rates of older people and women will increase)

(Source) The Japan Institute for Labor Policy and Training, *Projections of Labor Demand and Supply* (2023)

이와 같은 고령화가 가장 크게 미치는 영향은 노동력의 감소입니다. 일본의 노동력 예측을 예시로 들어 설명드리겠습니다. 그림 4를 살펴보시면, 2023년 약 6900만 명의 노동력이 2040년에는 6000만 명으로 약 900만 명 감소할 것으로 예측됩니다. 이는 경제와 사회에 심각한 부정적인 영향을 미칠 수 있습니다.

이렇게 노동력이 급격히 감소하게 되면, 생산이 줄어들고, 전체 소비도 감소하게 될 수 있습니다. 이는 노동자 한 명당 생산성 증가 없이는 경제 성장에 큰 어려움을 겪게 된다는 것을 의미합니다. 또한, 사회 보장 시스템의 지속 가능성에도 큰 영향을 미칩니다.

이러한 문제에 대응하기 위한 중요한 해결책 중 하나는 고령층의 노동력 참여를 촉진하는 것입니다. 즉, 고령자들의 의지와 능력을 최대한 발휘할 수 있는 '평생 활동적인 사회'를 구축하는 것이 중요합니다.

고령층의 노동력 참여 증가와 소비 증가는 경제 성장의 핵심 동력입니다. 또한, 고령자들이 계속해서 노동 시장에 참여함으로써 사회 보장 시스템의 부담을 줄일 수 있습니다. 그림 4의 B 사례를 보시면, 고령자와 여성의 노동력 참여를 늘리면 약 6800만 명 정도로 노동력을 유지할 수 있다는 예측이 나옵니다. 이는 100만 명 이상 감소하는 수준에 불과하며, 이렇게 노동력을 유지할 수 있다면 생산과 소비를 지속할 수 있을 뿐만 아니라 사회 보장 시스템의 지속 가능성도 확보할 수 있습니다. 물론, 고령자들에게 강제로 일을 시킬 수는 없습니다. 그러나 한국과 일본은 이 점에서 유리한 조건을 가지고 있습니다.

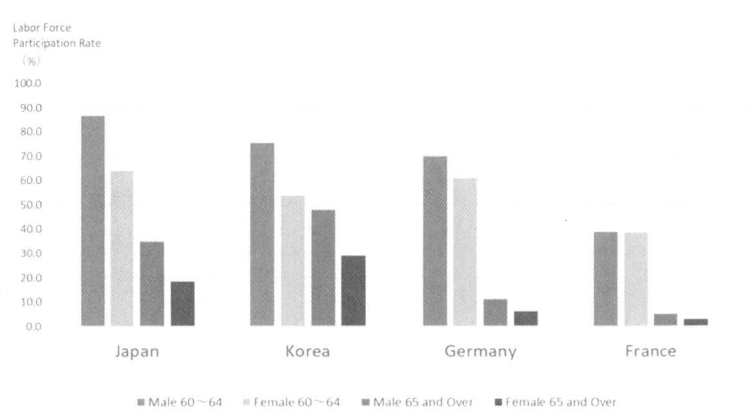

Figure5 Labor Force Participation Rates of Older People in East Asian Countries and European Countries in 2022

(Source)OECD, *OECD Database*

그림 5를 보면, 한국과 일본의 고령자 노동력 참여율이 유럽 국가들에 비해 현저히 높다는 것을 확인할 수 있습니다. 이는 고령자들이 여전히 일할 의욕을 가지고 있다는 것을 의미합니다.

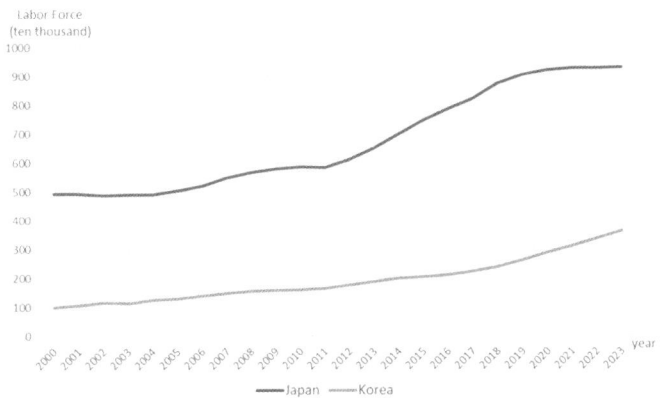

Figure6 Labor Force Aged 65 and Over in Japan and Korea

(Source) Statistics Bureau of Japan, *Labor Force Survey*
Statistics Korea, *Economically Active Population Survey*

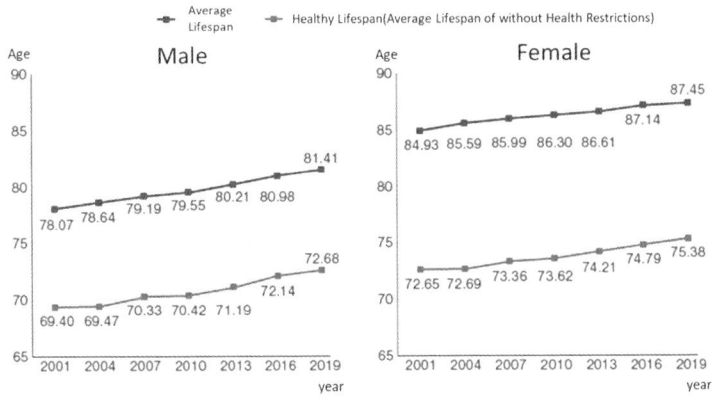

Figure7 Trends in the Average Lifespan and Healthy Lifespan

(Source) Ministry of Health, Labour and Welfare, *e-Health-net*

따라서, 한국과 일본은 고령화 사회에 직면하고 있으나, 고령자들의 강한 의지를 활용할 수 있는 유리한 조건을 가지고 있습니다. 이를 바탕으로 평생 활동적인 사회를 구축할 수 있는 기회가 존재합니다. 이를 어떻게 실현할 수 있을까요?

첫째, 고령자들의 건강 상태를 개선하는 것이 가장 중요합니다. 경제학적 분석에 따르면, 고령자들의 노동력 참여에 가장 중요한 변수는 건강 상태입니다.

그림 7을 보면, 건강한 수명은 증가하고 있지만, 여전히 남성은 평균 수명보다 약 8년, 여성은 약 12년 짧습니다.

건강한 수명을 연장하는 데 있어 예방 의학은 중요한 역할을 합니다. 정기 건강 검진, 생활 습관병 예방, 백신 접종, 구강 건강 관리 등은 모두 건강한 수명을 늘리는 데 효과적입니다. 이러한 예방 의학에 대한 투자는 고령자들의 노동력 참여를 촉진하고, 경제와 사회의 지속 가능성 증대에 기여하는 좋은 투자라고 할 수 있습니다.

둘째, 퇴직 제도의 개선이 필요합니다. 일본에서는 60세 이상 퇴직 연령을 법적으로 설정할 수 있으며, 고령자들이 계속해서 일할 수 있는 계획을 마련해야 합니다. 그러나 퇴직 후 고령자들의 임금이 급격히 하락하는 문제가 발생하고 있습니다. 이를 해결하기 위해서는 퇴직 제도와 연공 서열 중심의 임금 체계를 근본적으로 개혁할 필요가 있습니다.

셋째, 공적 연금 제도에 대한 개혁이 필요합니다. 일본의 연금 제도에서는 퇴직 연령 이후 일하면 연금 혜택이 감소하는데, 이는 고령자들이 일자리를 줄이거나 완전히 그만두게 만드는 요인이 됩니다. 이를 해결하기 위해서는 연금 제도를 고령자들이 계속 일할 수 있도록 개선해야 합니다.

고령자들의 노동력 참여를 촉진하는 것이 청년들의 일자리를 빼앗는다는 우려도 있을 수 있습니다. 그러나 현재 청년 인구가 줄어들고 있는 상황에서 일본에서는 이러한 의견이 점차 사라지고 있습니다. 그림 9를 보면, 2010년대 동안 청년층의 구인구직 비율이 고령층보다 항상 높았다는 것을 알 수 있습니다.

고령자들의 고용을 촉진하는 것은 청년들의 적정 근무 시간 단축에도 효과적이며, 고령자들이 계속 사회 보장 기여금을 납부하고 세금을 납부함으로써 청년들의 사회 보장 부담을 경감시킬 수 있습니다.

마지막으로, 청년들의 삶을 개선하기 위한 가장 중요한 과제는 육아 지원을 강화하는 것입니다. 저는 한때 일본 사회 보장 시스템 개혁위원회의 의장을 맡았으며, 2013년 일본 정부에 육아 지원 강화를 권고하는 보고서를 제출한 바 있습니다. 이후 일본 정부는 육아 지원을 개선해 왔지만, 여전히 부족한 부분이 있습니다. 육아 지원 강화를 위한 정책은 일본뿐만 아니라 한국에도 중요한 과제라고 생각합니다.

한국은 일본과 중요한 이웃 국가이며, 두 나라의 경제는 밀접하게 연관되어 있습니다. 그리고 두 나라는 고령화라는 공통의 문제에 직면해 있습니다. 앞서 말씀드린 것처럼, 일본과 한국이 고령화 문제에 대응하기 위한 해결책은 거의 동일하며, 고령화 문제 해결을 위한 연구 협력과 상호 학습이 더 활발히 이루어져야 합니다.

오늘 컨퍼런스는 그러한 협력의 중요한 기회가 될 것입니다. 두 나라가 '평생 활동적인 사회' 모델을 함께 구축한다면, 이는 미래에 고령화 문제를 겪을 다른 국가들에게 큰 참고가 될 것입니다. 오늘 이 중요한 자리를 만들어 주신 모든 분들께 깊은 감사의 말씀을 전하며, 제 발표를 마치겠습니다. 감사합니다.

# 특별연설

**정운찬** 동반성장연구소 이사장/前 국무총리, 서울대 총장

---

안녕하십니까. 오늘 이렇게 뜻깊은 자리에 초청해 주신 세계경제연구원과 KB금융그룹에 진심으로 감사인사를 드립니다. 바로 본론으로 들어가겠습니다.

한국은 커다란 나라가 되었습니다. 인구가 5천만 명이 넘으면서 1인당 국민소득도 3만 달러가 넘는 세계 7개 국가 가운데 하나입니다. 우리와 어깨를 나란히 한 다른 6개국은 미국, 일본, 독일, 영국, 프랑스 그리고 이탈리아입니다. 이러한 눈부신 성적에도 한국은 저성장과 양극화란 위기에 직면해 있습니다.

한국은 1997년 IMF 경제위기와 2008년 글로벌 금융위기 이후 경제 활력이 떨어지고 저성장이 고착됐습니다. 연평균 경제성장률을 보면 1960~1970년대에는 10%를 넘었고, 1980년대까지만 해도 8%대였으나, 김영삼 정부 이후(1993~) 장기성장률(10년 이동평균)이 정권이 바뀔 때마다 1%씩 떨어져 현재 2%대에 머물러있습니다. 산업화 시대의 모방형 인재 교육은 창조형 인적자원 축적으로 연결되지 못했고, 공동체 정신은 약화되었으며, 미래에 대한 희망도 희미해졌습니다. 소득분배를 보면 상위 1%가 전체 소득의 15%를, 그리고 상위 10%가 47%를 가져갑니다. 그뿐만 아니라 대기업, 특히 4대 기업의 경제력 집중은 세계 어느 나라에서도 찾아보기 힘들 정도로 심합니다.

이러한 상황은 어디에서 유래했을까요? 한국의 경제정책은 '재벌 중심·수출 주도'의 '선 성장·후 분배'가 기본전략입니다. 수출 및 중화학

공업과 같은 특정 부문을 먼저 육성하고, 그 성과가 경제 전체에 파급되기를 기대하는 이른바 낙수효과 모델에 의존해 왔습니다. 성장과 효율을 극대화하는 것이 지상 목표였고, 분배와 형평은 부차적 고려 사항이었습니다. 불균형 성장의 결과 소수 대기업에 편중된 산업구조가 고착되었고, 국민 대다수의 고용과 소득을 담당하는 중소기업은 대기업과의 수직적 관계 속에 불공정거래를 감수해야 하는 위치로 전락했습니다.

기업의 양극화는 필연적으로 소득과 자산의 양극화와 성장의 부진을 가져왔습니다. 수출 대기업의 훌륭한 성과도 별 도움이 되지 않았습니다. 지난 4반세기(즉 25년) 동안 급속히 진행된 세계 경제의 개방화와 정보화, 그리고 한국 사회 특유의 갑을관계 문화로 인해 국내 산업 간 연계가 단절되었고, 그 결과 수출과 내수 간, 그리고 대기업과 중소기업 간에 고용과 소득을 만들어 내는 선순환 연결고리가 크게 약화되었기 때문입니다.

저는 지난 10여 년 동안 동반성장이 한국경제의 재도약을 가져오는 동시에 경제적 양극화를 해결할 수 있는 최선의 대안이라고 역설해 왔습니다. 그러나 기업 양극화에서 시작된 경제적 양극화로 다른 여러 문제가 터져 나오기 시작했습니다. 그 가운데 하나가 출산율 저하에 따른 인구감소 문제입니다.

우리나라 합계출산율(여성 1명이 평생 낳을 것으로 예상되는 평균 출생아 수)은 1983년 인구대체수준인 2.1명을 밑돌기 시작하더니 작년 2023년 역대 최저 수치인 0.72명을 기록했습니다. 잘 사는 나라의 합계출산율이 감소해 가는 추세이긴 하지만, 그중에서도 1명 이하 출산율은 현재 한국이 유일합니다.

저출산의 원인은 크게 4가지로 분류할 수 있습니다. 첫째, 미래 소득의 불안정성에 기인한 소득 요인, 둘째, 자녀의 편익과 비용에 기인한 자녀 요인, 셋째, 생활양식의 변화에 따른 가치관 요인, 넷째, 양성 불평등으로 인한 사회 요인 등이 있습니다. 한국에서는 IMF 구제금융 이후 2000년대 초반부터 저출산이 시작되었고 그 원인은 주로 소득이나 고용 불안, 즉 경제적 양극화에 기인한 것으로 판단됩니다.

'동반성장(Shared Growth)'이란 '더불어 성장하고 함께 잘살자'라는 사회 철학입니다. 사회공동체를 구성하는 개인, 집단, 국가 사이를 '동반자' 관계로 조성하여, 공동체가 지속 가능하도록 운영하자는 것입니다. 만약 한국 사회가 10년 전부터 동반성장을 적극적으로 추진하여 대기업과 협력하는 중소기업의 근무 여건이 좋아지고 생활에 여유가 생겼다면 중소기업에 다니는 대다수 국민이 짝을 만나 결혼하고 자녀를 출산했을 것입니다. 혹은 고령층이 모아둔 연기금을 청년 벤처 창업 생태계에 적극적으로 투자했다면 청년들의 경제 상황도 개선되고 자연스럽게 결혼과 출산으로 이어질 수 있었다고 생각합니다. 그러나 우리는 양극화를 방치했고 초저출산으로 이어졌습니다.

지금 많은 지방 도시가 소멸 위험에 직면했고 학령인구 감소로 2023년에 신입생이 10명도 되지 않는 초등학교는 전국에 1,587교나 됩니다. 세계 유일 분단국가인 한국에 병역자원 감소가 얼마나 큰 안보적 위협이 될지는 말할 필요도 없습니다. 한반도미래인구연구원의 '2024 인구보고서'에 따르면 2031년에는 국민 절반이 50세 이상이 되고, 2044년에는 경제성장의 핵심 기반인 생산가능인구가 1천만 명이나 줄어듭니다. 필연적으로 정부 차원에서 저출산에 대한 예산과 정책은 적극적으로 지원하고 개발해야 합니다.

저출산·고령사회위원회와 국회 예산정책처에 따르면 지난 2006년부터 2023년까지 17년 동안 정부가 저출산 예산이라며 발표한 사업의 총예산액은 국비 기준 379.8조 원에 이릅니다. 저출산 대책이 처음 발표된 2006년 2.1조 원이었던 저출산 예산이 2023년 48조 원으로 22.9배 증가했습니다. 그러나 이 기간 출산율은 꾸준하게 떨어졌습니다. 지금까지 추진했던 정부의 저출산 정책은 실패했다는 사실을 인정해야 합니다.

저출산 예산으로 책정된 사업의 내용들을 보면 수긍하기 어려운 부분이 많습니다. 예를 들어 관광 활성화 기반 구축, 국내 관광 역량 강화, 게임산업 육성, 인공지능 융합형 기술인력 역량 강화, 만화산업 육성, 해양수산 신산업 육성 및 기업 투자 유치 지원 등등, 이 모든 사업이 전부 저출산 대응 사업에 포함되어 있었습니다. 저출산 문제 해결에 직접적으로 관련되지 않은 사업들이 너무 많이 포함되어 있습니다.

가장 알기 쉬운 저출산 정책으로 한국도 프랑스·스웨덴·일본처럼 자녀양육가구에 현금을 직접 지원하는 방법을 채택할 수 있습니다. 다만 예산 사업별로 효율성을 따져보지 않고 재정만 쏟아붓는 것은 밑 빠진 독에 물 붓기에 불과합니다. 앞으로는 사업별로 저출산 문제 해결에 효과가 있는지 측정하고 평가하는 시스템을 갖추어나가야 합니다. 그러나 저출산 문제를 정부 노력과 예산만으로 해결하기는 어렵습니다. 정계, 재계, 학계, 종교계가 모두 지혜와 힘을 모아 해결해야 합니다. 저출산의 핵심적인 원인 중 하나가 출산의 주체인 엄마와 아빠, 부모가 느끼는 육아와 교육 부담입니다.

정부는 한 아이를 낳은 부모가 다시 아이를 낳아보자고 자연스럽게 결심할 수 있는 환경을 만들어야 합니다. 그리고 국민들에게 아이를 낳기만 하면 국가와 공동체가 키워준다는 믿음을 심어주기 위해서 법과 제도로 하루빨리 명확한 신호를 주어야 합니다.

이상으로 제 발언을 마치겠습니다. 경청해주신 여러분 감사합니다. 오늘 컨퍼런스의 성공을 기원합니다.

# 특별 대담

## 조셉 스티글리츠(Joseph Stiglitz)
노벨경제학상 수상자/컬럼비아대 석좌교수

---

**전광우 이사장:** 스티글리츠 박사님, 다시 뵙게 되어 반갑습니다. 뉴욕에서 이렇게 늦은 시간에도 저희와 함께해 주셔서 진심으로 감사드립니다. 현재 우리는 두어 달 뒤 트럼프 2기 행정부 출범을 앞두고 더 큰 지정학적 긴장과 거시경제적 도전에 직면해 있습니다. 이처럼 중요한 시점에 스티글리츠 박사님을 특별 기조연사로 모실 수 있게 되어 매우 뜻깊게 생각합니다.

스티글리츠 박사님께서는 2001년 노벨 경제학상을 수상한 세계적인 경제학자로 학문과 정책 분야에서 탁월한 성취를 이루신 분이며, 지속 가능 성장과 책임 있는 세계화를 지지하는 가장 존경받는 학자입니다. 세계은행의 수석 이코노미스트 및 수석 부총재를 역임하셨으며 빌 클린턴 정부에서는 경제자문위원회 의장직을 맡으신 바 있습니다. 뿐만 아니라 약 20여년 전에는 한국이 아시아 금융위기를 성공적으로 극복하는 데 중요한 기여를 한 공로를 인정받아 한국 정부로부터 국민훈장 목련장을 수여받기도 했습니다.

그럼 이제 스티글리츠 박사님의 특별 연설을 청해 듣겠습니다. 박사님, 감사합니다.

**조셉 스티글리츠 박사:** 따뜻한 소개 말씀에 감사드립니다. 저도 여러분과 컨퍼런스 현장에서 직접 만나 뵐 수 있었으면 정말 좋았을 텐데 아쉽습니다. 미국이 선거를 비롯해 많은 일들로 매우 분주한 시기인 관계로 이번에는 화상으로 참여를 하게 되었지만, 다음에 기회가 되면 꼭 직접

뵙기를 바랍니다.

이번 컨퍼런스의 대 주제가 "글로벌 대전환"인데요. 현 시점에서 더없이 적절한 주제라고 생각합니다.

우리는 막 도널드 트럼프가 승리한 미국 대선을 치렀습니다. 코로나 팬데믹, 러시아의 우크라이나 침공, 가자와 레바논에서 벌어지는 대학살, 그리고 이에 대해 아무런 조치를 취하지 못하는 국제사회의 무능함 위에 덧붙여진 또 하나의 큰 사건입니다.

예상대로, 국내외를 막론하고 민주주의와 법치주의, 다자주의에 대한 의문이 제기되고 있습니다. 본격적으로 말씀드리기에 앞서, 제가 현 시점에서 가장 깊이 우려하는 것은 바로 민주주의와 다자주의의 미래라는 점을 먼저 강조하고 싶습니다.

그럼 이제 미국 경제 전망부터 시작해 보겠습니다. 미국은 여전히 세계 최대의 경제 대국입니다. 미국에서 벌어지는 일은 전 세계에 영향을 미칩니다. 단기적, 장기적 관점으로 나눠 말씀드리겠습니다. 트럼프가 자신의 대선 공약을 실행에 옮기고 의회를 설득해 이를 통과시키고 그것이 법적 정당성을 확보한다는 가정하에 경우 어떤 일이 벌어질 지, 그리고 이러한 가정 보다는 보다 현실에 기반해 실제로 어떤 일이 일어날 가능성이 있는지를 신중히 살펴보려 합니다. 트럼프의 첫 임기를 되돌아보면 트럼프가 많은 공약을 내세웠지만 상당 부분은 실현하지 못했기 때문입니다.

우선 트럼프가 이번 대선 과정에서 내세운 공약들은 미국 경제에 매우 해로울 것이며, 국제 경제에도 부정적인 영향을 줄 것이 분명합니다. 이는 현재 전개되고 있는 거의 모든 경제적·정치적 측면에 파장을 일으킬 것입니다. 조금 체계적으로 정리해보자면, 유권자들을 가장 괴롭힐

경제적 문제는 아마도 인플레이션일 것입니다.

제가 보기에는 트럼프의 대선 공약들이 실제로 정책으로 시행된다면 또 한 차례의 인플레이션을 유발할 위험이 있으며, 이는 특히 더욱 문제가 될 것입니다.

코로나 팬데믹에 따른 공급망 붕괴와 그 뒤를 이은 러시아의 우크라이나 침공 등 공급 충격이 수요 구조에도 변화를 초래하면서, 결국 우리는 지난 세기 동안 겪지 못했던 수준의 인플레이션을 경험했습니다. 다행히 연준을 비롯한 각국의 중앙은행과 정부의 노력으로 우리는 이제 막 인플레이션의 고비를 가까스로 넘어서고 있습니다. 인플레이션은 놀라울 정도로 빠르게 하락했습니다. 현재 인플레이션 수준은 대부분의 중앙은행과 은행가들이 안심할 수 있는 수준에 이르렀습니다.

그런데, 우리가 인플레이션을 가까스로 통제한 바로 이 시점에, 트럼프는 이를 다시 자극하겠다고 공언하고 있습니다. 그의 여러 정책들 가운데는 인플레이션을 유발할 가능성이 매우 높은 것들이 있습니다.

그중 가장 우려되는 것은 중국산 제품에 대해 100%에 달하는 고율 관세를 부과한다는 것입니다. 미국은 다른 많은 국가들과 마찬가지로 의류, 가전제품, 컴퓨터, 아이폰 등 다양한 물품을 중국에 크게 의존하고 있기 때문에 중국산 제품에 대한 고율 관세는 파괴적인 결과를 초래할 것입니다.

물론 일부 기업들은 생산 거점을 중국에서 다른 나라로 옮길 수 있겠지만, 이는 매우 혼란스럽고 비용이 많이 드는 일이며, 그러한 변화가 인플레이션으로 이어지지 않을 것이라고 보기 어렵습니다.

세계화의 물결 속에서 많은 국가와 기업들이 중국에서 생산하기로 선택한 이유는 중국이 생산비가 가장 저렴한 곳이기 때문이며, 그것이 자본주의의 본질입니다. 따라서 대규모 관세를 부과하는 것은 결국 수입품에 대한 또 다른 형태의 세금이며, 이는 곧 인플레이션으로 이어질 수밖에 없습니다. 실제로 대부분의 경제학자들은 고율 관세를 인플레이션을 유발하는 조세 방식으로 간주합니다.

그런데, 이는 다른 어떤 집단보다 중하위층에 더 큰 고통을 안기는 세금입니다. 왜냐하면 이들의 소비 중 수입 제품이 차지하는 비중이 더 크기 때문입니다. 대부분의 경제학자들은 특히 저소득층에 훨씬 더 큰 피해를 줄 것이라는 데 의견을 같이합니다. 뿐만 아니라, 다른 국가들이 트럼프의 고율 관세에 보복 관세를 취할 가능성이 높기 때문에 여기에서 파생되는 추가적인 피해도 있을 수 있습니다. 보복 관세를 전략적으로 시행할 수 있는데, 그렇게 되면 우리는 최악의 상황에 처하게 될 것입니다. 미국산 제품에 대한 수요는 줄어들고, 동시에 물가는 오를 것입니다. 이 경우 미국은 경기 침체와 인플레이션이 동시에 나타나는 스태그플레이션에 직면하게 될 것입니다.

개인적인 견해로는, 과거 경험으로 미루어 이번 트럼프 2기 정책도 '거래 중심적 접근'이 지배적일 것으로 보입니다. 지난 2017년부터 2020년까지의 트럼프 1기처럼 이번에도 우여곡절 끝에 어떻게든 넘길 수 있을지도 모르지만, 이번에는 그 위험이 훨씬 더 크다는 사실을 인식해야 합니다. 이 트럼프의 재임 기간에는 1기와는 다르게 여러 깊은 상처가 남게 될 가능성이 높습니다.

이번 미국의 역사적 선거 결과로 인해 미국뿐 아니라 한국을 비롯한 전 세계도 엄청난 도전에 직면해 있습니다. 감사합니다.

**전광우 이사장:** 박사님, 훌륭하고 큰 영감을 주신 연설 진심으로 감사합니다. 이제 몇 가지 질문을 드리겠습니다. 첫 번째 질문은 관세 관련입니다. 한국을 포함해 미국으로 수출하는 많은 국가들에 있어 '관세'라는 단어는 매우 큰 우려로 다가옵니다. 그런데 박사님의 말씀을 듣고 보니, 트럼프가 여러 사안에 있어 거래 중심적 접근을 취하는 경향이 있다는 점을 고려할 때, 실제로는 선거 기간 중 약속한 것만큼 심각하지는 않을 수도 있다는 조심스러운 기대도 갖게 됩니다. 어떻게 보시나요?

**조셉 스티글리츠 박사:** 그렇습니다. 두 가지 측면에서 말씀드릴 수 있습니다. 우선은 트럼프를 지지한 미국 기업들과 정치 후원자들이 트럼프의 관세 정책에 대해 강하게 이의를 제기할 것이고, 그 중 많은 사례가 성공적으로 관철될 것으로 생각합니다. 이는 트럼프의 관세 정책이 우려만큼 나쁘지 않을 수 있음을 시사합니다.

다른 한 측면은, 트럼프가 협상을 아주 좋아하기 때문에 한국이나 중국 등 주요국들이 "트럼프가 관세를 낮춘다면 보복 관세로 대응하지 않겠다"고 말하며 협상에 나설 것이라는 점입니다. 트럼프의 첫 임기에서 이미 봤듯이, 트럼프의 발언은 언제나 협상의 시작일 뿐입니다.

그래서 이 협상이 어디로 향할지는 누구도 확신할 수 없지만, 제 생각에는 결국 트럼프가 선거 캠페인에서 말한 것만큼 실제는 나쁘지는 않을 것입니다. 다만, 제 생각대로 흘러간다 하더라도 미국 경제가 현재 상황보다는 훨씬 악화될 것이며, 국제적인 규범 기반의 무역 질서 또한 붕괴될 것입니다. 이것이 매우 중요한 핵심입니다. 다자주의와 규칙 기반 질서가 어떻게 훼손되고 있는지를 인식해야 합니다.

원래는 모든 거래마다 협상을 벌일 필요가 없어야 했습니다. 우리는 '최혜국 대우 원칙(Most Favored Nation Principle)'이라는 무역 규범을 기반으로 움직여 왔습니다. 하지만, 트럼프 정권에서는 이 원칙이 무시되고 있으며, 파괴되고 있습니다. 지난 70년간 쌓아올린 무역 질서의 구조 전체가 무너지고 있는 것입니다. 최혜국 대우 원칙 이전, WTO는커녕 GATT 이전의 세계로 되돌아가고 있는 셈입니다. 럼에도 불구하고 사람들은 이에 대해 충분히 논의하지 않고 있습니다. 이것은 정말 중대한 문제입니다.

트럼프가 처한 또 다른 딜레마에 대해 한 가지 더 말씀드리겠습니다. 그는 억만장자들과 대기업에 대한 감세 정책의 재원을 관세로 충당하고자 합니다. 하지만 그가 실제로 관세를 시행한다면 재정 적자는 급격히 불어날 것입니다. 제가 앞서 말씀드렸듯이, 7조 달러 규모의 적자가 예상되는데, 만약 관세 수입을 확보하지 못한다면 이 수치는 훨씬 더 커지게 됩니다.

결국 트럼프는 진퇴양난에 빠지게 되고, 재정적자에 민감한 정치세력들은 더욱 시끄럽게 반발하거나 스스로 우스운 처지에 놓이게 될 것입니다. 그들은 '동태적 추계(dynamic scoring)'라는 개념을 끌어와 "이 모든 정책은 더 많은 성장으로 이어질 것이다"라고 주장하겠지만, 그런 마술 같은 계산이 통할 수 있는 범위는 극히 제한적입니다.

**전광우 이사장:** 말씀 잘 들었습니다. 다음 질문은 바이든 행정부가 야심차게 추진했던 정책인 인플레 감축법(IRA) 및 반도체 과학법(CHIPS)에 관한 것입니다. 이러한 정책에 따라 한국을 포함한 세계 각국과 주요 글로벌 기업들이 미국에 대한 대규모 투자를 이미 결정하고, 사업도 진행되고 있는 상황입니다. 따라서 트럼프가 대선 공약을 실제로 이행하게 될 경우 이러한 법안들이 폐지될 가능성에 대한 우려가 커지고 있습니다. 이는 한국뿐 아니라 미국의 주요 동맹국 모두에게 큰 걱정거리라고 생각됩니다. 어떻게 보시는지요?

**조셉 스티글리츠 박사:** IRA에 대한 많은 논의는 이 법이 트럼프의 재집권에도 영향을 받지 않도록 설계되었다는 점, 혹은 사실상 그렇게 작동할 것이라는 데 초점이 맞춰져 있습니다. IRA로 인한 혜택 대부분은 공화당 우세 지역에 돌아갔고, 이들 지역에서 투자와 일자리 창출에 매우 효과적이었습니다.

그런데 여기서 트럼프에게는 또 하나의 충돌이 발생합니다. 한쪽에는 바이든에 대한 증오심이, 다른 한쪽에는 정치적 현실이 있습니다. 정치적으로 보면 트럼프 본인의 거점 지역 노동자들에게 그렇게 많은 혜택을 가져오는 법안을 없애는 것은 어리석은 일이지만, 트럼프가 바이든에 대해 품고 있는 극심한 악감정을 기억해야 합니다. 그는 실제로 선거 기간 중 밝힌 대로 IRA 폐지를 강하게 밀어붙일 가능성도 있습니다.

이 두 요인 중 무엇이 우위를 점할지는 저도 모르겠습니다. 합리적인 정치라면 당연히 정치적 현실, 즉 일자리가 우선되어야 할 것입니다. 하지만 우리는 지금 합리적인 인물과 상대하고 있는 것이 아닙니다. 그렇기 때문에 비합리적인 인물이 어떤 결정을 내릴지 이성적으로 예측하기는 어렵습니다. 그가 정치적으로 비합리적인 결정을 내린 사례는 이미 여러 차례 있었습니다. 그래서 한국을 비롯한 미국의 수요 교역 상대국들은 계속해서 트럼프의 정책 결정을 경계하고 대비하는 것이 맞다고 봅니다.

여기서 하나 더 강조하고 싶은 점이 있습니다. 제가 앞서 인플레이션에 대해 말씀드렸는데요. IRA는 이름 그대로 '인플레이션 감축법'으로 물가를 낮추기 위한 법안입니다. 이 법은 두 가지 방식으로 인플레이션을 완화시킵니다. 첫째, 저렴한 재생에너지의 공급을 확대함으로써 에너지 가격을 낮춥니다. IRA가 폐지된다면 이들 가격은 다시 오르게 되고, 이는 또다시 인플레이션을 유발할 것입니다.

따라서 IRA 폐지와 관련해 제가 우려하는 또 다른 측면은 그 인플레이션 유발 효과입니다. 무엇보다 이 법안이 폐지된다면 이는 미국이 기후 변화 대응을 위해 내디딘 거의 유일한 전진에서 대대적인 후퇴를 하는 것을 의미하게 됩니다. 한국은 기후 변화 대응에 있어 정말로 선도적인 국가 중 하나입니다. 수소 에너지 정책도 추진하고 있고, 실질적으로 기후 변화에 대응하고 있습니다. 반면 미국은 화석연료 업계의 로비로 인해 기후 대응에 별다른 행동을 취하지 못했기에, IRA는 미국에 있어 매우 중요한 조치였습니다.

따라서 IRA가 폐지된다면 이는 엄청난 후퇴가 될 것이며, 참으로 가슴 아픈 일이 될 것입니다. '가슴 아프다'는 표현은 단지 경제학자인 제 개인의 감정만이 아니라, 기후 위기 대응에 힘써온 한 사람으로서, 그리고 이 문제를 가장 중대한 사안으로 인식하고 있는 젊은 세대를 생각해서 드리는 말입니다. 그들은 자신들이 불타는 지구를 물려받고 있다는 사실에 큰 분노와 슬픔을 느끼고 있습니다.

**전광우 이사장:** 네, 답변 감사합니다. 트럼프 2기 출범을 앞둔 미국과 세계경제의 주요 현안, 그리고 전망에 대해 깊이 있는 통찰을 공유해 주셨습니다. 훌륭한 강연과 대담이었습니다. 오늘 늦은 시간까지 저희와 함께 해 주셔서 다시 한번 진심으로 감사드리고, 다음에는 꼭 현장에서 직접 뵐 수 있기를 고대하겠습니다.

**조셉 스티글리츠 박사:** 함께할 수 있어서 영광이었습니다. 감사합니다.

세션 I

# 미 대선 이후의 세계경제 및 지정학적 변화와 전망

**좌장**
신성환 한국은행 금융통화위원회 위원

**기조발표**
니콜라스 라디(Nicholas Lardy) Senior Fellow, PIIE

**패널**
후카가와 유키코(Fukagawa Yukiko) 와세다대 교수
윌리엄 페섹(William Pesek) Nikkei/Forbes 수석 칼럼니스트
이종화 고려대 교수/前 한국경제학회 회장, ADB 수석이코노미스트
최병일 이화여대 국제대학원 명예교수

**신성환 위원:** 존경하는 내외귀빈 여러분, 좋은 아침입니다.

영국의 전설적인 총리이자 전시 영웅으로 잘 알려진 윈스턴 처칠은 "비관주의자는 모든 기회에서 어려움을 보고, 낙관주의자는 모든 어려움 속에서 기회를 본다"고 말했습니다. 오늘 우리는 글로벌 경제의 중요한 전환점에 서 있습니다. 미국 대선 결과와 중국이 직면한 지속적인 경제적 도전들이 결합된 시점으로, 자본주의와 중상주의의 극단적인 형태로 변화할 가능성을 예고합니다.

이제 우리는 변화하는 세계 경제 환경 속에서 어떻게 헤쳐 나갈 것인지, 그리고 그 속에서 어떻게 기회를 창출할 수 있을지 논의해야 할 시점에 있습니다. 우리가 직면한 변화는 매우 크고 중요합니다. 미중 경제 분리가 글로벌 공급망에 큰 혼란을 일으킬 수 있으며, 미국 시장에서 배제된 중국 제품들이 우리의 비미국 수출 시장을 차지하게 만들 수 있습니다. 또한 IRA 보조금 종료와 세금 부과 등의 조치가 우리 기업들에 큰 어려움을 줄 수 있습니다. 더불어, 높은 시장 수익률과 강력한 미국 경제로 인해 강한 달러가 지속되면서 우리의 경제 정책에 제약을 가할 수 있습니다.

외교적인 측면에서도 글로벌 지정학적 갈등과 역학 관계가 급변하고 있습니다. 한미 방위비 분담 협정도 재조정될 가능성이 있습니다. 한국은 수출이 GDP의 40% 이상을 차지하는 작은 개방 경제입니다. 참고로 미국은 10% 미만, 일본은 20% 미만, 중국은 25% 미만입니다. 따라서 외부 환경의 변화에 어떻게 적응하느냐가 우리의 지속 가능한 번영을 위해 매우 중요합니다.

이에 본 세션에서는 몇 가지 핵심적인 질문들에 답해보고자 합니다. 예일대학교 교수를 지내시고 현재는 피터슨 연구소의 선임 연구원으로 계시는 니콜라스 라디 박사는 중국 경제가 내수 수요 부진과 어려운 무역 환경 속에서도 정말 괜찮은 상태인지에 대해 다룰 예정입니다. 또한, 중국이 투자 중심의 경제에서 소비 중심의 경제로 성공적으로 전환할 수 있을지, 그리고 그 과정에서 부실 자산 문제를 어떻게 해결할 수 있을지에 대한 논의를 이어갈 것입니다.

KDI의 조동철 원장님께서는 장기적인 생산성 감소라는 큰 도전에 대해 설명하실 것입니다. 이에 대해 우리는 경제 생산성을 높이기 위한 어떤 정책이나 정책적 틀을 도입해야 할지, 또한 현재의 외부 환경을 어떻게 유리하게 활용할 수 있을지에 대한 방안을 모색할 것입니다.

와세다대학교의 후카가와 유키코 교수님은 경제 및 지정학적 갈등이 고조되는 상황에서 동맹국들과의 협력 체계를 구축하는 것이 얼마나 중요한지에 대해 이야기하실 것입니다. 전면적인 경제 통합은 현실적으로 어려운 점이 많아 많은 나라들이 특정 분야부터 협력하려는 노력을 기울이고 있는 상황인 만큼, 한국과 일본, 그리고 우리의 동맹국들 간에 어떤 분야에서 협력할 수 있을지에 대한 논의할 예정입니다.

세계적인 경제 금융 전문 칼럼니스트인 윌리엄 페섹 씨는 미중 간의 갈등과 미국과 다른 국가들 간의 긴장이 극단적으로 고조될 가능성에 대해 다룰 것입니다.

고려대학교의 이종화 교수님은, 현재의 달러 지배 체제를 대체할 수 있는 다른 경제 체제가 우리 생애 내에 등장할 수 있을지에 대해 논의하실 것입니다.

마지막으로, 이화여자대학교 명예 교수이신 최병일 교수님께서는 새로운 공급망과 경제안보 체계 재편에서 우리가 어떻게 대응할 수 있을지, 그리고 핵심 기술과 산업 분야에서 경쟁력을 강화할 수 있는 정책적 방안을 제시해 주실 것입니다.

이번 세션 동안 각 연사들의 핵심 논점들을 염두에 두시고 발표를 경청해 주시기 바랍니다.

그럼 먼저 니콜라스 라디 박사님의 기조발표를 듣고 이어서 차례로 연사들의 발표를 듣도록 하겠습니다.

**니콜라스 라디 박사:** 먼저, 이렇게 시의적절하고 매우 흥미로운 주제로 초청해 주신 주최 측에 감사의 말씀을 드립니다. 오늘 제 발표는 크게 두 가지 주제로 나누어 진행하겠습니다. 첫 번째는 미국 대선 이후의 새로운 지정학적 상황에 대해 간략히 설명드리고, 두 번째는 중국 경제에 대한 몇 가지 오해를 바로잡는 시간을 갖겠습니다.

미국의 대통령 당선인에 대해 이야기하자면, 그가 실제로 어떤 정책을 펼칠지는 정확히 예측하기 어렵습니다. 그는 자주 일관되지 않은 발언을 하고, 입장을 바꾸는 경우가 많기 때문에 아시아 국가들이 그의 정책 방향을 예측하기는 매우 어려울 것입니다. 대통령 당선인은 세 가지 주요 주제를 일관되게 제시해 왔습니다. 첫 번째는 관세, 두 번째는 세금 감면, 세 번째는 이민자 추방입니다.

## Five Misconceptions

1. Convergence of GDP to advanced economy levels has stalled
2. Household income and spending remain weak post-pandemic
3. China faces a Japanese-style balance sheet recession
4. Property investment in China has collapsed
5. Government policy has depressed private investment

첫 번째로 주목할 점은 그가 관세 수입이 세금 감면을 재정적으로 뒷받침할 것이라고 주장하는 점입니다. 그러나 이는 매우 가능성이 낮습니다. 피터슨 연구소는 그가 중국에서 수입되는 제품에 60%의 관세를 부과할 경우, 수입량이 75% 감소할 것이라고 추정하고 있습니다. 결과적으로 세수 증가는 없을 것이며, 오히려 예산 적자는 커지고, 더 많은 인플레이션이 발생할 것입니다. 이러한 인플레이션은 많은 노동자를 추방하는 정책이 시행되면 더 악화될 것입니다. 특히 건설업과 식품 가공업에서 가격 상승을 초래할 수 있습니다.

인플레이션이 상승하면 연방준비제도(이하 연준)은 금리를 인상할 가능성이 높습니다. 금리가 오르면 미국으로의 자본 유입이 증가하고, 달러는 강세를 보일 것입니다. 하지만 높은 관세에도 불구하고 무역 적자는 크게 줄어들지 않을 것입니다. 따라서 대통령 당선인의 정책이 계획대로 추진된다면, 미국은 더 높은 인플레이션, 여전히 큰 무역 적자, 금리 인상이라는 상황을 맞이할 것입니다.

그런데 금리 인상은 두 가지 주요 결과를 초래할 수 있습니다. 첫째, 주요 주식 시장에서 조정이 일어날 가능성이 커집니다. 주식 시장은 금리가 계속 낮을 것이라는 기대에 의해 급등했으나, 금리가 오르면 이 기대는 무너질 것입니다. 둘째, 금리가 상승하면 미국 경제 성장률이 둔화될 가능성이 큽니다. 금리가 오르면 기업들이 투자를 줄이고, 주택 시장도 약화될 것입니다.

이러한 쟁점들이 어떻게 전개될지는 지켜보는 것이 중요합니다. 관세를 통해 감세에 따른 세수 부족을 충당하겠다는 공약은 거의 불가능하다고 생각합니다.

이제 중국 경제에 대해 말씀드리겠습니다. 중국이 여러 가지 이유로 경제적 어려움을 겪고 있다는 사실은 잘 알려져 있습니다. 지정학적 상황, 탈세계화, 미국 시장에서의 높은 관세 가능성, 인구 구조 변화, 노동력 감소, 생산성 저하 등 여러 가지 도전 과제가 있습니다. 이 문제들은 중요한 문제지만, 이미 널리 알려진 만큼 저는 이를 깊이 다루지 않겠습니다. 대신, 중국 경제에 대해 흔히 잘못 이해되고 있는 몇 가지 부분을 짚어보겠습니다.

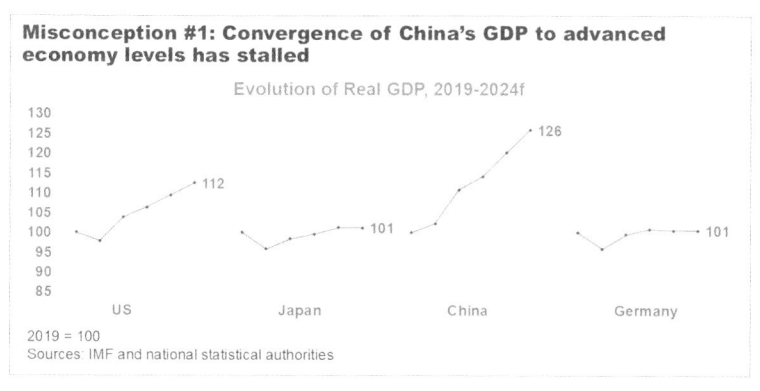

첫 번째 오해는 중국이 선진 경제 수준에 도달하는 과정에서 정체되었거나 '피크 차이나(Peak China)'에 도달했다는 주장입니다. 예를 들어, 경제전문매체 이코노미스트 지난해 봄과 최근 몇 주 사이에 중국의 경제 성장이 둔화되었고, 미국의 GDP 대비 중국의 GDP가 감소하고 있다고 보도했습니다. 하지만 저는 이것이 잘못된 이해라고 생각합니다. 미국의 GDP가 중국에 비해 증가한 이유는 지난 몇 년 동안 미국에서 고물가가 지속되었기 때문입니다. 2021년부터 2023년까지 미국의 GDP 디플레이터 기준 인플레이션은 약 16%였고, 중국은 6% 미만이었습니다. 즉, 미국의 명목 GDP는 인플레이션이 3배 더 높았기 때문에 증가한 것입니다.

하지만 실질 성장률을 보면 다른 그림이 나옵니다. 이 슬라이드에서 보시는 바와 같이, 유럽과 일본은 지난 5년 동안 거의 성장하지 않았습니다. 반면 미국은 다른 선진 산업 국가들에 비해 상대적으로 잘 성장했습니다. 그러나 중국은 여전히 미국보다 두 배 이상 빠르게 성장하고 있습니다. 따라서 '피크 차이나'라는 개념과 중국의 성장 정체 주장은 현재까지의 증거로는 뒷받침되지 않는다고 생각합니다.

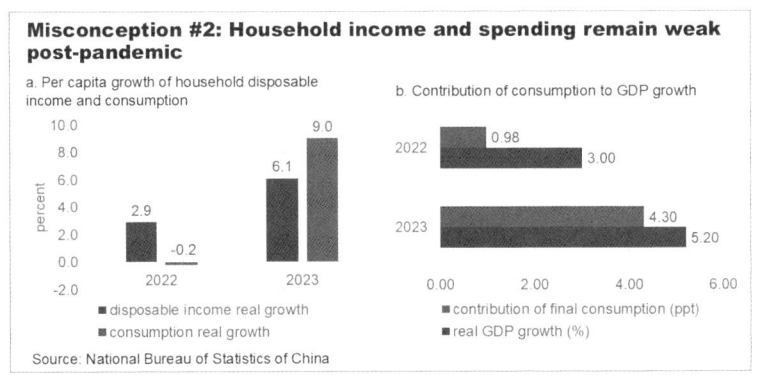

두 번째 오해는 COVID-19 팬데믹 이후 중국에서 소비자 신뢰가 약화되었고, 소비 수요가 약하다는 주장입니다. 그러나 이것이 사실인지에 대한 증거는 그리 확실하지 않습니다. 2023년 실질 가처분 소득은 6% 이상 증가했지만, 가계 소비는 9% 증가했습니다. 이는 소비자들이 이전보다 더 많이 소비했다는 의미이며, 이 경우 저축률이 감소했을 것입니다. 만약 소비자들이 신뢰를 잃었다면, 미래에 대한 우려로 저축률이 상승했을 것입니다. 그러나 데이터는 그와는 반대되는 결과를 보여줍니다.

같은 방식으로, 2024년 첫 세 분기 동안 가처분 소득은 약 5% 증가했지만, 가계 소비는 6% 증가했습니다. 이는 소비가 경제 성장에 큰 기여를 하고 있다는 것을 보여줍니다. 2023년에는 최종 소비가 경제 확장의 중요한 부분을 차지했습니다.

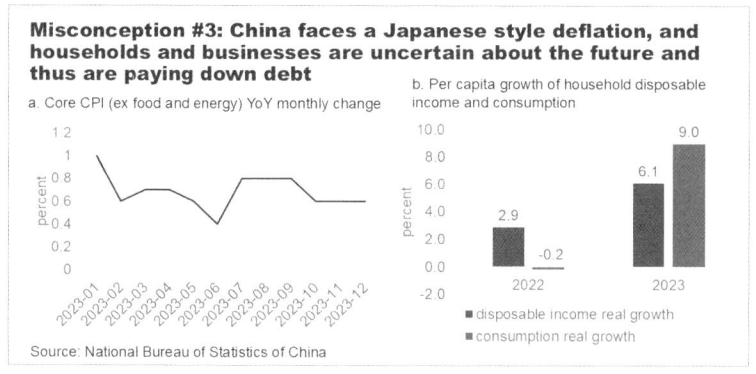

세 번째 오해는 디플레이션에 관한 문제입니다. 일부는 중국이 1990년대 초 일본과 같은 디플레이션 경로를 따르고 있다고 주장합니다. 일본식 디플레이션은 일반적으로 저성장, 가계와 기업의 부채 축소, 차입 감소, 불확실성 등이 특징입니다. 그러나 중국의 경우 물가는 매우 낮지만, 이는 일본의 디플레이션처럼 경제를 위축시키는 요소로 작용하지 않고 있습니다. 실제로 가계 소비는 증가하고 있고, 저축률은 감소하고 있습니다. 이는 부채 축소로 인한 경기 둔화가 아니라는 것을 보여줍니다.

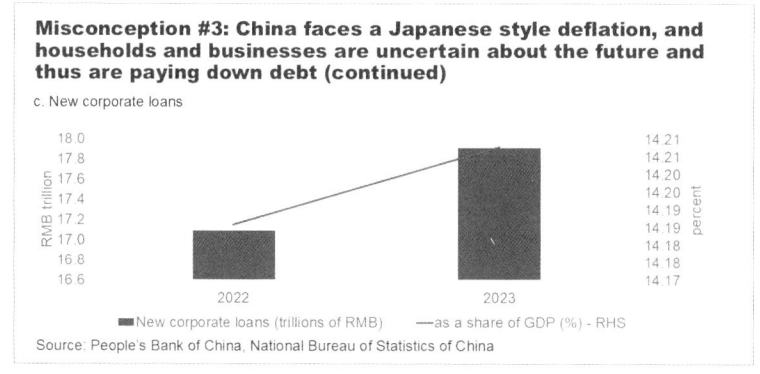

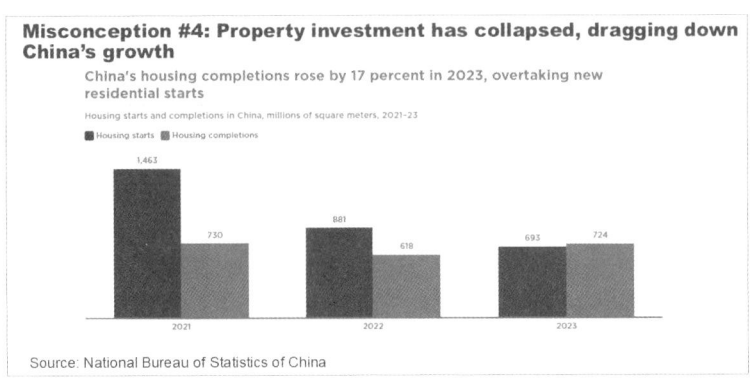

네 번째 오해는 부동산 부문에 대한 것입니다. 부동산 투자 감소는 사실입니다. 하지만 중요한 점은 부동산 투자 감소가 주택 착공 감소보다 크지 않다는 점입니다. 예를 들어, 2021년 주택 착공은 급격히 감소했고, 2022년에도 계속 감소했습니다. 그러나 완공된 주택 수는 증가했습니다. 2023년에는 처음으로 완공된 주택 수가 신규 착공 수를 초과했습니다. 이는 중국 부동산 시장을 안정시키고, 가계의 자산에 대한 신뢰를 회복하는 데 중요한 기여를 할 수 있습니다. 정부는 기존 프로젝트를 완공하는 데 집중하고 있습니다. 이를 위해 은행들이 자금을 계속 대출할 수 있도록 '화이트리스트'를 만들어 완료가 가까운 프로젝트에 우선적으로 지원하고 있습니다.

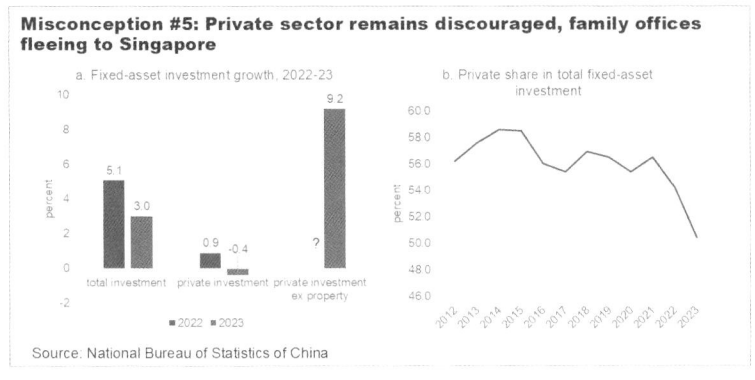

마지막으로, 민간 부문에 대한 오해가 있습니다. 저는 지난 몇 년 동안 중국 경제의 민간 부문에 대해 많은 연구를 해왔는데, 결과적으로 민간 부문이 중국 경제 성장에 매우 중요한 기여를 했다고 생각합니다. 최근 민간 투자 감소가 있긴 했지만, 이는 주로 부동산 부문에서 발생한 문제입니다. 2023년에는 부동산을 제외한 분야에서 민간 투자가 9% 이상 증가했습니다. 즉, 민간 부문은 여전히 매우 강력하고 중국 경제 성장에 중요한 기여를 하고 있습니다. 또한 민간 기업은 혁신의 대부분을 이끌고 있습니다.

결론적으로, 중국은 인구 문제와 지정학적 어려움 등 여러 역풍을 맞고 있지만, 중국 경제에 대한 부정적인 시각은 과장된 부분이 많습니다. '피크 차이나'와 소비 위축, 일본식 디플레이션 경로, 부동산 투자 급감 등의 주장은 데이터로 뒷받침되지 않으며, 민간 부문은 여전히 중요한 역할을 하고 있습니다.

이상으로 제 발표를 마치겠습니다. 감사합니다.

**후카가와 유키코 교수:** 우선, 이렇게 뜻깊은 행사에 초대해 주셔서 진심으로 감사드립니다. 또한 전광우 박사님을 비롯한 세계경제연구원의 모든 임직원분들께 깊은 감사의 말씀을 전합니다. 저는 세계경제연구원의 준 가족으로서 다시 이 자리에 오게 되어 매우 기쁩니다.

오늘 저는 일본-한국 관계에 대해 말씀드리게 되었습니다. 최근 1~2년 동안 일본과 한국 간의 관계는 중요한 자산으로 발전해왔습니다. 오늘 제 발표는 일본-한국 협력의 잠재력에 대한 내용입니다.

## Global Trading System in the Crisis

- Negative cycles: Increasing protectionist measures=>distorting resource allocation, decreasing efficiency and reducing resilience of supply chains, discouraging innovation, => slow down economic growth
- Economic security, geopolitical tensions
- Dysfunction of the World Trade Organization (WTO): Distorting trading measures, Politicization of trade rules,
  Virtually not dispute settlement (≠ Market power)
- Need for consensus decision making

글로벌 차원에서 두 나라가 직면한 도전은 점점 더 유사해지고 있습니다. 일본은 한때 주요 경제 강국 중 하나로, 미국, 유럽과 함께 세계 3대 경제국으로 자리잡았으나 현재 그 영향력이 점차 줄어들고 있습니다. 한국 역시 수출 의존도가 높아지는 등 비슷한 상황에 놓여 있습니다. 비록 그 속도는 느리지만, 보호무역주의, 경제 안보, 지정학적 긴장, WTO(세계무역기구) 체제의 기능 불능 등 글로벌 경제의 부정적인 순환은 두 나라 모두에게 큰 도전 과제가 되고 있습니다.

## Alternative Approaches: RTAs and Plurilateral Trade Agreements

- Liberalize trade policy and set up new trade rules with like-minded members of the WTO and establish a rules-based trade system
- Regional trade agreements: comprehensive issue coverage such as trade liberalization with limited number of members
- Plurilateral trade agreements (Joint statement initiatives): single issue with a large number of members
- MPIA: dispute settlement
- Expected impacts
- (Positive) Complement the WTO, trade creation
- (Negative) Divide the WTO members, trade diversion

▶ 3

이와 같은 상황에서 중요한 점은, 우리가 협력할 수 있는 신뢰할 수 있는 파트너를 찾는 것입니다. 한 가지 방법은 지역무역협정(RTA)을 통한 협력입니다. 이는 유럽이나 한국을 비롯한 여러 경제권에서 과거에 주로 채택한 방식입니다. 하지만 일본과 한국은 두 나라 간 공식적이고 제도화된 RTA가 없는 유일한 국가들입니다. 두 나라는 모두 OECD의 일원이지만, 공식적인 RTA를 체결하지 않았다는 점에서 독특한 상황에 처해 있습니다. 그렇다면 우리는 어떻게 협력할 수 있는 틀을 마련할 수 있을까요?

## Comprehensive Issue Coverage: WTO+, WTO-X

- CPTPP(TPP): WTO+(plus), WTO-X(extra), 27 issues including trade in goods and services, investment, e-commerce, state-owned enterprises (SOEs), labor, etc
- RCEP: WTO+, WTO-X, excluding SOEs, labor, transparency and corruption, etc

| | TPP | RCEP | WTO |
|---|---|---|---|
| Market Access for Goods | ● | ● | ● |
| Rules of Origin and Origin Procedures | ● | ● | ● |
| Textiles and Apparel | ● | | |
| Customs Administration and Trade Facilitation | ● | ● | ● |
| Trade Remedies | ● | ○ | ● |
| Sanitary and Phytosanitary Measures | ● | ● | ● |
| Technical Barriers to Trade | ● | ● | ● |
| Investment | ● | ● | ▲ |
| Cross Border Trade in Services | ● | ● | ● |
| Financial Services | ● | ● | ● |
| Temporary Entry for Business Persons | ● | | ● |
| Telecommunications | ● | ● | ● |
| Electronic Commerce | ● | ● | |
| Government Procurement | ● | | ▲ |
| Competition Policy | ● | ● | |
| State-Owned Enterprises and Designated Monopolies | ● | | |
| Intellectual Property | ● | ● | ● |
| Labor | ● | | |
| Environment | ● | | |
| Cooperation and Capacity Building | ● | ● | |
| Competitiveness and Business Facilitation | ● | | |
| Development | ● | ● | |
| Small and Medium-Sized Enterprises | ● | ● | |
| Regulatory Coherence | ● | | |
| Transparency and Anti-corruption | ● | ● | |
| Administrative and Institutional Provisions | ● | ● | |
| Dispute Settlement | ● | ● | ● |

　일본은 CPTPP(포괄적이고 점진적인 환태평양경제동반자협정)와 같은 다자간 협정에 참여하고 있으며, 한국 역시 이러한 협정에 참여하고 있습니다. 미국이 TPP에서 탈퇴했음에도 불구하고, 우리는 이 네트워크를 강화하려는 노력을 계속하고 있습니다. 또한, 일본, 한국, 중국이 참여하는 RCEP(역내포괄적경제동반자협정)과 같은 다른 지역 경제 협력 네트워크도 있습니다. 이 협정은 사실상 일본, 한국, 중국 간 자유무역협정의 형태를 띠고 있으며, 기본적인 구조는 TPP와 크게 다르지 않습니다. 이미 중국이 TPP 가입 의사를 밝혔기 때문에 한국, 대만, 또는 중국 중 어느 국가를 우선적으로 다뤄야 할지에 대한 고민이 필요합니다.

# Japan and Korea in the changing globalization: (1) Trade Regime

- Threats for Free Trade (Malfunctioning pluri-literalism): Geopolitics, Economic security, Technology
- Change of competition environment: Innovation, Industrial policy, Trade rule making
  - ☞ Significance of domestic market (US, EU, China)
  - ☞ Significance of friends (IPR protection, Data rules, Rule of origins, Investor protection> Market
    - ☞ Korea: Still the "Export-led growth"?
    - ☞ Japan: Still the stagnant home market?
      - ☞ Common needs for deep integration:
        Quasi home market for Korea (ex. Entertainment)
        Better competition for Japan (ex. DX/GX)

세계화가 변화함에 따라 일본과 한국이 직면한 외부 환경도 달라졌습니다. 일본은 한국과 같은 지역 파트너와의 심화된 통합을 통해 새로운 기회를 모색해야 하며, 한국 역시 전통적인 수출 주도형 및 제조업 중심의 경제 모델을 넘어 엔터테인먼트, 콘텐츠 및 서비스 산업 등의 분야에서 일본과 협력할 수 있는 가능성을 찾아야 합니다. 일본 역시 주변국으로부터 긍정적인 경쟁적 압력을 받을 필요가 있습니다. 이는 두 나라 모두에게 전략적 협력의 목적을 제공할 수 있습니다.

## Japan and Korea in the changing globalization: (2) Technology

- Change of competition environment: Rise of China
  - ☞ Games for emerging economies:
    (Infrastructure investment + Capital accumulation (Borrowings) + Learning + Economy of scale → Innovation without legacy cost + Movement of persons + Cyber space (Networking, Crypt currency) + Regulation architecture (home market)
  - ☞ Common constraints in human capital, Pool potentials
    Labor/ Pension fund reform for Korea
    Re-skilling and labor mobility for Japan
  - ☞ Economic security information exchange with friends

기술 분야에서도 협력할 수 있는 기회가 많습니다. 앞서 조동철 회장님께서 정확히 지적하셨듯이, 미국 경제는 더 이상 내수 시장에만 의존할 수 없습니다. 내수 시장에서의 혁신은 글로벌 시장에서의 성공으로 이어지며, 이는 중국과 마찬가지로 일본과 한국에도 적용됩니다. 문제는 일본과 한국이 상대적으로 작은 내수 시장을 가지고 있기 때문에, 어떻게 혁신을 촉진할 수 있을지에 대한 고민이 필요합니다. 또한, 두 나라 모두 과학과 공학 분야에서 인적 자원 제약을 겪고 있습니다. 따라서 일본과 한국이 인적 자원을 통합하면, 우리는 큰 잠재력을 함께 발휘할 수 있을 것입니다.

## Japan and Korea: Heterogenous structure

**Japan**
- Gov. debt
- Deflationary pressures after the market bubble collapse
- No capital control, Settlement currency
- Capital account, Technology account surplus
- Long-term resource strategy
- Low wage, low unemployment
- Peaking out aging
- Gradual process in de-risking
- Lagged behind DX in public administration
- Geopolitical risk: N. Korea

**Korea**
- Household debt
- High property market, Inflationary pressures
- Short-term capital controls, Non settlement currency
- Deficit in technology account surplus
- Weak resource strategies with smaller reserve
- High wage. High unemployment
- Peaking aging
- Sudden de-risking
- Better DX interface in public administration
- N. Korea: Risk + Potential?

▶ 9

그런데 일본과 한국은 많은 공통점을 가지고 있지만, 미시적인 차이점도 존재합니다. 따라서 우리의 전략은 이러한 차이점과 공통점을 결합하여 시장 중심의 통합을 촉진하는 것이어야 합니다. 예를 들어, 일본의 주요 기업들은 대부분 서비스 중심인 반면, 한국의 주요 기업들은 여전히 제조업과 수출 중심입니다. 일본 경제는 점차 서비스 중심으로 변화하고 있지만, 혁신 능력에는 한계가 있는 상황입니다. 이 부분에서 한국이 도움을 줄 수 있을 것입니다.

## Korea's contents industry

- $132.4 billion (2022), 10<sup>th</sup> export item (Getting larger than LCD panel, mobile phones….)
- Large synergy effect with consumer goods export ($100 million export will boost $180 million consumer export → Production effect of $510 million, job creation of 2982)
- After all cultural matters: Dominant Chinese market (45%) followed by Japan (15%)
- Service trade has been boosted as income converges as the neighbor market: Tourism (+), IPR (-)

역사적으로, 한국이 세계의 부유한 경제국들을 빠르게 따라잡을 수 있었던 원동력은 제조업이었으며, 일본은 그 과정에서 중요한 경쟁국이었습니다. 그러나 이제 그 경쟁의 시대는 끝났습니다. 한국은 엔터테인먼트와 문화 콘텐츠 수출 분야에서 글로벌한 영향을 미치고 있으며, 전 세계 콘텐츠 시장에서 중요한 역할을 하고 있습니다. 이 과정에서 일본도 많은 혜택을 보고 있습니다. 또한, 일본은 고령화 사회 문제를 해결하는 데 있어 중요한 경험을 가지고 있습니다. 이는 한국에 큰 도움이 될 수 있습니다.

## Bi-lateral cooperation : From Growth to Sustainability (Homogeneity + Heterogeneity)

- Environment and Energy: Common resource investment for risk sharing, Energy efficiency by energy-mix and smart technologies, GX (ex. Power chips, Smart mobility、 Green Data center (From *Green by Digital to Green of Digital*)
- Aging society: DX in medi-care and public administration, Common basic research for aging, Evidence Based Policy Making (EBPM) and Implementation (Agriculture and Health)
- Local development: Smart city, Agricultural reform, Sight-seeing, Health care, Disaster management, Seamless logistics (ex. Global Food Value Chains for food export)
- Human capital: Common qualifications for professionals, Pension system for labor mobility, Foreign workers standards

▸ 15

따라서 양국 간의 협력은 글로벌 경쟁에서 벗어나, 지역적인 협력 관계로 발전할 가능성이 큽니다. 우리는 글로벌 협력 규칙에 대해 공동으로 협상하고, 전문가 교류와 국제기구에서의 공동 대표 활동 등을 통해 협력할 수 있는 많은 기회를 가지고 있습니다. 또한, 한국은 개발도상국에 대한 공식 개발원조(ODA)를 크게 확장하고 있어, 이 분야에서도 함께 협력할 수 있을 것입니다.

Bi-lateral cooperation : From Global competition to cooperation (Strategic use of Homogeneity)

- Global cooperation ① : Common bargaining for global rules (Exchange of professionals, International organization reform, Anti Economic state crafts (US/China, and Global south (ex. Beyond ISDs in TPP)
- Global cooperation ② : Fragile/ Conflict state supports (ODA reform in Project screening, Performance analysis, Data/Archive management), Common allocation
- Global cooperation ③ : Basic research for future pandemic (JK model for Asia), Public goods provision

▶ 16

결론적으로, 일본과 한국은 서로에게 많은 기회를 제공할 수 있는 협력의 파트너입니다. 우리는 많은 도전 과제를 공유하고 있지만, 서로의 차이를 보완하며 함께 성장할 수 있는 잠재력을 가지고 있습니다. 지역 무역 협정, 기술 협력, 고령화 및 환경 문제 해결 등 다양한 분야에서 협력할 수 있는 기회가 많습니다.

감사합니다.

**윌리엄 페섹 칼럼니스트:** 이 자리에 오게 되어 매우 기쁩니다. 저는 미 대선 결과와 관련해서 저널리스트 입장에서 몇 가지 말씀드리겠습니다.

앞서 기조발표를 해주신 라디 박사님과는 2015년 아제르바이잔에서 열린 아시아개발은행(ADB) 회의에서 뵙고 10년만에 이번에 다시 뵙게 되었는데요, 당시 저는 세션 좌장을 맡고 있었고 라디 박사님은 그 세션에서 발표를 했었던 것이 기억납니다.

그때를 생각하며 저는 지난 10년 동안의 전 세계의 큰 변화들에 대해 돌아보게 되었습니다. 아마 '립 밴 윙클(Rip Van Winkle)' 이야기를 아시는 분들이 많을 것입니다. 이 이야기는 워싱턴 어빙의 단편소설로, 한 남자가 오랫동안 잠을 자고 깨어나서 세상이 너무나 달라졌다는 것에 충격을 받는 이야기입니다. 오늘 아침 저는 2015년 아제르바이잔에서 만났던 라디 박사님이 놀랐을 법한 10가지 사항을 즉흥적으로 적어보았습니다.

첫번째는 중국이 디플레이션을 수출하고 있다는 점입니다. 두번째는 일본이 10년 만에 네 번째 총리가 등장했음에도 불구하고 일본은행이 여전히 금리를 0.2% 이상으로 올리지 못하고 있다는 점입니다. 또한, 인도의 인구가 이제 중국을 초과했고, 세계 경제는 거의 2년 동안 팬데믹에 의해 멈췄습니다. AI는 새로운 닷컴처럼 모든 것을 변화시키고 있으며, 비트코인은 이제 사기가 아니라고 여겨지고 있습니다. K팝은 이제 새로운 Motown이 되어 전 세계를 휩쓸고 있으며, 마르코스 가문은 필리핀에서 다시 권력을 잡았습니다. 또한, 한 명의 장군이 다시 인도네시아를 이끌고 있다는 사실도 놀랍습니다. 그리고 무엇보다도, 세 번 결혼하고 여섯 번 파산한 리얼리티 TV쇼 스타인 도널드 트럼프가 미국 대통령에 두 번이나 당선되었음을 깨닫는 것이 가장 충격적입니다.

저는 지난 9월 세계경제연구원의 초청으로 서울을 방문해 미국 대선 전망 시나리오에 대한 발표를 한 적이 있습니다. 그때 저는 트럼프가 패배하고 해리스가 승리할 것이라고 매우 자신 있게 이야기했었는데요, 결과적으로는 제가 틀렸습니다.

이제 트럼프 대통령의 두 번째 임기가 아시아에 어떤 부정적인 영향을 미칠지에 대한 제 생각을 나누어 보겠습니다.

트럼프는 분노하고 있습니다. 그는 2020년 대선에서 패배한 것에 화가 나 있고, 탄핵시도가 있었던 것, 기소된 것에 화가 나 있습니다. 첫 번째 무역 전쟁에서 중국과 싸운 결과가 기대와 달리 좋지 않았다는 것에 화가 나 있고, 일본과 한국이 대화하는 것에 불쾌감을 느끼고 있습니다. 그는 중국이 반도체, 재생 가능 에너지, 전기차, 항공우주, 생명공학, AI, 로봇공학, 그린 인프라 등에서 미국보다 더 많은 투자를 하고 있다는 것에 화가 나 있습니다. 또한 베트남이 미국으로 돌아오길 기대했던 모든 일자리를 차지했다는 사실에 분노하고 있습니다. 트럼프는 아시아가 10년 뒤로 퇴보할 것이라 생각했으나, 그게 이루어지지 않자 더욱 화가 나 있습니다. 이제 그는 정치적 제약 없이 자신만의 길을 가고 있으며, 아시아는 그가 표적으로 삼을 첫 번째 지역이 될 가능성이 큽니다.

트럼프의 경제 계획은 아시아의 시장을 빼앗는 것에 집중되어 있습니다. 그는 세금 인하와 규제 완화를 이야기하지만, 그의 정책은 1985년 시점에 갇혀 있습니다. 그 당시에는 관세가 효과적이었을 수 있었지만, 지금은 상황이 다릅니다. 아시아에서 일자리를 빼앗고 이를 트럼프 지지 지역으로 돌리는 것이 쉬운 일이 아니라는 점에서, 그는 실수를 하고 있습니다.

또한, 트럼프의 거래주의적 태도는 현실적이지 않습니다. 그는 협상보다는 무조건 이기려는 관철시키려는 스타일의 정치인입니다. 중국이 이를 받아줄 것인가에 대해 저는 회의적입니다. 그는 대만을 협상 카드로 사용할 가능성도 있기 때문에, 대만은 이를 두고 우크라이나와 같은 상황이 올 수 있다는 우려를 할 수 있습니다.

트럼프는 첫 번째 관세 60%를 시작으로 더 많은 관세를 부과할 계획을 가지고 있습니다. 그는 멕시코에서 제조된 모든 자동차에 대해 100% 관세를 부과하려고 하고 있으며, 일본과 한국은 그가 여기에 대해서도 같은 방식으로 협박할 것이라고 예상해야 합니다. 또한 그는 양자 무역 거래를 다시 부활시킬 것이며, 이 과정에서 일본과 한국은 불리한 상황에 처할 수 있습니다.

트럼프는 다시 한 번 방위비 인상을 강요할 가능성이 큽니다. 이전에도 서울과 도쿄에서 수십억 달러를 지불하라고 요구했던 것처럼, 이번에도 그럴 가능성이 높습니다. 또한, 그는 연준을 장악하려 할 것이며, 달러의 가치 하락을 유도하려 할 수 있습니다. 이는 경제에 큰 영향을 미칠 수 있습니다. 더 나아가, 그는 미국의 부채 문제를 해결하기 위해 디폴트를 고려할 수도 있습니다. 현재 미국의 부채는 36조 달러에 달하며, 이는 중국 경제의 두 배에 해당합니다.

마지막으로, 트럼프가 김정은을 백악관으로 초대할 가능성도 충분히 존재합니다. 이러한 일은 예상치 못한 상황이 될 수도 있지만, 그가 이를 실현할 가능성은 여전히 존재한다고 생각합니다.

이 모든 사항들을 고려할 때, 아시아는 트럼프 2기 정부 하에서 중요한 변화를 겪을 수 있습니다. 저는 정부들이 이에 대비하고 준비하는 것이 중요하다고 생각합니다. 이 시점에서 안전벨트를 매고 준비하는 것이 가장 좋습니다. 제 예측이 틀리기를 바라지만, 그럼에도 불구하고 아시아는 많은 도전에 직면할 것이라고 생각합니다. 감사합니다.


**이종화 교수:** 존경하는 전광우 이사장님과 내외 귀빈 여러분, 오늘 이 자리에 서게 되어 매우 영광입니다. 오늘 저는 최근 미국 대선 결과에 따른 글로벌 경제의 주요 변화에 대해 말씀드리고자 합니다. 긍정적인 의견을 가진 사람들도 있고, 부정적인 의견을 가진 사람들도 있지만, 저는 그 사이에서 현실적인 관점으로 현재 전세계에서 일어나고 있는 일들을 설명하려고 합니다.

우선, 10월에 발표된 IMF의 경제 전망을 바탕으로 글로벌 경제 전망을 살펴보겠습니다. 여러분이 아시다시피, 글로벌 경제는 COVID-19 팬데믹 이후 강한 회복을 보였지만, 그 회복 속도는 이후 다소 둔화되었습니다. IMF의 전망에 따르면, 2025년 글로벌 경제 성장률은 특히 미국에서 둔화될 것으로 보입니다. 그럼에도 불구하고 미국 경제는 여전히 견조한 성장세를 보일 것입니다. 반면, 중국의 경제 성장률은 내년에 다소 둔화될 것으로 예상됩니다.

한편, 인플레이션은 전 세계적으로 둔화하는 추세입니다. 이는 주로 에너지 가격의 하락과 긴축적인 통화정책의 영향 때문입니다. 최근 미국에서는 노동시장 긴축이 인플레이션을 주도하는 주요 원인으로 작용하고 있지만, 에너지 가격 하락으로 그 영향이 일부 상쇄되었습니다. 앞으로는 노동시장 공급이 안정되면서 임금 상승률이 둔화되고, 미국의 인플레이션도 점차 하락할 것으로 예상됩니다.

그런데 2023년 10월 IMF가 미국과 글로벌 경제 연착륙을 전망했을 당시와는 글로벌 경제 여건이 많이 달라졌고, 여러가지 다면적인 충격과 불확실성에 직면해 있습니다. 이제 우리는 도널드 트럼프가 미국 대선에서 승리한 이후, 글로벌 경제가 어떻게 진화할 것인지에 대한 중요한 질문에 직면해 있습니다. 트럼프 당선자는 대선 공약으로 더 높은 관세, 세금 인하, 규제 완화, 금리 인하 등을 포함하는 정책을 추진할 것이라고 밝혔습니다.

이번 대선 결과가 글로벌 금융시장에 미친 영향을 살펴보면, 주식 시장은 기록적인 수준으로 상승했고, 미국 달러화는 급등했으며, 채권 가격은 하락했습니다. 비트코인도 사상 최고치를 기록했습니다. 이러한 움직임은 트럼프 행정부가 시행할 정책들—세금 인하, 규제 완화, 고율 관세—에 대한 기대감에서 비롯되었습니다. 그런데 이는 미국 경제 성장에 대한 낙관적인 전망을 키운 반면, 인플레이션에 대한 우려를 증대시켰습니다. 채권 시장이 이 같은 우려를 대변합니다. 트럼프의 정책이 글로벌 경제에 미칠 영향을 두고 더 많은 불확실성과 위험을 예고하고 있습니다.

그렇다면 우리는 무엇을 주의 깊게 지켜봐야 할까요? 많은 요소가 있지만, 저는 오늘 여러분께 미국의 통화정책에 집중해서 말씀드리겠습니다. 이는 내년 글로벌 경제에 중요한 영향을 미칠 것입니다. 한국은 특히 미국의 금리 정책이 한국의 통화정책과 금융시장에 미치는 영향을 잘 알고 있습니다.

트럼프 2기 행정부는 세금 인하와 세금 개혁, 그리고 관세와 관련된 정책에 집중할 가능성이 큽니다. 이러한 정책은 인플레이션을 높이는 결과를 초래할 수 있습니다. 결과적으로 연준은 금리 인하를 늦추거나 인하 자체를 주저할 가능성이 높습니다. 많은 예측이 있지만, 일부 전문가들은 연준이 트럼프의 경제 정책이 미국 인플레이션에 미치는 구체적인 영향을 확인하면서 금리 인하에 신중을 기할 것이라고 전망하고 있습니다. 과연 연준의 통화정책이 어떻게 전개될지 두고 봐야 할 시점입니다.

현재로서는 내년 글로벌 경제, 미국 경제, 한국 경제가 어떻게 될 것인지 정확히 예측하기는 매우 어렵습니다. 그러나 IMF의 예측을 하나 소개하고자 합니다. IMF의 시뮬레이션은 미국과 글로벌 경제에 대해 하방리스크를 제시합니다. IMF 시뮬레이션은 다섯 가지 주요 충격을 고려하고 있습니다. 첫 번째는 미국 대부분의 수입품에 10%의 관세를 부과하고, 이에 대해 유로 지역과 중국이 보복성 관세를 부과하는 것입니다. 중국은 10%의 추가 관세를 부과할 것으로 보이며, 이는 미국 수출에 큰 영향을 미칠 것입니다.

두 번째는 이로 인한 무역 정책의 불확실성이 증가하는 것입니다. 이는 글로벌 투자에 부정적인 영향을 미칠 것이며, 특히 제조업 분야에서 투자 감소를 초래할 수 있습니다. 세 번째는 사업 소득세를 10년 연장하는 세금 개혁안입니다. 네 번째는 미국과 유럽으로의 이주 흐름 감소입니다. 현재 약 1%로 추정되지만, 이는 상당한 영향을 미칠 수 있습니다. 다섯 번째는 긴축적인 글로벌 금융 환경입니다. 금리 인하 속도 둔화와 함께 국가 및 기업의 부채 프리미엄 상승이 주요 요인입니다.

이 다섯 가지 충격이 결합될 경우, 2025년과 2026년 동안 미국 GDP는 약 0.4% 감소할 것으로 예상됩니다. 중국의 GDP도 0.2~0.3% 감소할 것입니다. 이 다섯 가지 충격이 모두 결합될 경우, 미국 GDP는 약 1% 감소하고, 중국 GDP도 1% 감소하는 결과를 초래할 것입니다. 이는 미국과 중국 경제 모두에게 큰 충격이 될 것입니다. 트럼프 정책이 미국에 긍정적인 영향을 미칠 가능성은 낮고, 중국과의 관계에서 더 큰 부정적인 충격이 예상됩니다. 물론 세금 인하 효과에 따른 긍정적 측면이 이러한 충격을 일부 상쇄할 수 있긴 합니다.

장기적으로 보면, 보호무역주의, 경제적 고립, 경제 분열이 계속될 가능성이 큽니다. 각국은 이러한 경제적 수단을 정치적 동기를 위해 사용할 것입니다. 우리는 지금도 리쇼어링, 자원 확보, 교역 및 금융 흐름의 변화가 일어나고 있음을 목격하고 있습니다. 미국과 중국 간의 무역 및 기술 관련 긴장은 앞으로 더 심화될 것으로 보입니다. 중국은 자국 경제를 되살리려는 노력과 함께, 기술적 자립을 추구할 것입니다. 이는 특히 중요합니다. 중국은 AI 관련 특허 신청 수에서 미국을 추월했습니다. 이는 중국이 AI 부문에서 큰 성과를 올리고 있다는 것을 시사합니다.

결국 두 나라 간의 경제 및 기술적 탈동조화는 더욱 심화될 것이며 중국의 경제 성장률은 계속해서 둔화될 수밖에 없습니다. 인구 감소와 기술적 생산성 향상의 둔화가 주요 요인입니다. 앞으로 몇 년 동안 5% 이상의 성장률을 유지할 수 있을 것으로 보이지만 장기적으로는 성장률이 1~2% 수준으로 낮아질 것입니다.

관건은 미달러의 기축통화 지위가 지속될 수 있을지에 대한 의문입니다. 미달러는 여전히 글로벌 시장에서 중요한 자산으로 간주되고 있지만, 중국과 브릭스(BRICS) 국가들은 미국 달러에 대한 의존도를 줄이기 위한 노력을 기울이고 있습니다. 트럼프 2기 행정부 하에서 미국 달러의 안정성은 약화될 가능성이 높습니다. 이는 달러의 기축통화 지위에 위협을 가할 수 있습니다. 달러의 기축통화 지위가 50% 이하로 떨어질 경우, 그 네트워크 외부성(network externality)이 사라질 수 있습니다. 이러한 변화는 향후 몇 십 년에 걸쳐 일어나겠지만, 달러의 지배력은 점차 감소할 것으로 보입니다.

결론적으로, 트럼프노믹스는 글로벌 경제에 중요한 영향을 미칠 것입니다. 특히 고율의 관세와 세금 인하가 트럼프 2기 초반 충격으로 작용할 것이며, 그 영향은 미국 통화정책과 무역 정책을 통해 전 세계로 확산될 것입니다. 특히 미중 갈등이 어떻게 전개될지, 그리고 그로 인한 한국 경제에 미칠 영향에 대해 지속적으로 주목해야 할 필요가 있습니다. 또한, 미국 달러의 기축통화 지위가 향후 크게 감소할 가능성도 충분히 염두에 두어야 할 것입니다. 경청해 주셔서 감사합니다.

**최병일 교수:** 전체적인 맥락에서 한 걸음 물러서서 보면, 현재 세계적으로 글로벌리스트와 포퓰리스트 간의 중요한 경쟁이 벌어지고 있음을 알 수 있습니다. 이 경쟁에서 포퓰리즘이 2:1로 우세를 보이고 있으며, 이는 2016년 여름의 브렉시트 국민투표와 밀접하게 연결되어 있습니다. 브렉시트와 2016년 도널드 트럼프 대통령 선거를 돌아보면, 이 두 사건은 세계 정치와 정치 경제의 근본적인 변화를 상징한다고 할 수 있습니

다. 많은 분석가들이 이를 '시대정신(zeitgeist)의 변화'로 해석하고 있습니다.

하지만 그럼에도 불구하고, 트럼프 대통령의 경제 정책, 특히 무역 정책은 그의 목표와 완전히 일치하지 않는 부분이 많습니다. 그는 보편적인 관세를 주장하며, 특히 중국에 60%의 고율 관세를 부과해 미국 내 투자와 일자리 창출을 도모하려 했습니다. 그러나 우리의 분석에 따르면, 이러한 접근 방식은 예상한 결과를 가져오지 못한 것으로 보입니다.

그럼에도 불구하고, 저는 트럼프가 미국의 국경을 강화하려는 전략을 계속해서 추진할 것이라고 확신합니다. 그의 무역 정책에서 두 가지 중요한 측면을 짚어보겠습니다. 첫째, 그는 미국 제조업, 특히 자동차 산업의 부흥을 목표로 했습니다. 이는 미국 대선에서 중요한 역할을 하는 분야입니다. 둘째, 그는 중국과의 경제적 결별을 목표로 했습니다. 트럼프는 첫 임기 동안 중국에 대해 관세를 이용해 압박을 가했으나, 그 결과는 엇갈렸고, 코로나19 팬데믹이 그의 임기 말에 발생하면서 결과를 예측하기 어려웠습니다.

결국 트럼프는 '1단계 무역 협정'을 남기고, 더 복잡한 문제는 후속 협상으로 미뤄두었습니다. 제 생각에 2단계 협상은 이루어지지 않을 가능성이 크고, 오히려 트럼프는 중국을 미국 시장에서 더욱 배제할 것입니다. 이런 점을 고려할 때, 한국의 정책 입안자들과 정치인들, 기업 지도자들에게 다음 네 가지 정책 제안을 드리고자 합니다.

먼저 종합적인 협상 전략 수립이 필요합니다. 트럼프는 선거 캠페인에서 방위 예산의 대폭 증액과 무역 적자 문제를 중요 의제로 삼았습니다. 그는 수출을 장려하고 수입은 줄여야 한다고 주장했습니다. 이에 따라, 미국과 큰 무역 적자를 가진 국가들, 특히 자동차 산업에서 적자가 큰 멕시코, 한국, 독일, 일본 등이 주요 타깃이 됩니다. 각 문제를 개별적으로 다룬다면 큰 그림을 놓칠 위험이 있습니다. 따라서 방위와 무역 문제를 연결한 종합적인 협상 전략을 마련하는 것이 중요합니다. 우리는 양보할 준비가 되어 있지만, 그 대가로 반드시 무엇인가를 확보해야 합니다. 예를 들어, 한국과 미국 간의 원자력 협정은 일본에 비해 재처리 문제 등에서 상대적으로 불리합니다. 이는 협상에서 중요한 고려 사항입니다.

두번째는 지속 가능한 투자 전략 채택입니다. 미국에 대규모 투자를 하는 한국 기업들은 트럼프 임기 이후(2025~2028년)에도 지속 가능한 투자 전략을 수립해야 합니다. 특히 배터리, 반도체, 전기차 등 분야의 투자 대부분이 테네시, 오하이오, 노스캐롤라이나 등 공화당 '레드' 지역에 집중되어 있습니다. 연방 정부가 트럼프 행정부에서 체결된 협정을 취소하려 하더라도, 지역 차원의 풀뿌리 정치와 협력하는 것이 중요합니다. 이것이 장기적인 투자 확보와 해당 지역에서 긍정적인 사업 환경을 만드는 데 필수적입니다.

세번째는 인력 개발 및 기술 향상에 주력해야 합니다. 미국에 제조 시설을 설립한 글로벌 CEO들은 숙련된 노동력을 확보하는 데 어려움을 겪고 있습니다. 수년간 미국은 많은 제조업을 동남아시아로 이전했으며, 이제 미국 내 공장을 설립하더라도 고도로 숙련된 노동력을 확보하고 유지하는 데 어려움이 있습니다. 이는 한국 기업과 정책 입안자들이 해결해야 할 문제로, 주법 제정자들에게 노동력 개발을 강화할 것을 요구해야 합니다. 성공적인 시장 진출을 위해서는 현지 노동력을 강화하는 노력이 필요합니다.

네번째는 글로벌 무역 기구의 재구성을 위해 노력해야합니다. 현재 WTO와 같은 기존의 글로벌 무역 기구들이 무역 분야에서 제대로 기능하지 못하고 있다는 점은 이미 잘 알려져 있습니다. 2008년 글로벌 금융

위기 이후 선진국과 신흥국 간의 격차를 좁히기 위해 설립된 G20은 그 목적을 달성하지 못하고, 사실상 사진 촬영을 위한 자리가 되어버렸습니다. 저는 수년간 G7의 재구성을 주장해왔습니다. G7은 과거의 유산이지만, 이제는 그 형식만으로는 효과적이지 않습니다. 한국, 호주, 인도 등을 초대해 G7을 재편성하고, 글로벌 경제의 균형 잡힌 이익을 대표하며, 글로벌 정책을 형성하는 역할을 강화해야 합니다.

이러한 점들을 고려할 때, 우리는 당면한 문제들을 넘어, 더 긴 안목에서 미래를 준비해야 합니다. 위기 속에서도 기회는 존재하며, 역사는 변화를 실현할 용기와 능력을 가진 사람들이 그 기회를 잡고 현실로 만드는 법입니다. 트럼프의 첫 임기 동안, 그는 중국의 고도 기술 분야 부상을 저지하는 데 집중했습니다. 한국은 이를 기회로 삼아 반도체 분야에서 중국에 대한 경쟁 우위를 더욱 강화하고, 전기차와 배터리 기술에서의 최근 어려움을 극복할 수 있는 절호의 기회를 맞이하고 있습니다.

과거 한국은 미국의 안보와 중국의 경제 성장에 의존하는 패러다임을 따랐지만, 이제 그 방식은 더 이상 유효하지 않습니다. 한국은 이제 더 효과적인 동맹을 구축하고, 뜻이 맞는 국가들과의 협력을 강화해야 합니다. 이를 위해 G10과 같은 기존 제도의 개편도 필요합니다. 이를 통해 한국은 변화하는 세계 질서 속에서 경쟁력을 유지하며, 글로벌 무대에서 여전히 중요한 역할을 할 수 있을 것입니다. 감사합니다.

**신성환 위원:** 모든 연사분들 발표 감사드립니다. 이제 제가 몇가지 질문을 드리고자 합니다.

한국과 관련된 내용입니다. 경제 이론에 따르면, 자본은 저성장 국가에서 고성장 국가로 이동한다고 합니다. 즉, 우리의 생산성이 예를 들어 미국보다 낮으면 자본이 한국에서 미국으로 이동하게 되고, 그로 인해 미국 달러는 강세를, 원화는 약세를 보이게 됩니다. 이렇게 되면 수출이 증가하고, 결국 수출 증가로 국내 생산도 늘어나는 구조입니다. 그러나 현실에서는 이와 같은 메커니즘이 제대로 작동하지 않는 것 같습니다. 예를 들어, 일본을 보면, 일본의 잠재 성장률은 지난 30년 동안 미국보다 낮았고 여전히 낮은 수준입니다. 그로 인해 일본 엔화는 약세를 보였고, 일본 중앙은행은 내수 경제가 침체된 상황에서도 금리를 올릴 수 없었습니다.

이러한 상황을 고려할 때, 생산성 향상이 우리 경제 정책의 최우선 목표가 되어야 한다는 점에 전적으로 동의합니다. 이는 현 정부 뿐만 아니라 차기 정부, 그리고 그 이후에도 오랜 시간 동안 중요한 과제가 되어야 할 것입니다. 하지만 이를 달성하는 것은 결코 쉬운 일이 아니며, 생산성을 높이는 중요한 요소 중 하나는 바로 규제 완화입니다. 규제 완화는 트럼프 경제 정책의 핵심 요소 중 하나였습니다.

따라서 저는 한국에서 규제 완화를 어떻게 추진하고, 그 속도를 어떻게 가속화할 수 있을지에 대한 여러분의 의견을 듣고 싶습니다. 우리는 이미 오랜 시간 동안 규제 완화에 대해 이야기해 왔지만, 실질적인 변화로 이어지지는 않았습니다. 이를 어떻게 실현할 수 있을지에 대해 의견을 주시면 감사하겠습니다.

**최병일 교수:** 제가 이 질문에 답할 수 있을 것 같습니다. 10년 전 한국정책연구원장으로 근무할 때, 우리가 마주했던 질문과 똑같은 질문이 여전히 계속해서 반복되고 있습니다. 그리고 조동철 회장님께서 말씀하신 것처럼, 이명박, 박근혜, 문재인, 그리고 현재 윤석열 대통령에 이르기까지, 이 네 차례의 정부는 모두 경제의 강력하고 탄탄한 기반이 없으면 미래가 없다는 점을 제대로 인식하지 못한 채 여러 가지 문제를 해결하지 못한 것 같습니다. 이는 결국 정치적 용기와 관련이 있다고 생각합니다. 제 지인들 중 일부는 트럼프의 당선이 한국에 긍정적인 영향을 미

칠 수 있을 것이라고 이야기했습니다. 왜냐하면 한국은 외부에서 큰 충격을 받았을 때, 갑작스럽게 모든 갈등과 차이를 극복하고 다시 일어설 수 있는 능력을 여러 차례 증명해왔기 때문입니다. 이번에도 그런 일이 일어날 수 있기를 바랍니다.

**신성환 위원:** 감사합니다. 제가 마지막으로 드리고 싶은 질문은, 중국이 향후 부실 자산 문제를 처리할 수 있을지에 관한 것입니다. 중국이 일본의 경로를 따르고 있는 이유 중 하나는, 미국과 달리 일본은 시장 가격을 즉시 반영하지 않고, 그 고통을 시간이 지남에 따라 분산시킨 반면, 미국은 문제를 즉각적으로 해결하고 그에 따른 고통을 비교적 짧은 시간 안에 감내했다는 점입니다. 정치적으로, 자국민에게 고통을 주는 것은 쉽지 않은 일인데요, 중국이 부실 자산 문제를 해결할 수 있을까요? 짧은 시간 안에 모든 부실 자산을 정리할 의지와 능력이 있다고 보시나요?

**니콜라스 라디 박사:** 이 질문은 정말 중요한 질문이라고 생각합니다. 첫 번째 문제는 부실 자산의 규모에 대해 정확한 추정이 어렵다는 점입니다. 중국은 약 20년 전, 은행 시스템에서 부실 자산을 처리하는 데 상당히 성공적이었지만, 현재 부실 자산은 주로 지방정부 금융 차량과 일부 중소형 은행에 쌓여 있습니다. 이 자산의 규모와 품질에 대한 정보는 부족한 상황입니다. 자산의 품질은 천차만별로, 일부는 괜찮지만, 다른 일부는 부채 이자도 감당하기 어려운 상황입니다.

정부는 최근 이 문제를 해결하려는 첫 번째 작은 조치를 발표했습니다. 바로 기존 채권을 상환할 수 있도록 새 채권을 발행하는 것입니다. 새 채권은 금리가 낮고 만기도 길어 지방정부의 채무 부담을 일정 부분 완화할 수 있을 것입니다. 그러나 초기 평가에 따르면, 이 새로운 프로그램이 가져올 구제 효과는 매우 제한적일 것으로 보입니다. 이는 큰 미봉책에 불과하며, 근본적 해결을 위해서는 훨씬 더 많은 노력이 필요할 것입니다.

이 문제는 정치 경제적인 성격도 강합니다. 중앙정부는 지방정부의 미상환 부채에 대해 책임을 지고 싶어하지 않습니다. 지방정부는 1994년 재정 개혁 이후 제한된 재정 자원으로 다양한 사회 프로그램과 투자 프로그램을 수행해야 했기 때문에 많은 차입을 하게 되었습니다. 이로 인해 중앙정부와 지방정부 간에는 큰 갈등이 존재합니다. 지방정부는 결국 중앙정부가 이 부채에 대한 책임을 질 것이라고 보고 있지만, 중앙정부는 이를 피하려고 하고 있습니다. 이 문제는 해결까지 오랜 시간이 걸릴 것으로 보입니다.

만약 경제 성장률이 다시 높아지고, 더 많은 경제 개혁이 이루어진다면 부실 자산을 흡수할 수 있을 것입니다. 그러나 성장률이 계속해서 하락하고, 생산성 증가가 둔화되며 국가와 당의 개입이 더 강화된다면, 이 문제는 더욱 해결하기 어려워지고, 아마도 해결이 불가능할 수도 있습니다.

**윌리엄 페섹 칼럼니스트:** 저도 간단히 첨언하겠습니다. 지난 금요일 이후, 시진핑 주석은 2017년과 마찬가지로 다시 한번 중국을 트럼프 2.0 시대의 세계화 수호자로 자리매김하고자 하고있습니다. 중국이 이제 단순한 주주를 넘어, 세계 금융 시스템의 중요한 이해당사자가 되려는 모습을 보이는 것은 긍정적인 변화입니다. 하지만 저는 시 주석이 세계 경제에서 이해당사자가 되는 것의 비용을 충분히 이해하고 있는지에 대해 의문을 가지고 있습니다.

현재 시 주석은 집권 3기로 마오쩌둥 이후 가장 강력한 중국 지도자로 평가받고 있습니다만, 그가 부동산 위기를 해결할 실현 가능한 계획과 이를 위한 충분한 시간이 있는지 궁금합니다. 디플레이션 문제, 지방정부의 부채 문제가 여전히 해결되지 않고 있는데 이는 2020년 기준으로 이는 일본의 연간 GDP의 두 배에 달합니다. 뿐만 아니라 사상 최악의 청년 실업 문제, 고령화 문제 등 인구 구조 변화에서 오는 구조적 문제를 해결할 정책 수립도 필요합니다.

그런데 실상은 매년 GDP 목표 설정을 위해 결국 인센티브를 왜곡시키는 결과를 낳고있습니다. 국유기업(SOE)에 대한 보조금을 중단하고, 과잉 생산에 따른 디플레 수출 행위를 중지할 계획이 있는지도 궁금합니다. 더 나아가 중국이 더 자신감 있는 국제사회의 리더로서 서고자 하는 계획이 있는지에 대해서도 질문을 던지고 싶습니다.

중국이 인공지능 분야에서 글로벌 리더로 자리 잡으려면, 자국 최고의 혁신가들이 나라를 떠날 위험을 무릅쓰지 않도록 해야 할 것입니다. 또한, 현재 중국의 혁신가들이 글로벌 커뮤니티와 온라인으로 상호작용하며 아이디어를 교환할 수 없는 상황에서, 중국이 어떻게 인공지능 분야에서 선도적인 역할을 할 수 있을지 의문이 듭니다.

마지막으로, 시진핑 주석이 3기 집권 중에 중국 소비자들이 더 많이 소비하고, 덜 저축할 수 있도록 돕는 안전망 시스템을 마련할 충분한 시간이 있을지에 대해서도 고민해 봅니다. 글로벌 경제의 중요한 이해당사자가 되기 위해서는 중국이 최소한 수출과 수입의 균형을 맞추는 적극적 노력을 시작해야 할 필요성이 있습니다.

시진핑 주석은 매우 똑똑하고, 강력한 리더입니다. 트럼프도 그를 매우 높게 평가합니다. 이제 시 주석이 중국을 더 안정적인 기반 위에 올려놓을 전략을 마련할 수 있어야 할 때라고 봅니다. 3기 집권을 하고 있는 만큼 이미 시간을 많이 흘려보냈지만, 아직 늦지 않았다고 생각합니다.

**신성환 위원:** 감사합니다. 훌륭한 강연과 토론에 함께해 주신 모든 연사분들께 진심으로 감사드립니다. 오늘 컨퍼런스가 성공적인 논의의 장이 될 수 있기를 기원합니다. 경청해주셔서 감사합니다.

## 세션 II

# 지속가능성장을 위한 기후금융 및 상생금융의 혁신

**좌장**
홍종호 서울대 환경대학원 교수

**기조연설**
비노드 토마스(Vinod Thomas) Senior Fellow,
Institute of Southeast Asian Studies, Singapore/前 세계은행 수석 부총재
산제이 팻나익(Sanjay Patnaik) Director of the Center on
Regulation and Markets, The Brookings Institution
구본재 Deloitte Consulting 부사장/파트너

**패널**
이형희 SK SUPEX추구협의회 Communication 위원장
이 진 금융감독원 금융시장안정국 국장

**홍종호 교수:** 오늘 컨퍼런스의 두 번째 세션을 시작하겠습니다. 이번 세션은 "지속가능성장을 위한 기후금융 및 상생금융의 혁신"이라는 타이틀과 같이 기후 금융, 포용적 금융, 지속 가능한 성장에 초점을 맞출 예정입니다. 금융은 지속 가능한 경제의 필수적인 부분입니다. 효과적이고 시의적절한 금융이 없다면 혁신이나 투자가 이루어질 수 없고, 결국 지속 가능한 성장을 달성할 수 없습니다.

이 시의적절하고 중요한 주제를 다루기 위해 오늘 세 분의 저명한 연사분들과 세 분의 토론자분들을 모셨습니다.

먼저, 전 세계은행 수석 부총재를 지내신 비노드 토마스 박사님의 기조연설을 듣겠습니다. 현재는 싱가포르 소재 동남아시아 연구소 선임 연구원으로 활발히 활동하고 계십니다. 토마스 박사님을 박수로 환영해 주십시기 바랍니다.

**비노드 토마스 박사:** 다시 만나 뵙게 되어 반갑습니다. 그리고 오늘 이 귀한 자리에 초청해주신 전광우 이사장님께 감사드립니다. 오늘은 효율적인 발표를 위해 파워포인트를 보면서 4가지 요점에 대해 말씀드리겠습니다.

### A Super Wicked Problem

1. State of Play
2. Ramp up Climate Finance
3. Complement with Carbon Pricing
4. A Proactive Central Bank

기후 변화는 사실 많은 부분이 한국을 포함한 전 세계 사람들에게 이제 매우 친숙합니다. 그런데 중요한 것은 기후 변화 관련 어떠한 일이 벌어지고 있는지 현실을 제대로 인식하는 것이 중요합니다. 이것이 오늘 제가 말씀드리고자 하는 첫번째 요점입니다.

**The Wild Card: US Elections and Fallacy of Composition**

- Trump rollbacks would add 4 billion metric tons of carbon dioxide emissions by 2030, the annual emissions of Japan plus EU (Carbon Brief).
- Universal tariffs on all imports from all countries, with a 60% rate on China will provoke retaliatory tariffs, inflation and little room for climate investments.
- If following the US, India burns more coal, oil and gas, and Russia, Brazil, Indonesia, the Middle East—and South Korea—do the same, carbon emissions will approach 430 ppm, temperatures exceed 2 degrees and derail economic growth.

그 중에서도 중요한 것은 기후 변화에 대한 미국의 정책의 영향력이 압도적이라는 점입니다. '프로젝트 2025' 문서에 등장한 정책들을 감안한다면 미국의 탄소 배출량은 매년 증가할 것이며 이는 유럽연합과 일본을 합친 수준을 넘어설 것입니다. 이러한 상황이 되면 한국을 비롯한 다른 국가들이 아무리 탄소중립을 위한 정책을 현실적으로 달성한다고 해도 효과를 보지 못할 것입니다. 미국의 탄소 배출량 증가가 그만큼 막대한 수준이기 때문이며, 전 세계에는 재앙이 닥칠 수 있습니다.

미국이 배출량을 늘리면 인도, 인도네시아, 러시아, 브라질 등이 따라서 배출량을 늘릴 것입니다. 관세도 마찬가지입니다. 한 국가가 탄소 배출량과 관세를 인상하면 전 세계적인 문제로 이어집니다. 단순히 한 국가가 배출량을 늘리고 관세를 늘리면 자국 산업에는 도움이 될 것이라고 생각할 수 있지만, 결국 다른 나라들도 같은 행보를 보일 경우 "구성의 오류"로 인해 모두에게 부정적인 결과에 직면하게 됩니다. 현실적으로 생각할 필요가 있습니다.

## 1. State of Play: Record Emissions and Temperatures

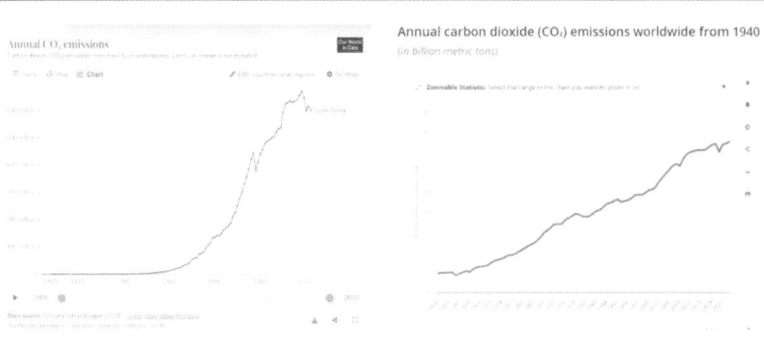

보시는 바와 같이 탄소 배출량은 꾸준히 증가하고 있습니다. 한국의 경우도 배출량이 20~30년 동안 계속해서 증가해왔지만 지난 몇 년 동안은 대폭 감소하는 모습을 보이고 있습니다. 물론 한국은 여전히 세계에서 13번째로 큰 탄소 배출국입니다. 따라서 오늘 우리가 말하는 모든 내용은 한국의 정책 결정과 매우 밀접한 관련이 있습니다.

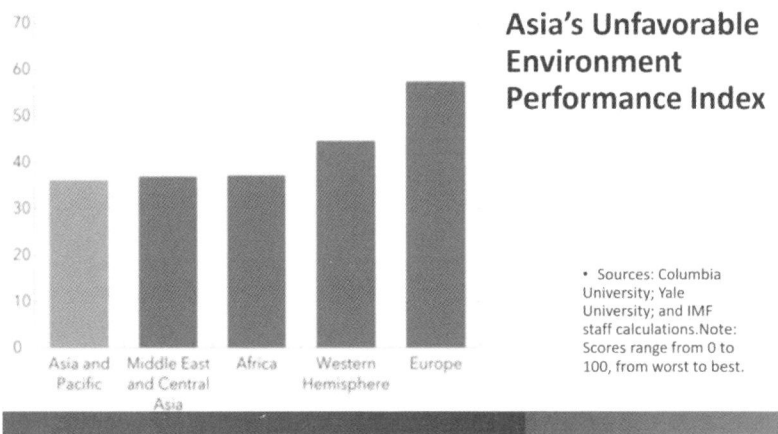

다음 슬라이드에서는 아시아 태평양 국가들이 다른 지역에 비해 환경 보호와 관련해서는 크게 잘 하고 있는 점이 없다는 것을 알 수 있습니다. 동아시아가 이뤄낸 기적과도 같은 경제 성장은 대단한 업적이지만 그에 비해 환경보호 측면에서는 유럽이나 서구에 비해 상대적으로 뒤처져 있습니다. 시간이 얼마 남지 않은 만큼 우리는 경제적 성장뿐 아니라 환경을 보호하며 지속가능한 성장을 이어가기 위한 자격을 갖추어야 합니다.

다음은 한국의 기후 프로필에 대해 말씀드리겠습니다. 여기 계신 분들은 잘 알고계시겠지만, 슬라이드의 두번째 불릿을 보시면 한국 탄소배출의 40%가 전력 생산 과정에서 나오고, 26%가 산업, 18% 가 교통 관련 부문에서 탄소가 배출되고 있습니다. 따라서 해당 부문의 배출량 저감을 위한 조치가 필요하다는 점을 강조하고 싶습니다.

하지만 각 부문에서 $CO_2$를 줄이기 위한 제약 조건이 상당히 뚜렷하다는 것을 알고 계실 겁니다. 그리고 정치, 경제와 심지어 문화적인 측면에도 영향을 미치기 때문에 각기 다른 도전 과제를 안고 있습니다. 그럼에도 불구하고 저는 외부인으로서 한국이 과연 석탄에 세금을 부과하고 풍력, 태양광 등 한국이 가능성이 높은 재생에너지와 향후 수소를 급격하게 늘리는 것이 우선순위가 될 수 있는지 묻고 싶습니다.

다음으로 기후 금융과 관련하여 한 가지 요점을 말씀드리고 싶습니다. 파이낸싱이 매우 중요하지만 기술도 마찬가지입니다. 사람들이 이 문제를 최우선 과제로 인식한다면 기후 문제를 해결하기 위한 기술적 도전을 위한 자금 조달은 자연스럽게 따라올 것입니다. 코로나19 당시를 떠올려 보세요. 전세계 모든 사람들이 이 문제를 최우선 과제로 여겼기 때문에 코로나 19 대응을 위해 단 1년 만에 19조 달러를 모을 수 있었습니다. 기후 변화 대응을 위한 자금 조달, 기술의 혁신, 그리고 이를 실현하기 위한 기술들 모두 매우 중요합니다.

## Financing to Avert a Catastrophe

- An estimate to avert a 2°C global warming is around US$ 5 trillion annually through 2030.
- Asia's financing gap is some US$600 billion a year for mitigation, and US$200 billion a year for adaptation, most public but private approaching 40%.
- A huge role of top-down financing must be complemented by a bottom-up process.
- Financing and technology will follow if but only if public sentiment calls for climate action.

(Recall US$ 15 trillion was raised in 2020 to fight COVID-19).

하지만 기후 금융에 우선순위를 두지 않는 한, 이러한 가정은 성립하지 않을 수 있습니다. 일례로 이번 미국 선거에서는 이 문제가 전혀 논의되지 않았습니다. 젊은 세대조차도 마찬가지였습니다. 따라서 한 가지 중요한 점은 하향식 및 상향식 금융이 필수적이라는 것입니다. 우리는 현재 하향식 접근 방식에 대해 많이 논의하고 있습니다. 이는 코로나19 모델과 유사합니다. 하지만 상향식 접근 방식은 마찬가지로 중요합니다.

왜냐하면 디지털 혁명에 이미 수조 달러가 투자되었기 때문입니다. 정책적으로 디지털 금융이나 인터넷 투자를 늘려야 한다는 논의는 전혀 없었음에도 불구하고 많은 혁신은 크라우드소싱을 통해 자금을 모으거나, 배당금을 얻기 위해 자금을 투자하는 방식을 통해 이루어졌습니다. 이것은 기술 세계에서 비롯된 것으로, 사람들이 이것이 경제 성장과 일치하며 경제 성장에 해로운 것이 아니라고 믿기 때문에 가능했습니다.

기후 변화는 불행히도 스펙트럼의 잘못된 쪽에 위치해 있습니다. 사람들은 이것이 지속 가능한 발전에 해로운 것이라고 잘못 생각합니다. 따라서 이 문제는 금융과 관련되어 있지만, 정보 확산과 사람들의 인식 변화를 이끌어내는 것이 우리가 직면한 가장 중요한 과제라고 말할 수 있습니다. 기후 금융에 우선순위를 두는 사고방식의 전환이 없다면 기후 대응을 위해 코로나 때와 같은 수준의 발빠른 광범위한 대응을 기대하기란 어려울 수 있습니다.

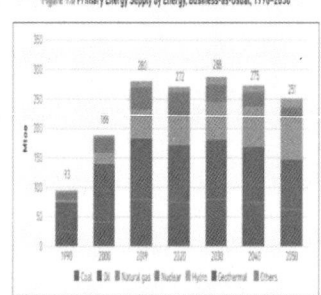

한국의 경우 다시 한번 강조하자면 해상 풍력 터빈, 태양열, 그리고 친환경 수소와 같은 재생에너지 확대가 핵심이 될 수 있습니다. 싱가포르는 에너지의 96%를 화석 연료에서 얻으면서도 2050년에 탄소 배출량을

제로로 만들겠다는 매우 야심찬 계획을 세우고 있는 데요, 핵심은 수소입니다. 하루빨리 실현될 수 있기를 바라는데, 한국에서도 가능한 시나리오일지 의문입니다.

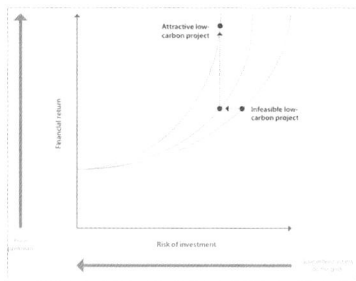

**HOW TO AUGMENT RENEWABLES**
Creating attractive risk/reward profiles for green investment

이 슬라이드는 우리가 직면한 문제를 명확히 보여줍니다. 즉, 태양광, 풍력 등 재생에너지에 투자할 경우 투자 위험이 너무 높고, 다른 축의 수익률은 너무 낮다는 점입니다. 따라서 수익률을 높이고 위험을 줄여야 합니다. 만약 우리가 이른바 '부정적 외부성'을 논의한다면, 이는 나쁜 경제학이 아니라 좋은 경제학입니다. 사회가 개인의 이익을 합친 것보다 더 많은 이익을 얻는다면 재생에너지에 보조금을 지원하는 것은 잘못된 것이 아닙니다.

# PRINCIPLES FOR AUGMENTING RENEWABLES

Creating attractive risk/reward profiles for green investment

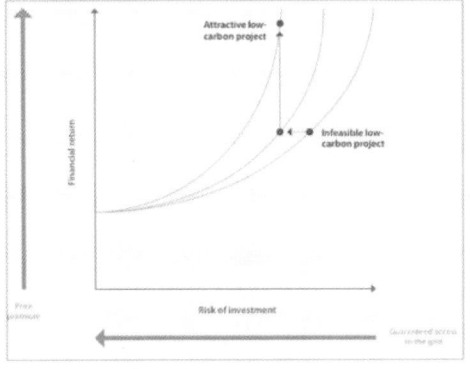

여기서 질문은 한국에서 관세나 요금을 재도입할 수 있느냐의 여부인데, 왜 안되겠습니까? 이는 좋은 경제 정책입니다. 예산 균형을 맞추는 데 따른 재정적 문제 등이 있을 수 있지만, 이 슬라이드는 다시 한번 재생에너지에 대한 두 가지 접근 방식이 필요하다는 점을 강조하고 있습니다.

## 2. Climate Finance: US$5 TR a Year (5% of GDP)?

Janak Raj & Rakesh Mohan 2024 "An Assessment of Climate Finance" a CSEP paper.

Table 1: Climate Finance Requirements - Key Global and EME Estimates

| S.No. | Source | Annual climate finance requirement (USD trillion) | Cumulative climate finance requirement (USD trillion) | Target year | Objective/Scenario | Sectors included |
|---|---|---|---|---|---|---|
| 1 | Bhattacharya et al. (2016) | 5.4 | 80 | 2030 | Paris Agreement goals (Global) | Power, transport, water and waste, and telecommunications |
| 2 | New Climate Economy (2016) | 6 | 90 | 2030 | Paris Agreement goals (Global) | Urban, transport, water, telecommunications, and energy systems |
| 3 | OECD (2018) | 6.9 | 104 | 2030 | Paris Agreement goals (Global) | Energy, transport, building, and water |
| 4 | IPCC (2018) | 2.4 | 48 | 2035 | 1.5°C temperature goal (Global) | Energy related |
| 5 | IEA (2021) Bouckaert et al. | 5 | 50 | 2030 | Net zero emissions by 2050 scenario (Global) | Energy |
| 6 | Grantham Research Institute (2021) Turner et al. | 7.4-7.9 | 74-79 | 2030 | Global | Energy, transport, water and sanitation, and telecom |
| 7 | Bhattacharya et al. (2022) | Additional 1.3 / 3.5 | Additional 7 / 35 | 2025 / 2030 | Net zero transition and climate resilience (EMDCs excluding China) | Human capital, sustainable infrastructure, agriculture forestry and other land use (AFOLU), and adaptation and resilience |
| 8 | Songwe et al. (2022) | 2-2.8 | 20-28 | 2030 | 1.5°C temperature goal (EMDCs excluding China) | Energy system, loss and damage, adaptation and resilience, natural capital, and mitigating methane emissions |

이번 세션에서 포용적이고 지속 가능한 금융에 대해 논의하고 있는데, 전 세계적인 상황을 살펴보면 우리가 익숙한 'B'로 표시되는 수십억

달러 단위가 이제는 'T'로 표시되는 수조 달러 단위로 급증하고 있습니다. 이 슬라이드는 아시아개발은행(ADB)을 위해 작성된 자료를 요약한 내용입니다. 보시면 기후 금융을 위해서는 연간 5조 달러가 향후 10년간 필요할 것으로 추정됩니다. 아제르바이잔에서 진행 중인 COP29에서는 7조 달러를 언급하고 있습니다.

그런데, 현재 단계에서는 5조 달러를 조달할 수 있다면 합리적이라고 생각하지만, 아직 이 또한 실현 가능성은 요원합니다. 7조 달러에 있어서 핵심 질문은 '증가분(incremental)', 즉, 국가가 저축과 투자를 그 만큼 늘려야 한다는 의미인가의 여부인데요. 만약 그렇다면 현실적으로 실현되기 어려울 것입니다. 전쟁을 포함한 수많은 다른 문제들이 존재하기 때문입니다. 화석 연료 대체만을 의미한다면 논의할 수는 있습니다. 하지만 재생 에너지가 화석 연료를 대체할까요? 현재로서는 그럴 듯 해보이지 않고 주요국들은 현재 그럴 계획이 없습니다. COP29 당사국인 아제르바이잔도 많은 화석 연료 계약을 체결하고 있기 때문에 화석 연료는 감소가 아니라 증가할 것입니다. 문제가 있습니다.

### Right and Wrong Climate Finance

- Global climate finance flows were US$803 billion per year in 2019-2020.
- Most finance in 2019–2020 went to renewable energy (US$336 billion per year) and sustainable transport (US$169 billion). Agriculture, forestry and other land use were only US$16.5 billion.
- But US$892 billion a year went to fossil fuels, US$450 billion to fossil fuel subsidies and US$1.89 trillion to ecologically harmful subsidies.

https://www.lse.ac.uk/granthaminstitute/explainers/what-is-climate-finance-and-where-will-it-come-from/

그런데 여기서 명확히 해야할 것은 우리가 필요로 하는 좋은 기후금융이 있는 반면, 피해야 할 나쁜 금융도 있다는 사실입니다. 국제통화기금(IMF)에 따르면, 이러한 나쁜 금융에 최근 몇 년간 10조 달러 넘는 자금이 동원되었습니다. 작년에도 5조 달러가 투입된 것으로 추정되었습니다. 여기서 말하는 '나쁜, 잘못된 자금 조달'은 화석 연료에 대한 보조금을 의미합니다. 즉, 매우 엄격한 경제학자라면 경제학 101에서 배운 것과 정반대의 일을 하고 있는 것입니다. 나쁜 것에 세금을 부과하고 좋은 것을 보조하는 대신, 좋은 것에 세금을 부과하고 나쁜 것을 보조하고 있습니다. IMF의 추산은 명확히 말해 건강 영향을 포함하기 때문에 개인적이 아닌 사회적 비용을 의미합니다. 만약 사적 비용이라면 5000억 달러를 넘는 수준일 것입니다.

Global Innovative Approaches

- ADB: Innovative Finance Facility to leverage balance sheets via guarantees; an Energy Transition Mechanism to help phase out coal through guarantees.
- The World Bank: Development Policy Loans tackling climate change; green bond funds to leverage private capital, for example, the Climate-Amundi $2 billion.
- Climate Funds: The GCF in Songdo especially for the Pacific islands.

한편, 재정 지원을 논의할 때에는 다양한 형태의 재정 지원을 층별 접근 방식으로 결합해야 합니다. 재생에너지에 적합하지 않은 단순한 부채와 자본 투자에는 시의적 ADB의 예시 중 일부를 보시면, 에너지 전환 메커니즘이 있습니다. 보증을 통해 재무제표를 활용하는 것은 당연한 선택처럼 들립니다. 재무 상태가 건실하다면, 왜 그 자원을 활용해 불확실한 상황에 처한 이들을 지원하고 보증하지 않을까요? 바로 이것이 ADB가 시도하고 있는 것입니다.

세계은행의 그린 본드도 증가하고 있습니다. 하지만 전체적인 맥락에서 보면 여전히 미미한 수준입니다. 그리고 한국 송도에 본사를 두고 있는 기후 기금(GCF)는 태평양 섬 국가들과 보조금 대출에 의존해야 할 국가들에게 특별한 의미를 지니고 있습니다. 적절하고 목적에 맞는 재정 지원이 보완되어야 합니다.

### South Korea's Climate Finance

- Launched the green finance scheme in 2009, a disclosure system in 2013, and ETS in 2015.
- SK has committed to carbon neutrality by 2050 but needs far stronger climate finance.
- Five financial institutions, including the KDB, have pledged 420 trillion won ($313 billion) in loans for decarbonization.
- KDB and others will establish a 9 trillion won ($8 billion) fund for new green energy facilities.
- 70% of GHG emissions are subject to the ETS, with a rising share of auctioning, with a modest impact.

현재 한국의 경우, 매우 중요한 여러 가지 이니서티브가 진행 중이라는 점을 강조하고자 합니다. 2025년 탄소 중립 목표를 달성하는 것뿐 아니라, 이를 2045년으로 앞당길 수 있기를 희망합니다. 재생에너지로 이를 추진하는 것은 한국에 좋고, 세계에도 이롭습니다. 또한 산업은행의 녹색 에너지 시설에 대한 자금 조달 확대 노력과 배출권 거래 제도(ETS)도 중요합니다.

ETS에 대해 잠시 설명드리자면, 이는 자금 조달의 보완 수단입니다. 간단히 말해, 배출과 같은 부정적인 요소에 가격을 매기는 것입니다. 우선 배출량에 세금을 부과하는 것이 가장 간단합니다. 저는 세금에 찬성하지만 원칙적으로 상한선이 있고 그 안에서 원하는 것을 하고 거래할 수 있다고 말하는 거래인 ETS에 찬성합니다. 한국은 이미 그렇게 하고 있고 여러 면에서 다른 나라보다 앞서 있습니다.

## 3. Carbon Pricing: Far Greater Ambition

- Three ways: (i) carbon tax, as in Japan and Singapore; (ii) emission trading system, as in Korea and China; (iii) an import tariff on the carbon content as EU is proposing.
- Some 46 countries price carbon, covering 30% of GHGs and at an average price of only US$6 a ton of carbon, but ranging from Japan's US$2.65 a ton of $CO_2$ to Denmark's US$165 (2030).
- EU, British Columbia, Canada, and Sweden show emission response and net benefits, but this needs strong pricing and complementary investments.
- IMF's has a sound proposal for price floors of US$75, US$50, and US$25 per ton of carbon for the US, China, and India which countries can apply using existing fiscal arrangements.
- Australia illustrates the power of special interests: a conservative government repealed the 2012 tax two years after it was instituted.

배출량이 많은 수입품에 관세를 부과하는 방법도 있습니다. 이에 대해서는 장단점을 길게 논의할 수 있습니다. 한국을 포함한 모든 국가가 그렇게 할 수 있다고 생각하며, 가장 좋은 시나리오는 이미 ETS를 하고 있거나 탄소세를 하고 있기 때문에 아무도 세금을 내지 않는 것입니다. 제가 탄소세를 찬성하는 이유는 경매를 통하지 않고도 쉽게 세수를 확보할 수 있고, 이를 기후 변화와 관련된 사회 보장에 사용할 수 있기 때문입니다.

Economists' Preferred Solution

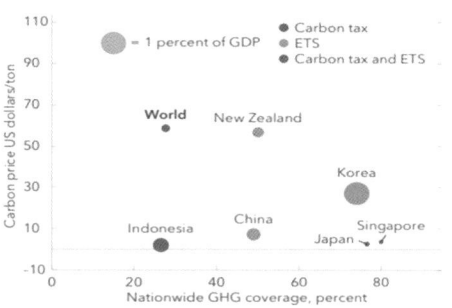

**Figure 10. Asia-Pacific: Carbon Pricing**
*(Bubble size shows value of pricing initiative)*

Source: Parry, Black, and Zhunussova (2022).
Note: The figure shows only countries that have implemented carbon pricing schemes. Bubbles denote government revenues in percent of GDP and linked to the respective carbon pricing initiative for the country. ETS = emissions trading system;

이 슬라이드는 IMF자료를 보여주는데요. 현재의 상황을 잘 요약해줍니다. 한국은 우측 아래에 위치해 있는 데요. 온실가스 배출량이 상당하고 배출 부문별 커버리지도 우수하다고 표시되어 있습니다. 매우 중요한 위치를 차지하고 있는 것입니다. 전국적인 배출량 커버리지가 높으며, 싱가포르와 일본과 유사합니다. 하지만 탄소 가격은 뉴질랜드에 비해 상대적으로 낮습니다. 그런데, 다양한 시나리오를 가정해 보면 커버리지가 매우 높지만 탄소 가격이 낮으면 효과적이지 않을 수 있습니다. 반대로 커버리지가 매우 낮고 탄소 가격이 높으면 역시 효과적이지 않습니다.

따라서 북동쪽에 위치하는 것이 바람직합니다. 제 개인적인 의견으로는 한국이 이를 실현할 수 있는 국가 중 하나입니다. 한국은 자체 이익을 위해 동북쪽 사분면에 위치할 수 있습니다. 뉴질랜드, 카자흐스탄, 한국, 중국을 비교할 때, 한국은 배출권 거래 제도와 관련된 여러 지표에서 유리한 방향으로 강하게 나타납니다.

## 4. Central Bank: Disengaged to Proactivity

- Price signals and low real interest rates needed to boost clean energy, grid replacement and battery storage.
- Actual incentives, however, are perverse: fossil fuel subsidies (figure); CBs having to raise interest rates; falling clean energy/oil & gas price index.
- Extreme natural disasters and reduced demand encourage higher savings and *lower* real interest rate.
- But mounting disasters and disaster policies *raise* real interest rates.

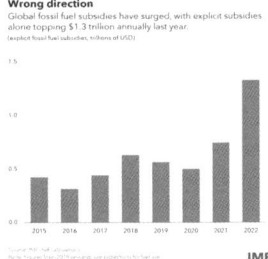

**Wrong direction**
Global fossil fuel subsidies have surged, with explicit subsidies alone topping $1.3 trillion annually last year.
(explicit fossil fuel subsidies, trillions of USD)

IMF

　마지막으로 가장 중요한 점은, 이 모든 과정에서 우리는 다음과 같은 질문을 던져야 한다는 것입니다: 금융 부문이 민간 부문이 개별적으로 할 수 있는 것을 넘어 어떻게 도움을 줄 수 있을까요? 이 질문을 제기하는 이유는 부정적 외부성(negative externality) 때문입니다. 슬라이드를 보시면 제가 언급한 위험과 보상 때문에 자금 조달이 제약받는 경우, 이는 통화 정책 결과의 한 부분입니다. 따라서 이러한 관점에서는 중앙은행이 덜 관여하는 것보다 더 관여하는 것이 합리적입니다. 중앙은행의 독립성이 훼손되지 않는 경우라면 중앙은행은 관여할 필요가 있습니다. 기후금융과 관련하여 중앙은행의 관여와 독립성은 서로 반대되지 않습니다. 따라서 중앙은행이 탈탄소화를 위한 공정한 경쟁 환경을 적극적으로 지원해야 합니다. 방어적 접근도 필요한데, 한국은 현재 다양한 공개 감독 및 위험 관리 메커니즘을 갖추고 있습니다.

**Defensive: Disclosures, Risks & Oversight**

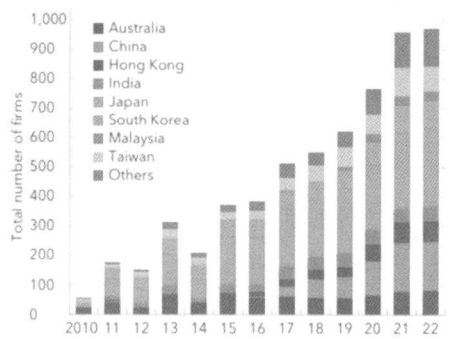

1. Asia-Pacific Firms Reporting Carbon Emissions
(Number of firms)

Sources: Capelle and others 2023 based on data from ICE Data Service

**Proactive: Interest Rates & Green Finance**

- Extreme heat and rainfall contributed to 10% of SK's inflation in 2023, while reducing industrial growth by 0.6 % points (BoK).
- Physical risks raise the default probability of the credit portfolios.
- Can Bok support proactive steps to level the playing field for decarbonization, while maintaining independence.
- For example, include green finance intermediary loans, climate impact assessments for collateral and green bond purchases in monetary policy.

이제 이 슬라이드를 보여드리면서 저의 발표를 마치고자 합니다. 우리는 기후 금융을 위해 많은 투자가 필요하며, 이를 위해 디지털 분야와 마찬가지로 상향식 및 하향식 자금 조달이 필요합니다. 한국은 이 두 가지를 결합하는 매우 유리한 위치에 있으며, 이는 한국의 복지뿐만 아니라 순수한 경제 성장에도 긍정적인 영향을 미칠 것입니다. 감사합니다.

**홍종호 교수:** 토마스 박사님, 훌륭한 발표 감사합니다. 이제 제가 한 가지 질문을 드리겠습니다. 2년 전 제가 인도의 한 대학에서 학부생들을 대상으로 강의를 했을 때, 강의가 끝난 후 세 명의 학생이 저에게 질문을 했는데 모두 똑같은 내용의 질문이었습니다. 그들은 우리가 직면한 기후 위기는 인도의 책임이 아니라, 오히려 미국과 유럽 등 선진국의 책임이라고 주장했습니다. 그들은 선진국들의 재정적 지원과 기술 이전이 없다면, 현재 경제 성장에 집중하고 있는 인도에 배출량 감축에 대한 인센티브나 의지가 없다고 강조했습니다.

아제르바이잔에서 기후 금융과 기후 기금 설립에 관한 주제를 다루는 제29차 유엔기후변화협약 당사국 총회(COP29)에 대해 언급하셨습니다. 트럼프 대통령이 재집권 할 정치 상황을 고려할 때, 선진국들이 기후 변화에 대처하는 데 있어 인도와 같은 개발도상국을 지원할 수 있는 기금을 조성하고 자금을 조달할 수 있는 가능성을 얼마나 된다고 보시나요?

**비노드 토마스 박사:** 아주 간단하게 답변을 드려야 할까요? 이 질문은 매우 광범위합니다. 인도는 1인당 국민소득이 한국의 극히 일부에 불과하지만, 총 소득은 한국보다 훨씬 높기 때문에 탄소 배출량이 많습니다. 인도는 1인당 또는 GDP 기준이 아니라 총 배출량 기준으로 세계에서 세 번째로 큰 배출국입니다. 따라서 인도와 중국이 온실가스 감축에 나서지 않는다면, 모든 것이 끝날 것입니다. 선진국들의 개도국 지원을 위한 기금 조성 등의 노력은 기대할 수 없게 될 것이라는 말입니다.

그러나 이 대화의 핵심은 완화(mitigation)와 적응(adaptation)입니다. 완화는 추가적인 피해를 방지하는 것을 의미하는 반면, 적응은 더 나은 방법으로 그 피해를 받아들이는 것을 의미합니다. 인도는 상대적으로 완화보다는 적응에 더 중점을 두고 있습니다. 제가 가르치는 수업에서도 이 주제가 자주 등장합니다. 적응을 지지하는 사람들은 완화보다 적응을 우선시하는 경향이 있습니다.

그런데 완화 조치에 대한 더 강력한 행동을 촉발할 수 있었던 한 가지 요인은 바로 재정 문제였습니다. 그리고 이것이 바로 아제르바이잔의 상황이 중요해질 수 있는 이유입니다. 아제르바이잔의 상황은 주로 석유 이익에 의해 좌우되기 때문입니다. 미국은 2025년에는 완화 조치에 초점을 맞추지 않고 그 반대 방향으로 나아갈 것이라는 점을 공식화했는데, 이는 인도가 완화 대신 적응을 우선시 하게하는 그럴듯한 구실을 만들 수 있는 좋은 핑계가 됩니다. 미국이 완화 조치를 취하지 않는다면 인도는 자국 경제 성장을 희생하면서 완화 조치에 나서지 않을 것입니다.

힘든 상황이지만, 저는 낙관적입니다. 민간 부문이 중요한 역할을 할 것이라고 믿습니다. 그들이 태양열과 풍력 에너지를 확장한다면, 배출량을 압도할 수 있는 수준으로 비용을 낮출 수 있을 것입니다.

**홍종호 교수:** 감사합니다. 다음으로 두 번째 연사인 브루킹스 연구소의 규제 및 시장 센터 소장인 산제이 팻나익 박사를 소개합니다.

**산제이 팻나익 박사:** 안녕하세요. 오늘 직접 참석하지 못해 아쉽지만, 이렇게 화상으로나마 여러분과 함께하게 되어 기쁩니다.

미국의 새 행정부 출범으로 미국과 그 행정부가 세계 기후 정책에 미칠 영향에 많은 관심이 쏠리고 있습니다. 저는 리더십의 변화에도 불구하고 여전히 관련성이 있을 것으로 생각되는 세 가지 영역과 이 영역을 활용하여 기후 위기를 해결할 수 있는 방법에 초점을 맞추고자 합니다.

첫 번째 영역은 기후와 AI의 교차점입니다. 이것은 혁신의 관점과 에너지 소비의 관점에서 점점 더 중요한 주제가 되고 있습니다. 기후와 AI는 두 가지 방식으로 검토할 수 있습니다. 첫째, AI와 데이터 센터의 에너지 소비를 살펴보고 이것이 탈탄소화에 어떤 영향을 미칠지. 둘째, AI가 기후 변화 완화와 적응에 어떻게 도움이 될 수 있는지 검토하는 것입니다.

**AI and climate – energy demand**

- Energy use

    - Energy trends:
        - Energy efficiency improvements
        - Tech companies' renewable energy purchases
        - Decarbonization of grids

    - AI expected to increase energy demand
        - AI data centers are big consumers of energy
        - Data center power demand estimated to grow 160% by 2030

BROOKINGS

에너지 측면에서는 미국이 특히 바이든의 정책 하에서 탈탄소화를 향한 강력한 변화를 경험했습니다. 많은 기술 회사들이 재생 에너지에 막대한 투자를 하고 있으며, 전력망의 탈탄소화 추세가 있습니다. 그러나 이로 인해 특히 재생 에너지에 대한 에너지 수요가 증가했습니다. 동시에, 미국 전역, 특히 워싱턴 D.C. 인근에 AI 데이터 센터가 등장하고 있습니다. 예를 들어, 버지니아에는 새로운 데이터 센터가 많이 생겨나고 있으며, 이 데이터 센터들은 막대한 양의 에너지를 소비하고 있습니다. 데이터 센터 전력 수요는 2030년까지 크게 증가할 것으로 예상됩니다.

여기서 문제는 탈탄소화와 AI 데이터 센터의 급속한 성장이라는 두 가지 트렌드 사이의 충돌입니다. 에너지 공급이 그에 맞춰 증가하지 않으면, 이로 인해 가격이 상승하게 되고, 이는 기후 정책의 수용을 약화시킬 수 있습니다.

## AI and climate – demand for renewables

- Tech companies – major purchasers of renewable energy
    - Amazon, Microsoft, Meta, Google: 4 largest purchasers, equal to ~Sweden's generation capacity

- Incentives:
    - Protect against power price variability
    - Reduce environmental impact
    - Improve brand reputation

- Challenge: variability in wind/solar sources, energy demand

BROOKINGS

재생 에너지 수요를 살펴보면, 아마존, 마이크로소프트, 메타, 구글과 같은 거대 기술 기업들이 미국 재생 에너지 시장의 주요 주자로 자리매김하고 있음을 알 수 있습니다. 이 회사들은 스웨덴의 전체 발전 용량에 해당하는 에너지를 구매했습니다. 그들은 가격 변동에 대한 보호, 환경 영향 감소, 브랜드 평판 향상 등 에너지를 확보하기 위한 강력한 인센티브를 가지고 있습니다.

그러나 그들은 풍력 및 태양열의 변동성, 그리고 증가하는 수요를 충족하기 위해 고군분투하고 있는 에너지 공급의 현실로 인해 어려움을 겪고 있습니다. 예를 들어, 마이크로소프트는 최근 한 에너지 회사와 계약을 맺고 수십 년 전 심각한 원자력 재해의 현장인 스리마일 섬 원자력 발전소를 복원하기로 했습니다. 이 계약은 일부 회사들이 얼마나 신뢰할 수 있는 에너지를 갈망하고 있는지를 보여줍니다.

**AI and climate – mitigation and adaptation**

- Harnessing AI for combating climate change

- Digitalization of energy sector
    - Improve reliability of grids
    - Improve efficiency

- Predictions and tracking
    - Weather events
    - Deforestation

- But: fundamental challenges of climate change remains

BROOKINGS

반대로, AI는 기후 변화를 완화하고 적응할 수 있는 큰 잠재력을 가지고 있습니다. 저는 이와 관련하여 AI의 가능성에 대해 진심으로 기대하고 있습니다. 에너지와 같은 분야에서 혁신적인 AI 응용 프로그램이 그리드 신뢰성과 효율성을 향상시키는 데 사용되고 있습니다. AI를 사용하여 극단적인 기상 현상을 예측하는 회사도 등장하고 있습니다. 일부 회사는 최대 6개월 전에 기상 현상을 예측할 수 있어 공급망 및 위치 계획에 획기적인 역할을 하고 있습니다.

AI는 종종 위성 이미지와 결합하여 삼림 벌채 문제를 해결하는 데 사용되고 있습니다. 재료 과학 분야에서 AI는 더 나은 배터리와 같은 새로운 기술을 개발하는 데 중요한 역할을 할 수 있습니다. 기후 변화의 근본적인 문제는 여전히 남아 있지만, 저는 AI가 엄청난 잠재력을 가지고 있다고 생각합니다.

**Carbon pricing**

- US: only G7 country without national carbon tax or cap-and-trade system
- 12 US states operate their own cap-and-trade programs
- Unsuccessful attempts - national carbon pricing bills
- Inflation Reduction Act: "carrots"

BROOKINGS

제가 다루고 싶은 두 번째 영역은 토마스 씨가 이미 언급한 탄소 가격 책정과 탄소 관세입니다. 이는 2026년부터 탄소 국경 조정 메커니즘(CBAM)을 시행하기로 한 유럽연합(EU)의 결정을 고려할 때 특히 관련이 있습니다. EU는 이미 데이터를 수집하고 방법론을 개선하기 위한 시범 프로그램을 운영하고 있습니다. CBAM은 EU 외부의 기업들이 자국에서 EU와 동등한 탄소 가격을 책정했음을 증명하거나 국경에서 EU의 탄소 가격을 지불해야 한다는 것을 의미합니다. 이는 한국을 포함한 다른 국가들 사이에서 우려를 불러일으키고 있는데, 수출에 영향을 미칠 것이기 때문입니다.

미국을 살펴보면, 미국은 국가 탄소세나 배출권 거래제도가 없기 때문에 부유한 국가들 사이에서 여전히 예외로 남아 있습니다. 캘리포니아와 같은 일부 주에서는 자체 배출권 거래 프로그램을 운영하고 있지만, 국가 차원의 탄소 가격 책정 법안을 통과시키는 데는 거의 성공하지 못했습니다. 이에 대한 대응으로 바이든 대통령의 인플레이션 감소법(IRA)은 저탄소 전환을 촉진하기 위한 보조금과 세금 공제에 초점을 맞추고 있습니다. 그러나 그 효과를 측정하기에는 아직 너무 이릅니다.

의회에서 법을 완전히 폐지하지 않더라도 트럼프 대통령이 IRA 조항을 재검토하거나 변경할 가능성도 큽니다. 다만 기후 변화 대응에 지속적인 진전이 이루어질 것이라는 희망을 주는 추가 정책이 있습니다. 앞서 언급했듯이, 인플레이션 감소법(IRA)은 이미 통과되었으며, IRA의 많은 투자가 공화당 의원이 대표하는 지역에 집중되어 있습니다. 따라서, 이 법이 완전히 폐지될 가능성은 낮다고 생각합니다.

**US climate policy actions**

- Inflation Reduction Act
  - Incentives for climate investments
- PROVE IT Act
  - Study carbon intensity of certain industrial goods produced in / imported into US
  - Bipartisan support
- Carbon border adjustment mechanism (CBAM) bills – Republican and Democrat

BROOKINGS

일부 조항은 공화당에 의해 폐지될 가능성이 있지만, 행정부나 정부 기관을 통해 이러한 자금의 지출을 늦추는 조치가 취해질 가능성이 높습니다. 현재 검토 중인 또 다른 법안은 초당적 지지를 받고 있는 'Prove-It Act'입니다. 아직 통과되지 않은 이 법안은 주로 데이터 수집에 초점을 맞추고 있습니다. 구체적으로, 미국이 국내에서 생산되거나 수입되는 특정 공산품의 탄소 집약도를 연구하도록 의무화하고 있습니다. 이 법안은 유럽의 탄소 국경 조정 메커니즘(CBAM)에 대한 직접적인 대응입니다. 그 배경에는 다른 나라들, 특히 유럽에서 탄소 가격 책정 기준과 방법을 채택하는 상황에서 미국이 배제되는 것을 원치 않는다는 동기가 있습니다.

이것이 제가 다음으로 말씀드리고 싶은 중요한 요점입니다. 현재 탄소 국경 조정 메커니즘에 대한 상당한 양당의 지지를 얻고 있다는 것입니다. 제가 언급했듯이, 미국은 20년 이상 어떤 형태의 탄소 가격 책정을 통과시키려고 시도했지만 실패했기 때문에, 이 문제에 대한 관심이 높아지고 있다는 것 자체가 주목할 만한 발전입니다.

**Carbon border adjustment mechanism (CBAM)**

- More appealing in the US
  - Both Republicans and Democrats

Two proposed bills:
- Clean Competition Act
  - Senator Whitehouse, Democrat

- Foreign Pollution Fee Act
  - Senator Cassidy, Republican

BROOKINGS

이 잠재적 탄소 관세에 대한 접근 방식에서 공화당과 민주당이 공통적으로 가지고 있는 것은 중국에 대한 그들의 공통된 입장입니다. 양당은 중국에 대해 점점 더 강경한 태도를 취하고 있으며, 잠재적 탄소 관세를 탄소 집약도가 높은 중국에 대한 처벌의 수단으로 간주하고 있습니다. 탄소 집약도를 비교해 보면, 미국은 실제로 중국과 인도보다 훨씬 낮은 탄소 집약도를 가지고 있어 상대적으로 유리한 수치를 가지고 있습니다.

현재 의회에서 두 가지 법안이 검토되고 있습니다. 하나는 민주당 소속 쉘던 화이트하우스 상원의원이 발의한 청정 경쟁법입니다. 이 법안은 탄소 국경 조정 메커니즘을 확립하는 것을 목표로 하고 있으며, 국내 탄소 가격 책정도 제안하고 있습니다. 공화당 측에서는 카시디 상원의원이 발의한 해외 오염물질 배출세 법안이 있습니다. 이 법안은 국내 탄소 가격 없이 탄소 관세를 설정하는 것을 목표로 하고 있습니다. 특히 의회가 트럼프 시대의 감세 정책 연장을 논의하고 있는 상황에서, 어떤 형태로든 탄소 관세가 입법 논의에 포함될 수 있을지 내년에 지켜보는 것이 흥미로울 것입니다. 이러한 일이 일어날 가능성은 상당하며, 과소평가되어서는 안 됩니다.

**CBAM and spillover effects**

- Recent study by Resources for the Future (RFF): CBAM incentivizes exporting country to adopt carbon price

- July 2019: 57 carbon-pricing initiatives around the world

- May 2024: 75 implemented programs
  - ~24% of global emissions

마무리하면서 워싱턴 D.C.에 기반을 둔 싱크탱크인 리소스 포 더 퓨처(Resources for the Future)가 실시한 연구를 언급하고자 합니다. 이 연구에 따르면 CBAM은 수출국들이 국내 탄소 가격을 채택하도록 장려할 수 있는 것으로 나타났습니다. 그 이유는 간단합니다. 탄소 가격이 없는 국가가 유럽연합으로 수출할 때 비용을 부담해야 한다면, EU와 유사한 국내 탄소 가격을 도입하면 정부가 국내에서 수익을 올릴 수 있습니다. 이들 국가들은 자국 기업이 유럽연합에 돈을 지불하는 대신 자국 내에서 수익을 유지할 수 있습니다. 저는 이것이 전 세계적으로 도미노 효과를 일으킬 수 있다고 생각합니다. 왜냐하면 각국이 국내 탄소 가격 책정이 EU에 지불하는 것보다 더 유익한 선택일 수 있다는 것을 깨닫게 될 것이기 때문입니다.

전 세계 탄소 가격 책정의 성장을 살펴보면, 세계은행은 탄소 가격 책정 이니셔티브를 추적하는 훌륭한 대시보드를 보유하고 있습니다. 2019년에는 전 세계적으로 50개가 조금 넘는 탄소 가격 책정 이니셔티브가 있었습니다. 2024년까지 그 수는 75개 프로그램으로 증가하여 전 세계 배출량의 약 24%를 차지할 것입니다. 이러한 추세는 올바른 방향으로 나아가고 있으며, 미국의 행정부 변화로 인해 이러한 근본적인 역학관계가 크게 바뀔 것이라고는 생각하지 않습니다.

**Nature and financial markets**

- Challenge: externality problem
    - Markets do not recognize indirect costs borne by society
    - Damage to climate not incorporated
    - Difficult to price climate damage

BROOKINGS

마지막으로 제가 다루고 싶은 주제는 기후 금융입니다. 이 주제는 기조 연설에서도 핵심 주제로 다루어졌으며, 이전 연설자들도 이 주제에 대해 논의했습니다. 저는 미국이 자본 시장이 잘 발달되어 있지만, 민간 부문의 기후 완화 및 기후 적응에 대한 투자가 부족한 상황에 처해 있다는 관점에서 미국에 초점을 맞춰 말씀드리겠습니다.

최근에 저는 미국 내 기후 금융 증가에 대한 장애물을 조사하는 연구 논문을 발표했습니다. 많은 분들이 알고 계시겠지만, 자연과 금융 시장의 교차점에 관한 명확한 외부성 문제가 있습니다. 시장은 온실가스 배출로 인해 사회가 부담하는 간접 비용을 인식하지 못합니다. 기후 변화로 인한 피해는 시장 가격에 반영되지 않으며, 시장만으로는 기후 변화의 피해를 가격에 반영하기 어렵습니다.

장애물을 파악하기 위해 민간 부문의 다양한 이해관계자들과 협의했습니다. 이 협의 과정에서 기후 완화 및 적응 조치에 대한 투자가 부족한 이유를 알 수 있었습니다. 미국에서는 캘리포니아의 산불, 플로리다의 허리케인 증가, 노스캐롤라이나와 같은 지역에서 발생한 홍수 등 이전에는 경험하지 못했던 홍수 사건으로 인해 적응에 대한 필요성이 증가하고 있습니다. 피해가 상당하며 경제적 비용도 상당합니다.

**Innovative financial instruments**

- Sustainable investments / ESG / Green Bonds
    - High demand
    - Some empirical findings of poor track record

- Nature-based credits
    - Carbon credits, biodiversity credits

- Nature-preserving companies
    - Landowners lease or sell conservation easements
    - Third parties conserve land

BROOKINGS

지속 가능한 투자, ESG 채권, 녹색 채권 등 투자 가능한 수단을 살펴보면, 시장 수요가 여전히 상당합니다. 그러나 실증적 연구 결과에 따르면, 실적은 좋지 않습니다. 탄소 배출권과 생물 다양성 크레딧과 같은 자연 기반 크레딧은 종종 신뢰성 문제에 직면합니다. 토지 소유자가 제3자에게 보전 지역 사용권을 임대하거나 매각하는 등 자연 보호에 중점을 둔 새로운 기업이 등장하고 있습니다. 그러나 이러한 수단이 있음에도 불구하고, 기후 문제를 해결하는 데 필요한 규모의 투자가 이루어지지 않고 있습니다.

**Pain points of private climate finance**

Recent research from Brookings – 9 pain points:
1. Immature climate accounting.

2. Current information environment disadvantages small actors.

3. Limited government capacity incentivizes negative outcomes.

4. Climate-related benefits and costs are underpriced or unpriced, particularly due to lack of established cost-of-carbon metrics or similar measures.

BROOKINGS

저희 연구에서 확인된 주요 장애물 중 하나는 미성숙한 기후 회계 방법입니다. 많은 이해관계자들은 효과적인 투자를 위해 필요한 정교한 기후 회계 방법이 부족하다고 지적했습니다. 또한, 기후 투자와 관련된 정보 환경은 소규모 투자자들에게 불리하게 작용하는 경향이 있어, 자본의 동원이 제한됩니다. 특히 지방과 주 차원에서 투자를 촉진하거나 민간 부문의 참여를 장려할 수 있는 여건을 조성할 수 있는 정부의 역량도 제한적입니다. 게다가, 기후 관련 편익과 비용은 주로 확립된 탄소 가격 책정 지표가 없기 때문에 과소평가되거나 아예 평가되지 않는 경우가 많습니다.

**Pain points of private climate finance**

Pain points – continued

5. Current financing models often favor GHG-emitting projects that use established technologies.

6. Insurers, communities, and other partners are not yet capturing revenue streams to accelerate adaptation projects.

7. Fragmented political authority over projects often clashes, creating uncertainty among private investors.

BROOKINGS

그 밖의 문제로는 신기술보다는 기존 기술을 사용하는 온실가스 배출 프로젝트를 선호하는 자금 조달 모델이 있습니다. 또한, 방조제 건설이나 홍수나 허리케인으로부터의 인프라 보호와 같은 적응에 초점을 맞춘 프로젝트의 경우, 인센티브와 잠재적 수익의 불일치가 발생합니다. 민간 투자자들은 이러한 적응 노력에 대한 자금 확보가 어렵다는 것을 알고 있습니다. 또한, 프로젝트에 대한 정치적 권한이 분산되어 있기 때문에, 특히 연방, 주, 지방 정부 간의 조정이 허가 절차에서 상당한 지연을 초래하는 재생 에너지 부문에서 민간 투자자들에게 불확실성과 지연이 발생할 수 있습니다.

## Pain points of private climate finance

Pain points – continued
8. Public debates have struggled to balance need for new climate investments with ongoing demands to finance established economic activities where clean technologies are not yet available.

9. Political timelines (election results, terms of office, etc.) often misalign with project delivery timelines.

BROOKINGS

　마지막으로, 새로운 기후 투자에 대한 필요성과 기존 경제 활동에 대한 지속적인 자금 지원 요구 사이에서 균형을 맞추는 데 어려움을 겪는 경우가 많습니다. 특히 청정 기술이 아직 이용 가능하지 않은 경우 더욱 그렇습니다. 예를 들어, 산업 공정에서 기술은 탈탄소화를 가능하게 할 만큼 충분히 발전되지 않은 경우가 많습니다. 정치적 타임라인 또한 많은 기후 프로젝트의 장기적 특성과 일치하지 않는 경향이 있습니다. 선거 주기와 행정부의 변화는 기후 정책에 상당한 변화를 가져올 수 있습니다. 바이든 대통령이 기후 행동에 중점을 둔 후 트럼프 대통령 하에서 강조가 약화될 가능성이 있는 것처럼 말입니다. 이러한 불일치는 미국에 도전이 되지만, 그럼에도 불구하고 저는 시장, 특히 탄소 포집 및 저장, 전기 자동차와 같은 분야에서 긍정적인 추세를 낙관하고 있습니다. 이러한 추세는 행정부의 변화와 관계없이 계속될 것입니다. 관심을 가져 주셔서 감사합니다.

　**홍종호 교수:** 다양하고 중요한 이슈를 다룬 훌륭한 발표 감사합니다. 질문이 많이 있지만, 하나만 드리겠습니다. 발표에서 AI의 역할에 대해 언급하셨습니다. 한국의 일반 대중과 언론도 AI가 에너지 소비, 전력 수

요 및 탄소 배출에 미치는 영향에 대해 많은 관심을 가지고 있습니다. 상쇄 효과가 있을 수 있다고 언급하셨습니다. AI가 에너지 사용 효율성을 개선할 수 있다면 에너지 소비가 줄어들 가능성이 있습니다. 하지만 동시에, 데이터 센터와 AI 사용으로 인한 막대한 전력 수요 증가도 예견되고 있습니다.

이러한 상쇄 효과의 미래 전망에 대해 어떻게 생각하시는지 궁금합니다. AI의 효율성이 전력 소비 증가를 상쇄할 수 있을 것이라고 보시나요, 아니면 그 반대의 상황이 될 것이라고 예상하시나요?

**산제이 팻나익 박사:** 정확한 수치를 다룬 실증 연구는 아직 본 적이 없지만, 제 직관으로는 단기적으로는 효율성 향상이 전력 수요 증가를 상쇄하기에 충분하지 않을 것 같습니다. 그 이유는, 특히 미국에서 AI 데이터 센터의 성장 속도가 매우 빠르게 증가하고 있기 때문입니다. 동시에, 전력 수요는 전력화 및 탈탄소화를 위한 노력으로 증가하고 있습니다.

이 문제는 결국 경제적 문제, 국가 안보의 문제라고 봅니다. 기업들은 결국 데이터 센터를 구축하려 할 것이고, 이를 위해 상대적으로 저렴하고 접근 가능한 에너지를 제공하는 국가를 선택할 것입니다. 중동 지역의 많은 국가들이 대기업들에 에너지가 풍부하다고 제안하고 있습니다. 물론 대부분이 화석 연료에서 나온 에너지입니다. 만약 한국이나 미국과 같은 국가들이 충분한 에너지를 공급할 수 없다면, 일부 데이터 센터가 해외로 이전할 가능성이 있는데, 이는 우리가 피해야 할 상황입니다.

이 문제를 해결하기 위해서는 아마도 미국에서 개발 중인 소형 원자로와 같은 혁신적인 접근이 필요할 것입니다. 또한 가까운 미래에는 AI 데이터 센터의 성장을 지원하기 위해 여전히 화석 연료 발전소에 의존할 가능성도 있습니다. 이러한 전환은 단기간에 이루어지기 어려운 시간이 걸리는 과정이기 때문에, 이 문제를 해결하기 위해서는 시간이 필요할 것입니다. 질문에 대한 답이 되었기를 바랍니다.

**홍종호 교수:** 감사합니다, 팻나익 박사님. 이제 세 번째 연사로 딜로이트의 구본재 부사장님을 모시겠습니다. 큰 박수로 맞이해 주시기 바랍니다.

**구본재 부사장:** 안녕하십니까? 딜로이트의 구본재입니다. 제가 오늘 말씀드릴 내용은 앞서 언급된 기후 금융 관점과는 다른 시각에서, 개인사업자와 소상공인에 대해 말씀드리고자 합니다. 개인사업자들의 생존과 성장은 국가 경제의 지속 가능한 성장과 밀접하게 연관된 중요한 아젠다일 뿐만 아니라, 금융기관의 관점에서도 그들에 대한 파이낸싱은 포용적 금융(Inclusive Financing)과 관련이 있기 때문에 매우 중요합니다.

### 디지털 금융 경쟁 변화 - 금융업 신규 경쟁 법칙

빠른 디지털 변화에 대한 대응 및 금융업 내 성패를 규정 지을 새로운 Rule of Game이 형성되고 있으며, 이는 생존 게임화, 디지털의 영업채널화, 플랫폼 경쟁화임

**신규 경쟁 법칙**

| 구분 | 내용 |
|---|---|
| 성장 게임에서 생존 게임으로 변화 (變化) | • 산업의 업황 개선은 요원: Penetration 포화 및 저금리 장기화로 인해 지속적 성장 여력 제약<br>• 정부 규제 하 경쟁 강도를 높이는 신규 경쟁자들의 금융산업으로의 진입으로 인해 업권 경쟁 심화 및 수익성 지속 악화 전망 |
| 핵심 영업채널로서 대면 채널과 디지털 채널의 동기화 (同價化) | • 디지털 기술 기반 사업역량 고도화, 금융서비스 모델 재구성, 스마트 서비스 확산, 비대면 업무 방식 전환 등 금융기관들의 디지털 전환 및 언택트 사업 혁신 추진이 적극 요구됨<br>• 빠른 디지털 확산 및 고객의 다양한 니즈에 대응하기 위한 영업 모델과 운영 모델에 적합한 채널 혁신 필요 |
| 개별 회사 단위가 아닌 협업 기반의 플랫폼 경쟁화 (競爭化) | • 금융사들만의 경쟁이 아닌 유통, 통신, SNS 등 다양한 고객접점을 확보하고 있는 산업과의 Alliance 기반 플랫폼 단위 경쟁으로 경쟁의 성격 변화<br>• 이종 산업 서비스 제휴 기반 금융 및 비금융 서비스 복합 구매에 대한 할인 및 금리 혜택 중첩 등을 통해 플랫폼 내 고객 유입 및 Lock-In 필요 |

최근 디지털 기술의 빠른 발전과 함께 우리는 많은 변화를 경험하고 있습니다. 그 중에서도 금융업 내에서 새로운 성장 조건과 성공을 결정짓는 새로운 규칙이 형성되고 있습니다. 첫 번째는 성장의 게임에서 생존의

게임으로의 변화이고, 두 번째는 중요한 주요 채널로 비대면 디지털 채널이 등장하고 있으며, 세 번째는 개별 기업 단위가 아닌 협업 기관의 플랫폼화가 등장하여 경쟁을 벌이고 있다는 점입니다.

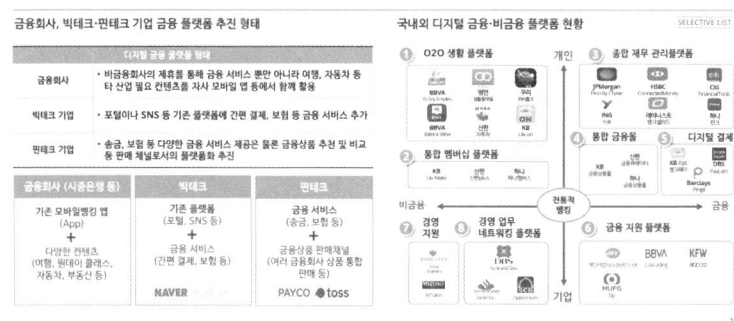

특히 고객 확보 및 유지를 위한 고객 경험의 혁신, 그리고 네트워크 효과를 극대화하기 위해 국내외 금융계의 빅테크 및 핀테크 기업들이 적극적으로 금융 산업에 진출하고 있으며, 다양한 디지털 금융 및 비금융 플랫폼을 출시하고 있습니다. 예를 들면, O2O 생활금융 플랫폼, 종합재무관리 플랫폼, 통합 멤버십 플랫폼, 디지털 결제 플랫폼 등 다양한 금융 및 비금융 플랫폼들이 출시되어 경쟁하고 있습니다.

### 개인사업자/소상공인 경쟁력 강화를 위한 정부 정책 동향

최근 금융당국을 중심으로 개인사업자/소상공인 디지털 경쟁력 강화를 위한 각 부처의 디지털-데이터 정책 확대 및 개인사업자 마이데이터 도입 본격화가 논의되고 있음

#### 개인사업자/소상공인 지원을 위한 주요 정책 방향

**소상공인 디지털 전환 정책** (중소벤처기업부)
지속적인 상권 발전을 위해 중장년 개인사업자/소상공인 및 전통시장 디지털 격차 해소
- 이커머스 개인사업자/소상공인 양성 (연 10만명)
- 스마트 상점 공방 공급 (5만개)
- 골목상권, 전통시장 내 디지털 전담 인력 및 배송 인프라 확충

**소상공인 개방형 빅데이터 플랫폼 구축** (소상공인시장진흥공단)
개인사업자/소상공인 경쟁력 제고 위해 전국 상권 빅데이터 기반 신사업 모델 발굴·지원
- 상권정보시스템, 내 가게 맞춤진단, 정책 통계 등 빅데이터 기반 정보 제공
  - 개인사업자/소상공인 개방형 빅데이터 플랫폼 1차 오픈 예정 ('24년 6월)

**개인사업자 마이데이터 신규 도입 논의** (금융위원회)
개인사업자 대상 마이데이터 도입으로 개인사업자/소상공인의 데이터 사각지대 해소
- 2023년 2월, 개인사업자 마이데이터 워킹그룹 발족
- 2024년 금융위원회의 주요 업무추진 계획 내 개인사업자 마이데이터 추가 후, 금융위·금감원·유관기관 킥오프 진행
  - 대다수 수요기관이 '개인 마이데이터 사업자의 업무 확대' 안 선호, '24.7월 중 신용정보법 개정 법안 발의 예정

---

이와 더불어 최근 금융당국을 중심으로 개인사업자와 소상공인의 디지털 경쟁력을 강화하기 위해 각 부처의 디지털 혁신 정책과 데이터 정책이 확대 추진되고 있습니다. 중소벤처기업부의 소상공인 디지털 전환 정책, 소상공인시장진흥공단의 소상공인 개방형 빅데이터 플랫폼 구축, 그리고 금융위원회의 개인사업자 마이데이터 신규 도입 논의들이 그것입니다.

### 개인사업자/소상공인 정의

개인사업자 및 소상공인은 국내 중소기업 사업자의 절대 다수로서, 자본 및 경기변동에 민감하여 자금 및 정보화 등 다양한 지원을 필요로 함

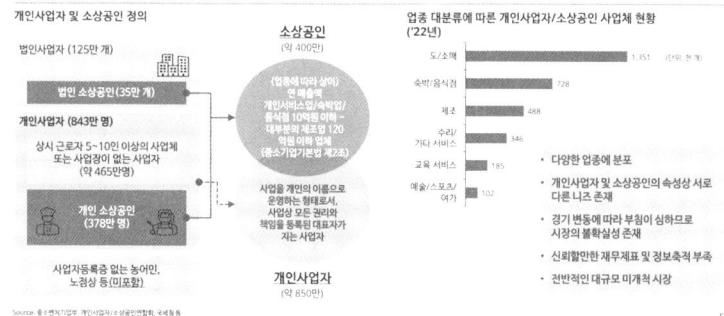

그렇다면 개인사업자와 소상공인은 누구일까요? 중소기업법에 따르면, 매출액 기준으로 연 매출 10억에서 120억 원 이하의 업종별로 분류되며, 기본적으로 제조업은 120억 원 이하, 기타 서비스업은 10억 원 이하의 기업으로 정의됩니다. 개인사업자와 소상공인은 법인 및 개인사업자를 포함하여 약 900만에서 천만 명 정도의 규모를 가집니다. 이들은 도소매업, 숙박업, 음식업, 제조업, 수리업, 교육 서비스, 예술, 스포츠, 여가 등 다양한 산업에 분포하고 있습니다.

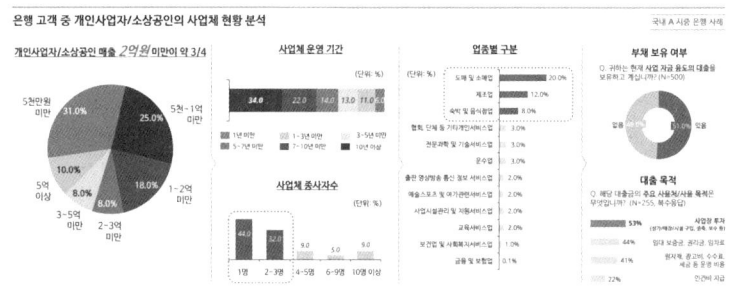

개인사업자/소상공인 정의
개인사업자/소상공인 매출 2억 미만이 ¾이며, 제조업과 도소매업에 편중되어 있고 종사자수는 3인 이하의 사업체가 대다수를 차지하며 신규 창업 고객의 비중이 낮은 편임

국내 개인사업자/소상공인은 대부분 종업원 3인 이하의 기업이며 연 매출 2억 미만의 특정 업종에 편중되어 있음

이들은 업종별, 규모별로 서로 다른 니즈와 애로사항을 가지고 있으며, 경기 변동에 따라 그 영향이 매우 크고, 상당히 높은 불확실성을 안고 있습니다. 또한 시장에서 신뢰할 수 있는 재무제표나 정보가 부족하기 때문에 금융권에서 다뤄지지 않는 경우가 많았습니다. 국내 일부 은행에서 소상공인과 개인사업자를 보면, 여신과 수신 상품을 이용하는 소상공인들은 대부분 종업원 3인 이하의 작은 기업이며, 매출액 2억 원 미만의 도소매업, 제조업, 숙박업, 음식점에 국한되어 있다는 점을 알 수 있습니다.

### 개인사업자/소상공인 Needs & Pain Points

개인사업자/소상공인의 Needs와 Pain Point에 대응하는 개인사업자/소상공인 전용 서비스 필요

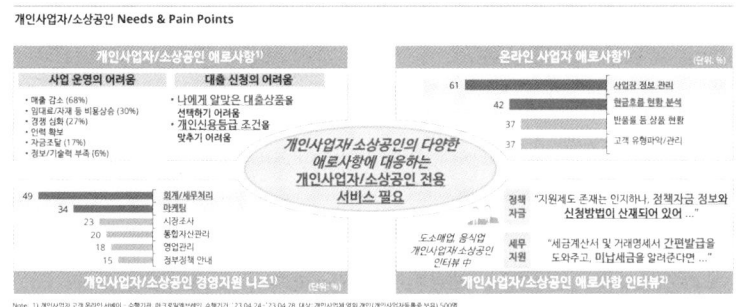

이들은 사업 운영에 여러 가지 어려움을 겪고 있습니다. 사업 운영의 어려움, 매출 감소에 대한 대응, 임대료와 비용 상승, 경쟁 심화, 인력 확보의 어려움, 자금 조달의 어려움, 기술 및 정보의 부족 등 다양한 문제를 겪고 있으며, 제 때 필요한 대출을 받기 어렵습니다. 대출 신청의 어려움, 사업장 운영을 위한 회계 관리, 세무 처리, 마케팅 및 고객 확보의 어려움을 느끼고 있으며, 사업장 운영과 관리에서 큰 어려움을 겪고 있습니다.

### 개인사업자/소상공인 서비스 플랫폼 구축을 위한 출발점

개인사업자/소상공인 서비스 플랫폼은 플랫폼에서 제공하는 서비스와 기능이 개인사업자/소상공인 니즈와 연계되어야 함

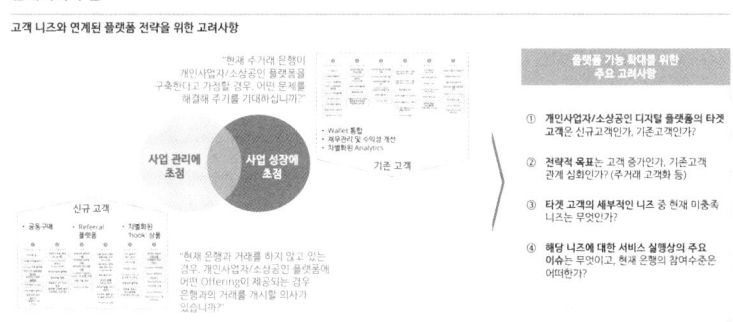

따라서 개인사업자와 소상공인을 위한 금융기관의 전용 서비스가 반드시 필요합니다. 그러면, 개인사업자와 소상공인들을 위한 서비스 플랫폼은 어떤 서비스를 제공해야 할까요? 서비스는 개인사업자들이 겪고 있는 애로사항을 잘 관리할 수 있도록 설계되어야 합니다. 이를 위해서는 몇 가지 고려 사항이 필요합니다. 첫째, 디지털 플랫폼의 타겟 고객이 기존 소상공인인지, 아니면 신규 고객인지 파악하는 것입니다. 전략적 목표가 새로운 고객을 확보하는 것인지, 아니면 기존 고객의 관계를 심화하는 것인지 정의해야 합니다.

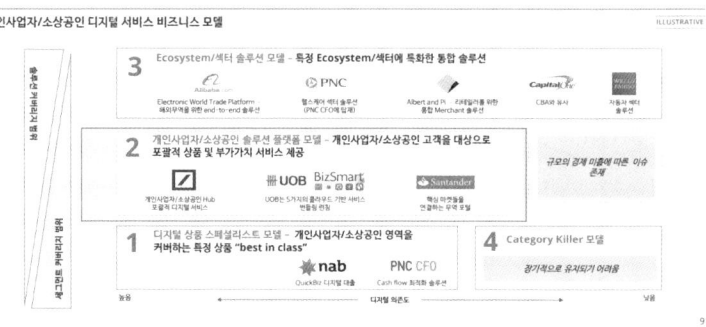

**개인사업자/소상공인 서비스 모델**
개인사업자/소상공인 디지털 서비스 모델은 디지털 의존도 및 커버리지 범위에 따라 다양한 형태가 존재하지만, 은행의 서비스 형태는 포괄적 개인사업자/소상공인 상품과 서비스를 제공해야 함

또한, 고객의 니즈, 특히 충족되지 않은 니즈를 파악하는 것이 중요합니다. 그렇다면 금융기관 관점에서 적합한 서비스 모델은 무엇일까요? 개인사업자와 소상공인을 위한 서비스는 특정 상품에 집중하는 모델이나 특정 카테고리에 집중하는 모델보다는, 포괄적인 상품과 서비스를 종합적으로 제공하는 개인사업자 소상공인 솔루션 플랫폼 모델이 적합해 보입니다.

**개인사업자/소상공인 솔루션 플랫폼을 통해 대응하고자 하는 가장 중요한 니즈**
개인사업자/소상공인 솔루션 플랫폼은 개인사업자/소상공인 니즈에 부합하는 다양한 코어 뱅킹 상품과 새로운 부가가치 기능을 종합적으로 제공하는 것을 의미함

개인사업자/소상공인 솔루션 플랫폼 코어 및 부가 서비스

이런 플랫폼은 금융기관의 전형적인 코어 뱅킹 서비스인 대출, 신용평가, 외환 서비스 외에도, 다양한 부가가치 서비스를 제공합니다. 예를 들어, 커머스 개선 서비스, 캐시플로우 관리 서비스, 매출·지출 관리 서비스, 물류 관리, 생산성 개선 서비스 등이 포함됩니다. 그러나 현재 한국에서는 은행이 제공하는 서비스가 주로 파이낸싱과 약간의 매출 지출 관리, 직원 근태·급여 관리 등으로 제한되고 있습니다.

**개인사업자/소상공인 솔루션 플랫폼을 통해 대응하고자 하는 가장 중요한 니즈**
개인사업자/소상공인의 자금 수요 및 이에 따른 대출수요는 지속적으로 발생함

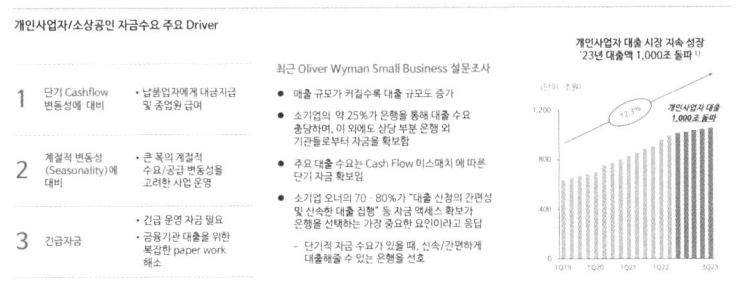

125

개인사업자와 소상공인에게 가장 강력한 니즈는 자금 수요입니다. 최근 글로벌 컨설팅사인 올리버와이만 조사 결과에 따르면, 소상공인의 매출 규모가 커질수록 대출 수요도 커지고 있습니다. 그러나 소기업의 25%만이 은행을 통해 대출을 받으며, 나머지는 제도권 밖에서 자금을 조달하고 있다고 합니다. 많은 소기업 오너들은 대출 신청의 간편성과 신속한 대출 집행을 이유로 은행을 선호합니다.

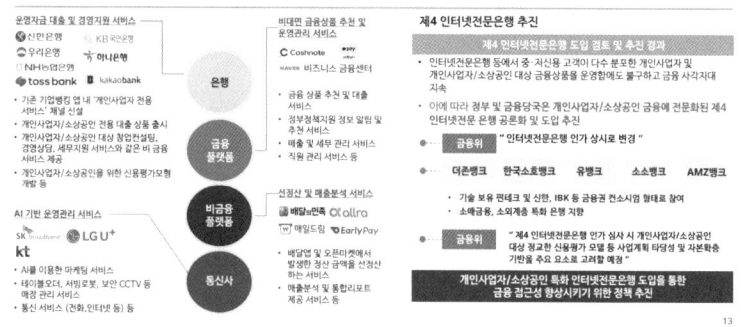

금융기관들은 이제 개인사업자와 소상공인을 중요한 고객군으로 인식하고, 기존의 뱅킹 앱을 활용한 금융 서비스 외에도 경영 지원 서비스 등을 제공하고 있습니다. 또한, 이동통신 사업자들도 결합 서비스를 통해 사업장 관리 서비스를 제공하고 있으며, 플랫폼 사업자들은 운영 관리 서비스를 제공하고 있습니다. 정부와 금융당국은 개인사업자 소상공인에 특화된 제4인터넷뱅크 도입을 논의하고 있습니다.

**해외 사례: 글로벌 선도 은행의 개인사업자/소상공인 부가가치 서비스 플랫폼**

글로벌 선도 은행은 Small Business 영역에서의 차별화를 달성하기 위하여 뱅킹 상품 뿐만 아니라 "Beyond Banking"의 부가가치 서비스를 제공함

**개인사업자/소상공인 플랫폼 서비스 스펙트럼**　　　　　　　　　　　　　　　　　　　　SELECTIVE LIST

| | 정보제공 중심 서비스 | | | 부가가치 제공 서비스 | |
|---|---|---|---|---|---|
| | 비즈니스 커뮤니티 | Advisory 서비스 | 마켓 플레이스 | 벤치마킹 및 Trade | 공동구매 | 솔루션 |
| | 개인사업자/소상공인 간의 정보공유 활성화 | Topic별 풍부한 자료 제공 | 개인사업자/소상공인 간의 상품/서비스 거래를 위한 플랫폼 제공 | Peer/Supplier/Client 비교, 글로벌 입찰기회 Alert 등 | 다양한 상품/서비스에 걸친 개인사업자/소상공인을 위한 discount 제공 | 비즈니스 개선을 위한 서비스 |
| RBS / bizcrowd | ✓ | | | | | |
| Bank of America | ✓ | ✓ | ✓ | | | |
| TEB | | ✓ | ✓ | ✓ | ✓ | |
| UOB / DBS | ✓ | | ✓ | | ✓ | ✓ |
| BARCLAYS | ✓ | ✓ | ✓ | | | ✓ |
| Santander | ✓ | ✓ | ✓ | | | ✓ |

해외 글로벌 은행들은 개인사업자와 소상공인에게 코어 뱅킹 서비스 외에도, 커뮤니티 서비스, 어드바이저리 서비스, 마켓플레이스 서비스, 공동 구매 서비스 등을 제공합니다. 예를 들어, 영국의 바클레이스, 스페인의 산탄데르, 독일의 도이치뱅크, 싱가포르의 DBS, 터키의 TB 은행 등은 트레이드 오브 파이낸싱 포털, 자금 관리, 오퍼레이션 툴, 비즈니스 분석 서비스 등을 제공하고 있습니다.

**군집 분석 (사례) – 군집 별 니즈 및 상세 니즈 강도 기반 우선위화**

군집별 매출액/ 영업기간/ 업종 분포 및 니즈 발현 정도를 고려하여, 최종적으로 5개 군집의 고객 프로파일 결정

| | | 군집별 샘플 수 및 니즈 강도 | | | | PRELIMINARY |
|---|---|---|---|---|---|---|
| 애로사항 | 애로사항 상세 | 군집 1 | 군집 2 | 군집 3 | 군집 4 | 군집 5 |
| 매출 확대 및 매출처 관리 | 판로개척 및 신규고객 확보 어려움 | 14.8265 | 117.8010 | 61.6162 | 230.1775 | 27.9221 |
| | 많은 고객수로 인한 복잡한 거래 관리의 어려움 | 9.7792 | 91.0995 | 44.4444 | 171.0050 | 17.5325 |
| 비용절감 및 생산성관리 | 원자재 및 인건비 등 비용의 상승 | 12.1451 | 73.2984 | 44.4444 | 10.6509 | 18.8312 |
| | 다수 벤더 사용으로 인한 벤더 관리의 어려움 | 8.3596 | 51.0471 | 29.2929 | 6.2130 | 12.6623 |
| 물류 및 재고관리 | 자재, 원료, 제품의 적시 조달 어려움 및 운송 관리가 복잡함 | 1.5773 | 17.2775 | 14.1414 | 1.1751 | 2.2727 |
| | 많은 재고 종류로 인해 재고 관리가 복잡함 | 1.5773 | 21.4660 | 14.1414 | 1.1834 | 2.2727 |
| 운전자금 또는 신규투자 자금 부족 | 현금 흐름 문제로 인해 운전자금 부족이 발생 | 219.8738 | 81.9372 | 138.3838 | 34.0237 | 49.3506 |
| | 신규 투자가 필요하나 자금이 부족 | 231.3880 | 89.7906 | 137.3737 | 35.2071 | 52.2727 |
| 인력 채용 및 생산성 관리 | 적합한 인력 채용 및 유지가 어려움 | 10.8833 | 146.3351 | 86.8687 | 14.4970 | 241.2338 |
| | 채용한 인력의 생산성을 높이는데 오랜 시간이 걸림 | 10.4101 | 140.5759 | 84.8485 | 13.6095 | 228.8961 |
| 중요한 의사결정 시 전문적인 정보 부족 | 적합한 전문가를 빠르게 찾기가 어려움 | 0.0000 | 27.7487 | 10.1010 | 0.0000 | 0.9740 |
| | 전문가의 의견 청취에 지나치게 높은 비용이 발생함 | 0.0000 | 24.8691 | 7.0707 | 0.0000 | 1.2987 |
| | 기획, 조사 업무 등을 수행하고 싶으나 마땅한 인력이 없음 | 0.0000 | 28.7958 | 9.0909 | 0.0000 | 0.9740 |
| 군집별 고객 프로파일 | | Death Valley 기업 | 성장기 제조업 | 정숙기 제조업 | B2C 고객 상대 기업 | 노동집약 기업 |

**고객 세분화 및 프로필 도출 (사례)**
정량조사 기반 군집분석을 통해 우선순위화한 5개 목표 고객의 프로필과 핵심 발현 니즈 정의

| | Death Valley 기업 | 성장기 제조업 | 성숙기 제조업 | B2C 고객 상대 기업 | 노동집약 기업 |
|---|---|---|---|---|---|
| 프로필 | · 평균 업력 3~5년<br>· 서비스업 비중 높음 | · 평균 업력 8~10년인 제조업<br>· 평균 매출액 50억+ | · 평균 업력 15년인 제조업 | · 평균 업력 7년, 도소매 및 완제품 B2C 판매 제조업 | · 인력 서비스업 (ex. 콜센터 등) |
| 핵심<br>발현<br>니즈 | · 운전 자금 부족의 해소 및 예방<br>· 신규투자 자금의 원활한 조달 | · 인력 채용 및 근속기간 증대 지원<br>· 판로개척 및 신규고객 확보 지원<br>· 다수 채널, 지불 수단 현금흐름 복잡성 해소<br>· 신규투자 자금의 원활한 조달 | · 운전 자금 부족의 해소 및 예방<br>· 신규투자 자금의 원활한 조달<br>· 인력 채용 및 근속기간 증대 지원<br>· 채용한 인력 생산성 향상 지원 | · 판로개척 및 신규고객 확보 지원<br>· 다수 채널, 지불 수단 현금흐름 복잡성 해소 | · 인력 채용 및 근속기간 증대 지원<br>· 채용한 인력 생산성 향상 지원 |

    최근 한국에서 개인사업자와 소상공인의 니즈를 분석한 결과, 다양한 유형의 고객군이 파악되었습니다. 이들 고객군은 각기 다른 애로사항과 니즈를 가지고 있습니다. 예를 들어, 운전자금 부족, 신규 투자 자금 부족, 인력 채용의 어려움, 판로 개척 등 다양한 니즈가 존재합니다. 금융기관은 이러한 니즈를 충족시키기 위해, 유사한 니즈를 가진 고객군을 분석하고, 그에 맞는 서비스 모델을 제공해야 합니다.

**3rd party 파트너사 선정**
3rd party 파트너쉽은 솔루션 소싱을 위한 효과적인 대안으로서, 이를 위해서는 "Provider Landscape"에 대한 심층적인 이해도 확보가 중요함

개인사업자/소상공인 디지털 서비스 파트너쉽 선정 – 외부 Service Provider Landscape

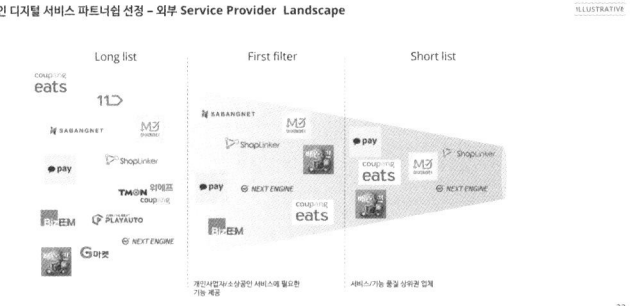

## 파트너간 가치교환 모델 설계

개인사업자/소상공인 플랫폼 솔루션 개발을 위해서는 서비스 모델이 "생존 가능"한 서비스 모델이어야 하며, 특히 참여하는 파트너들 간의 공정한 "Trade off" 보장이 중요함

### 파트너간 가치교환 모델 설계 – MVP Build의 일환으로서 정량화

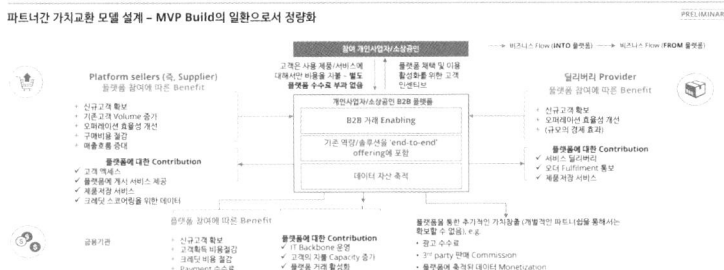

## 체계적 파트너쉽 구축 방안

체계적 파트너쉽 구축을 위해 실효성이 입증된 안정적이고 체계적 파트너십 구축 프로세스를 적용해야 함

### 파트너쉽 구축 프로세스

**캠페인 및 Promotion 방안**

개인사업자/소상공인 플랫폼 런칭 후 성공적인 안착을 위해서는 지속적 트래픽 증대를 위한 적극적인 프로모션이 수행되어야 함

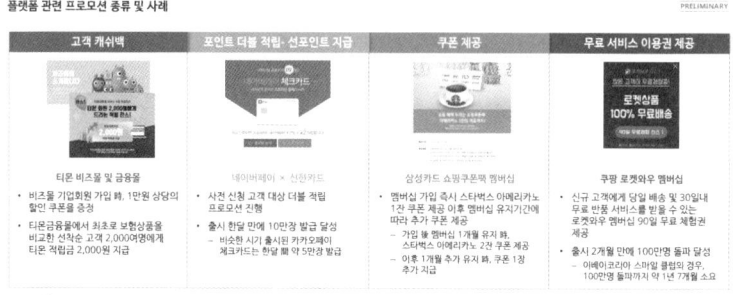

**개인사업자/소상공인 플랫폼 서비스 WIN-WIN 관계**

개인사업자/소상공인의 니즈를 해결하는 플랫폼 서비스와 강력한 로열티 프로그램을 통해 금융기관, 개인사업자/소상공인, Service Provider 간의 Win-Win 관계를 달성할 수 있음

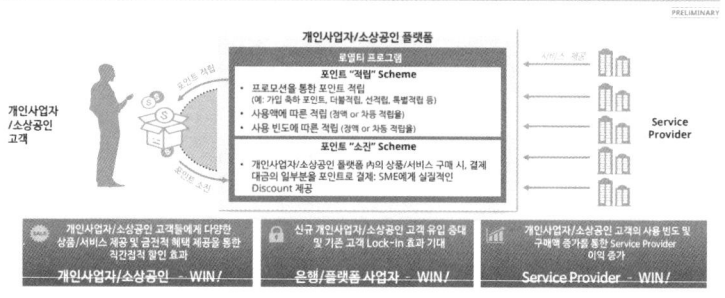

    이러한 서비스 모델은 경쟁 우위가 있는지, 개발이 용이한지, 그리고 제 3자 파트너십을 통한 서비스 제공 여부를 고려해야 합니다. 또한, 서비스 모델이 성공적으로 자리잡기 위해서는 트래픽 증대와 함께, 강력한 리워드 프로그램과 프로모션이 필요합니다. 고객의 애로사항을 해결하고, 금융기관과 플랫폼 사업자들이 윈-윈할 수 있는 관계를 구축해야 합니다.

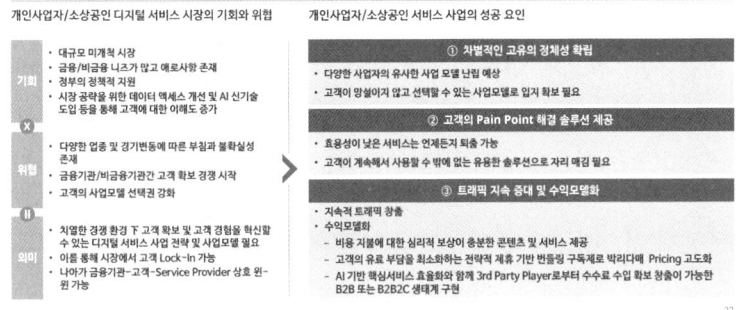

결론적으로, 약 천만 명에 달하는 개인사업자와 소상공인의 생존과 성장은 국가 경제의 지속 가능한 성장에 중요한 영향을 미칩니다. 금융기관이 이들의 애로사항을 해결할 수 있는 서비스 모델을 제공함으로써 이들을 더욱 중요한 고객 세그먼트로 자리매김할 수 있도록 할 필요가 있습니다. 이들은 미개척 시장에서 큰 잠재력을 가지고 있으며, 정부의 정책적 지원과 금융기관의 적극적인 서비스 제공이 필요합니다.

마지막으로, 성공적인 개인사업자와 소상공인 플랫폼 모델을 위한 세 가지 성공 요인은 차별화된 정체성 확립, 고객의 페인 포인트(pain point) 해결, 지속적인 트래픽 증대와 수익 모델화입니다. 이를 통해 금융기관과 서비스 제공자들은 상호 협력하여 더 큰 성과를 이끌어낼 수 있을 것입니다. 감사합니다.

**홍종호 교수:** 네, 구본재 부사장님, 열정적인 말씀과 흥미로운 주제 감사합니다. 오늘 두 번째 세션의 주제는 '기후 금융과 상생 금융'입니다. 구 부사장님께서는 특히 소상공인 자영업자에 대한 금융 서비스와 그 효과성에 대해 말씀해주셨는데요. 이를 기후와 연결 지어 질문을 드려보겠습니다. 앞서 비노드 토마스 박사님께서 기후 적응에 대해 언급하셨듯

이, 탄소를 줄이는 것뿐만 아니라 적응에 대한 이야기도 하셨습니다. 사실, 우리나라에서도 폭우로 인한 소규모 공장이나 가게 침수 피해가 빈번하게 발생하고 있습니다.

그렇다면, 앞으로 이러한 상생 금융의 방향이 기후와 관련된 분야로 확장될 수 있는 가능성, 그리고 이에 대한 금융기관의 입장은 어떤지 궁금합니다.

**구본재 부사장:** 사실 제가 말씀드린 내용은 기후와 관련이 있다고 볼 수 있습니다. 왜냐하면, 저는 개인사업자와 소상공인의 상생을 위한 금융기관의 역할과 서비스 모델에 대해 이야기했기 때문입니다. 우리가 경험한 바와 같이, 몇 년 전 코로나 사태로 많은 개인사업자와 소상공인들이 큰 위기에 처했습니다. 그때 정부는 적극적으로 나서서 긴급 자금을 지원했고, 그 창구가 바로 은행이었습니다. 앞으로 예상되는 급격한 기후 변화로 인해 특정 업종과 세그먼트들이 큰 위험에 직면할 가능성이 큽니다. 이러한 상황에서, 그들의 생존을 위한 지원과 금융기관의 역할이 매우 중요해질 것입니다. 이와 같은 지원이 이루어진다면, 국가 경제의 지속 가능한 상생 성장을 보장할 수 있다고 생각합니다.

**홍종호 교수:** 이해가 잘 되었습니다. 이제 세 분의 토론자분들을 모시겠습니다. 먼저, SK SUPEX추구협의회의 커뮤니케이션 위원장이신 이형희 위원장님께서 말씀해 주시겠습니다.

**이형희 위원장:** 네, 반갑습니다. 이형희입니다. 현재 저는 SK그룹에서 언론과 정부 정책에 대한 커뮤니케이션 업무를 맡고 있습니다. 하지만 이 일을 맡기 전, 6년 전부터 2년 전까지는 SK 그룹 내 ESG 관련 전략과 실행을 담당했습니다.

당시 EU의 그린딜 정책 발표와 금융기관들의 ESG 펀드, 그리고 국제기구의 ESG 관련 관심이 높아지던 시점이었기 때문에 저희의 가장 큰 고민은 ESG, 특히 기후 위기가 글로벌 아젠다로서 앞으로 지속될 것인데, 그렇다면 어떻게 선도적인 역할을 할 것인가였습니다. 당시 한국 기업 중에서는 RE 100이나 넷 제로 선언을 한 곳이 없었고, 그래서 SK 그룹 주요 회사들이 RE100 선언을 하고 국제기구에 신청하는 절차를 진행했습니다. 이후 넷 제로 목표를 설정하며, 각 회사는 2030년 혹은 2050년까지 제로를 달성하자는 선언을 했습니다.

또한, SK그룹의 주요 비즈니스 모델은 에너지, 반도체, 정보통신기술(ICT), 바이오 분야인데, 에너지 부문에서 석유화학과 카본 기반의 에너지를 사용하고 있어, 앞으로의 세계 변화에 잘 적응할 수 있을지에 대한 의문이 있었습니다. 이에 신재생 에너지, 에너지 효율화, 리사이클링 기반의 화학 산업 등으로 업의 주력을 전환하고, 배터리 분야에도 큰 투자를 했습니다.

이 이야기를 길게 한 이유는 자랑하려는 것이 아니라, 여기서 중요한 물음표가 생겼기 때문입니다. 저희는 퍼스트 무버 어드벤티지를 추구하며 변화에 앞장서기 위해 노력했으나, 최근 우크라이나 전쟁, 중동의 분쟁, 미국 대선 결과 등 다양한 사회적 사건들이 불확실성을 키우고 있습니다. 금융기관들에서도 과거와는 다른 목소리가 나오고 있으며, 기업은 룰 세터(rule-setter)가 아니기 때문에 룰 세팅(rule-setting)에서의 불확실성은 매우 큰 문제로 다가옵니다.

이러한 상황에서 기업은 어떻게 목표를 설정해야 할지 고민하고 있으며, 이제 기업이 맞닥뜨린 퍼스트 무버 리스크가 더 커졌습니다. 기후 위기 대응과 관련된 기술 개발에 어려움을 겪고 있는 회사들이 많아지고 있습니다. 이러한 문제는 세계적인 연구기관들이 함께 고민해야 할 문제이기도 하며, 금융기관들이 앞으로 어떤 목표를 설정할지에 대한 논의가 필요합니다. 각국 정부는 이제 바뀐 환경 속에서 기업들에게 어떤 목표를 제시해야 할지, 그리고 그것이 실제로 현실적인 목표가 될 수 있도록 더 치밀한 고민과 목표 설정이 필요하다고 생각합니다.

**홍종호 교수:** 이형희 위원장님께서 중요한 지적을 해주셨습니다. 기업은 시장에서 생존해야 하고 지속적으로 성장을 해야 하므로, 기후 위기에 대한 대응에서 균열이나 리스크가 생길 수 있다는 지적은 매우 적절합니다. 앞으로 기업이 이러한 리스크에 어떻게 대응할지, 그리고 기업이 룰 세팅을 어떻게 할 것인지는 매우 중요한 문제입니다.

다음으로, 실제로 룰 세팅을 하는 분을 모셨습니다. 금융감독원의 금융시장안정국 국장님이신 이진 국장님께서 발언해 주시겠습니다.

**이진 국장:** 네, 안녕하십니까? 저는 금융감독원의 금융시장안정국장 이진입니다. 오늘 이 자리에서는 간단히 저희 금융감독원에서 기후 위기 대응을 위해 수행하고 있는 업무에 대해 말씀드리겠습니다.

## 1. 국가별 기후위기 대응현황 비교

각국 기후변화 대응 동향을 ①저탄소 정책, ②일반기업 규제, ③금융회사 규제 측면에서 살펴본 결과, 우리나라는 **국제 추세에 발맞추어 대응 중**

| 구분 | | 중요도[1] | 국가 | | | | |
|---|---|---|---|---|---|---|---|
| 기후변화 대응 방안 | | | EU | 영국 | 일본 | 우리나라 | 미국 |
| 저탄소 정책 | 탄소중립 선언/법제화 | - | O/O | O/O | O/O | O/O | O/X[2] |
| | 저탄소 전환 지원 정책 | 높음 | 모든 국가에서 세제 혜택, 금융지원 등을 통해 **저탄소 산업 육성** | | | | |
| | 탄소국경조정제도 (CBAM) | | '23(시범) '26(본격) | '24(검토중) '27(시행) | 수출국 입장에서 기업의 부담 경감을 위한 대응 대비 중 | | '25(시범) '26(본격) |
| 일반기업 규제 | 기후·ESG일반 공시기준 제정 | 높음 | '23.7(확정) 시행중 | '24.7 '26년 | '25.3 '25년 | '24.4(초안) ~'26년 이후 | '24.3 미정 |
| 금융사 규제 | 기후리스크 자본규제 논의 | 낮음[3] | 적극 논의중 | | | 유보적 입장 | |
| | 저탄소 금융 분류 기준 | 중간 | 택소노미·전환금융[4] | | 전환금융[4] | 택소노미 | 없음 |
| | 공시 (금융회사 기후공시) | 중간 | 의무화 완료 | | | 의무화 검토 | |

1) 국내 산업에 미치는 영향 측면에서 중요도를 평가
2) 바이든의 행정명령 내용으로 포함
3) 향후 중요성이 높아질 수 있으나, 국제 논의가 완료되기까지 장기간이 소요될 것으로 보여 '낮음' 표기
4) 순수한 녹색(친환경) 분야는 아니나 온실가스 일부 감축 등 저탄소 전환에 기여하는 분야에 자금을 지원하는 금융

먼저, 우리나라가 기후 위기 대응에서 빠른 편인지, 아니면 늦은 편인지에 대해 간단히 답변 드리고자 합니다. 결론부터 말씀드리면, 우리나라는 기후 위기 규제에 대해 적절한 속도로 대응하고 있다고 생각합니다. 그 이유는 첫째, 2030년 목표와 2050년 넷 제로 목표를 2020년에 선언하고 이를 법으로 명시한 점입니다. 이 법적 조치는 글로벌 추세에 맞춰 마련되었습니다. 또한, 올해 4월에는 정책금융기관을 통해 약 300조 원 규모의 저탄소 투자 확대 기금을 마련하여 집행하기로 했습니다. 이는 저탄소 전환을 위한 금융 공급에 적극적으로 기여하고 있음을 의미합니다. 반면, 탄소 국경세나 공시 제도와 같은 대응은 EU에 수출을 하는 우리나라의 입장을 고려해, 기업의 부담을 최소화하는 적정 속도로 진행되고 있다고 판단됩니다.

### 2-1. 기후리스크 관리지침

동 지침서는 **금융회사 CEO**가 경영 전반에 걸쳐 기후리스크 요소를 반영하는데 도움을 제공

| 영역 | 주요 내용 |
|---|---|
| 사업환경 및 전략 | • 금융회사가 영위하는 사업에 어떤 기후리스크 요인이 단기, 중기 및 장기에 걸쳐 영향을 미치는지 주기적 점검 (§7)<br>• 사업전략 수립 및 실행에 있어 기후리스크의 영향을 고려 (§8) |
| 지배구조 | • 이사회와 업무집행책임자는 금융회사의 전략 등을 수립할 때, 기후리스크를 고려 (§9)<br>• 이사회와 업무집행책임자는 기후리스크를 평가, 모니터링, 보고하기 위한 정책을 포함한 효과적 감독을 유지(§10) |
| 리스크 관리 | • 사업부문별 명확한 역할과 책임, 고객·포트폴리오별 기후리스크 식별 및 평가, 내부통제 정책 등이 반영된 기후리스크 관리체계 구축(§13)<br>• 금융회사는 고객이 기후리스크 관리 방식을 개선할 수 있도록 유도 필요 (§21)<br>• 시나리오 분석 및 스트레스 테스트 실시 필요성과 결과 활용 등 (§26-§27) |
| 공시 | • 결산일로부터 적정한 시간 내에 기후리스크 관리 전반에 관한 정보를 공시 (§31)<br>• 공시내용은 금융안정위원회(FSB) 산하 기후변화 관련 재무정보공개 협의체(TCFD)의 권고사항'을 참고가능(§32)<br>  \*지배구조, 전략, 위험관리, 지표와 감축목표<br>• 공시의 정확성, 비교가능성, 적시성을 평가(§33) |

두 번째로, 저희 금융감독원의 역할에 대해 말씀드리겠습니다. 첫째, 저희는 '기후 리스크 관리 지침'을 제정하여 시행하고 있습니다. 이 지침의 목적은, CEO가 회사의 경영 전략을 수립할 때 탄소 절감을 위한 투자의 목표를 명확히 설정하고, 이사회에서는 CEO와 경영진이 이를 잘 이행하는지 관리 감독하며, 사업부에서는 이사회와 CEO가 설정한 목표를

이행하고 그 결과를 공시하도록 하는 것입니다. 저희는 금융회사가 이러한 기후 리스크 관리 지침을 전략에 반영하고 제대로 실행하는지 정기적으로 점검하고 있으며, 이를 통해 기후 리스크 관리에 대한 관심을 촉진하고 있습니다.

### 2-2. 기후 스트레스테스트

기후 스트레스테스트는 향후 기후변화 및 대응 시나리오에 따라 개별 금융회사가 감내해야 할 손실 규모를 추정하고, 금융안정에 미치는 영향을 평가하는 절차로 수행

1)기후변화 시나리오 생성, 2)금융리스크 전이 분석, 3)영향도 분석 과정을 통해 기후변화가 금융회사의 장기 자본적정성에 미치는 영향을 파악

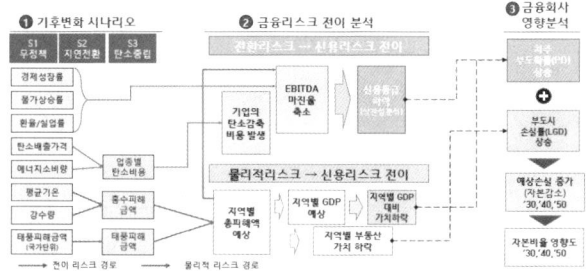

둘째, 금융감독원은 기후 스트레스 테스트를 금융회사와 공동으로 진행하고 있습니다. 기후 스트레스 테스트란, 지구 온난화로 인한 재해 발생과 관련된 손실을 기업이 측정할 수 있도록 돕는 작업입니다. 기업들은 탄소 배출권 거래로 인한 재무적 부담 때문에 채산성이 악화될 수 있으며, 이로 인해 부도 위험이 증가할 수 있습니다. 이러한 리스크를 금융회사의 여신 투자 포트폴리오에서 측정하도록 하여, 금융회사가 직면한 손실 위험을 계량적으로 계산하는 과정을 진행하고 있습니다. 이 테스트의 목적은 두 가지입니다. 첫째, 기후 금융 상품에 대한 프라이싱 역량을 강화하는 측면, 둘째, 금융회사가 저탄소 포트폴리오로 전환하도록 유도하는 의미를 가집니다.

## 2-3. 녹색여신 관리지침

[ 한국과 EU의 ESG금융 시장 규모 및 녹색금융 감독 대응 ]

| | ESG금융 시장 규모 | | 녹색금융 기준 | |
|---|---|---|---|---|
| 한국 | ESG 여신* | 340조원 | 녹색여신 | (관련기준 없음) |
| | 녹색여신 | 관련통계 없음 | | |
| | ESG 채권** | 98조원 | 녹색채권 | 녹색채권 가이드라인 |
| | 녹색채권 | 27조원 | | |
| | * '21년말 기준, ESG금융백서(이용우 의원) | | | |
| | ** '24.9월 기준, 한국거래소 | | | |
| EU | ESG 여신 | 약 1,500억 유로 | 녹색여신 | 녹색여신원칙(민간 규제) 자율 적용 중 |
| | 녹색여신 | 약 300억 유로 | | |
| | ESG 채권 | 약 3,000억 유로 | 녹색채권 | EU 녹색채권 표준 |
| | 녹색채권 | 약 2,500억 유로 | | |
| | ('22년말 기준, EBA) | | | |

⇨ 정부가 추진중인 탄소중립정책이 차질없이 이행될 수 있도록 「녹색여신 관리지침」을 연말까지 제정하여 녹색여신 활성화 추진

   세 번째로, 저희가 올해와 내년에 중점적으로 추진할 사업은 '녹색 여신 관리 지침'을 마련하여 녹색 여신을 활성화하는 것입니다. 현재 우리나라의 녹색 채권은 약 27조 원이 발행되어 있으며, 이는 증권거래소 산하의 녹색채권 가이드라인 기준에 맞춰 발행됩니다. 하지만 녹색 여신에 대한 명확한 기준은 없었기 때문에, 저희는 녹색채권 가이드라인에 준하는 녹색 여신 기준을 마련하여 내년부터 금융기관들이 이를 기반으로 녹색 여신을 많이 공급하도록 유도할 것입니다.

## 2-3. 녹색여신 관리지침

[ 여신과 채권의 감독체계 비교 ]

| 구분 | 여신 | 채권 |
|---|---|---|
| 녹색 금융 정책 특성 | · 녹색여신 관리지침<br>· 금융회사 내부통제에 반영<br>· 녹색여부는 차주(또는 금융사)가 판단 | · 녹색채권 가이드라인<br>· 발행인 공시 의무에 반영<br>· 녹색여부는 외부검증기관이 판단 |
| 거래 관계 | · 채무자·금융사간 쌍방 계약<br>· 녹색자금공급자는 금융사에 국한 | · 자본시장을 통한 중개<br>· 다양한 투자자가 녹색자금 공급 가능 |
| 정보 제공* | · 채무자 확인, 금융회사 검증 가능 | · 발행인 확인·공시, 제3자 검증 가능 |
| 감독 체계 | · 금융회사 내부통제 감독 (직접적)<br>· 약관 심사 | · 발행시장 공시 감독 (간접적) |
| 자금 사용자 | · 채무자 (대기업·중소기업 포함) | · 발행인 (대기업 및 금융회사) |
| 금융회사 장점 | · 여신의 저탄소 전환 (전 권역)<br>· 여신 실적을 금융회사가 홍보 | · 투자의 저탄소 전환 (보험, 금투)<br>· 발행 실적을 발행인이 홍보 |

* 자금 사용 확인에 대한 사항 포함

## 2-3. 녹색여신 관리지침

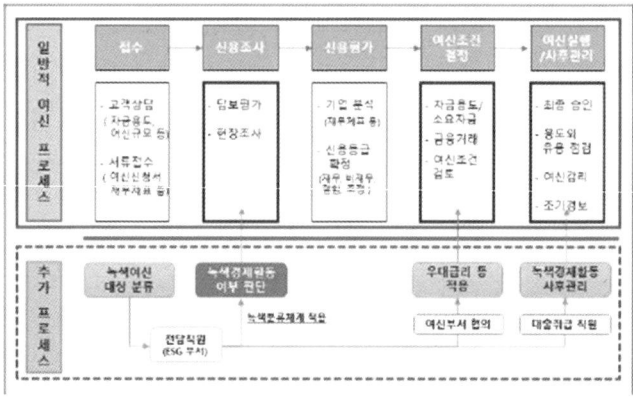

[ 녹색분류체계를 적용한 여신 프로세스 개요 ]

녹색 여신과 녹색 채권의 차이점은, 채권은 발행자가 스스로 인증을 받아 공시하지만, 녹색 여신은 금융회사가 차주에 대해 해당 여신이 녹색 경제 활동에 해당하는지를 판단하여 심사하고, 그에 맞는 금리 혜택이나 인증서를 제공하는 방식입니다. 녹색 여신 관리 지침은 금융회사의 여신 관리 프로세스에 내재되며, 차주가 대출을 신청할 때 제출한 서류를 은행의 전담 부서에서 녹색 경제 활동에 해당하는지 심사하고, 맞다면 금리를 인하하거나 인증서를 제공하여 혜택을 제공하는 방식입니다. 이후 이 자금이 실제로 녹색 활동에 활용됐는지에 대해 사후 관리도 진행됩니다.

### 2-4. 중소기업 ESG 지원

전세계적 탄소중립 추진에 따라, **탄소국경조정제도**가 '26년부터 EU 등에서 시행될 예정으로 국내 수출 중소기업 등에 부담 증가 전망 → 중소기업에 대한 금융권 공동 ESG 교육 및 컨설팅 지원 추진

| 금융권 ESG 교육과정 개설을 위한 MOU 체결 및 교육 진행 | ESG 컨설팅 지원 |
|---|---|
| • 금융회사(5대 지주), 지자체(서울시 등), 전문기관(기상청,환경산업기술원) 등과 업무협약식을 체결('23. 7월)하고, 금융회사 및 중소기업 담당자 100명을 선발하여 ESG 전문교육을 실시 중 | • 하나 금융지주, 인천시(인천자유경제구역청), 수출중소기업(10개사) 등과 업무협약식을 체결(23.7~8월중)하고, 해당 중소기업에 대한 맞춤형 ESG 컨설팅을 제공<br><br>- (컨설팅 내용) 단위 제품 생산당 온실가스 배출량, 원자재 구매·생산·납품 등 공급망내 지역별 기후리스크 산정 등 환경 부문 및 임직원의 근로조건 등 인권 부문<br><br>- (컨설팅 업체) 금융회사 직원 또는 환경 관련 스타트업 등 전문업체가 컨설팅을 실시하고, 금감원은 코디네이터로서 전체 과정을 조율 |

마지막으로, 중소기업들이 기후 위기에 대응하는 데 어려움을 겪고 있다는 점을 말씀드리겠습니다. 대기업들은 비교적 여력이 있지만, 대기업에 납품하는 중소기업들은 어려움을 겪고 있습니다. 이에 금융감독원은 은행이나 대기업과 협력하여 중소기업들에게 컨설팅을 제공하고 있으며, 작년 10월과 올해 10월에는 삼성전자와 함께 은행들이 2조 원 규모의 기금을 조성하여 녹색 탄소 저감 투자를 지원하는 프로그램을 운영하고 있습니다.

이상으로, 저희 금융감독원의 기후금융 관련 업무와 방향에 대해 말씀드렸습니다. 기후 위기 대응은 후대를 위한 필수적인 과제라고 생각하

며, 저희 금융감독원은 이에 대한 사명감을 가지고 적극적으로 업무를 추진하고 있음을 말씀드리며 마치겠습니다. 감사합니다.

**홍종호 교수:** 이진 국장님께서 우리나라 금융감독원의 기후 금융에 대한 역할과 향후 방향에 대해 잘 설명해 주셨습니다.

이제 이번 세션을 마무리하며, 세 분의 토론자께서 말씀하신 한국 상황에서의 기후 금융과 탈탄소화 관련 의견에 대해 비노드 토마스 박사님께서 마무리 정리 발언을 해주시겠습니다. 토마스 박사님 부탁드립니다.

**비노드 토마스 박사:** 감사합니다. 발표자 분들께서 너무 명확하게 기후금융과 한국이 취하고 있는 조치들, 그리고 그와 관련된 중요한 원칙들을 잘 전달해주셨습니다. 이 세션에 큰 찬사를 보냅니다. COP 29가 진행되고 있는 이 시점에 이 행사가 열리고 있다는 것이 정말 놀랍습니다. 이 세션에서 나온 논의들이 이 분야에서 중요한 역할을 하는 분들께 잘 전달되기를 바랍니다.

앞서 논의된 내용 외에 짧게 몇 가지 추가적인 포인트를 강조하고자 합니다. 첫째, 우리는 한국을 비롯한 전 세계에서 기후 위험이 증가하는 상황을 목격하고 있으며, 이에 대한 회복력이 이를 따라잡아야 한다는 점입니다. 예를 들어, 더 이상 단순히 홍수 이후 복구하는 것으로는 충분하지 않습니다. 우리는 앞으로 올 재해가 더욱 심각할 수 있기 때문에, '되돌리는' 것이 아니라 '앞으로 나아가는' 방식으로 대응해야 합니다. 이것이 첫 번째 핵심입니다.

둘째, 금융 구조에서 녹색채권 뿐 아니라 보증에 대한 강조도 매우 중요합니다. 이 부분은 상대적으로 덜 강조된 점이지만, 그 중요성을 간과해서는 안 됩니다. 또한, 한국이 배출권 거래제, 정량적 제한, 탄소세를 결합한 방안을 시도해 볼 수도 있다고 제안드립니다. 이러한 접근은 거의 손해를 보지 않으면서도 수익을 얻을 수 있는 방법입니다.

셋째, 마지막 토론에서 언급된 스트레스 테스트의 중요성은 매우 크다고 생각합니다. 전 세계 중앙은행들에게 독립성의 중요성을 내세워 기후 문제를 무시하는 이유로 삼지 않기를 촉구합니다. 기후 변화는 인플레이션, 성장, 고용에 큰 영향을 미칠 것이기 때문입니다. 만약 스트레스 테스트가 시행된다면, 기후 재해로 인해 금리가 상승할 가능성이 높아지는 한편, 재생 가능 에너지에 대한 장기 금융이 필요함에 따라 금리가 하락할 가능성도 있습니다. 결국, 이러한 상황에서는 분리된 금리 구조가 필요할 수도 있습니다. 이는 전통적인 접근법과 다르고 어려운 일일 수 있지만, 외부효과를 고려할 때 충분히 논의할 가치가 있습니다. 중앙은행은 이러한 스트레스 테스트를 진행하면서 중요한 역할을 할 것입니다.

다음으로, 한국에 대해 말씀드리고 싶습니다. 우리가 기후 변화 대응에서 완화, 예방, 적응, 그리고 기후와 함께 살아가는 방법에 대해 논의했습니다. 그렇다면 한국에서 무엇에 더 집중할지를 결정해야 할 시점입니다. 완화와 적응에 각각 얼마의 자원을 할당할 것인가 하는 문제입니다. 시간이 부족해 깊이 논의할 수는 없지만, 한국에 있어 50대 50의 비율이 적절한지 생각해볼 필요가 있습니다. 결국 재정 담당자들은 기후 금융이 단지 기후 변화 대응을 위한 것이 아니라 완화나 적응을 위한 것인지에 대한 명확한 답을 필요로 합니다.

한국은 그 역할을 훌륭히 해내고 있습니다. 전 세계는 한국을 모델로 보고 있으며, 이는 결국 한국의 이익을 위한 일입니다. 시간이 지남에 따라 재생 가능 에너지의 가격이 하락할 때, 한국은 기후 정책을 수립하는 데 어려움을 겪지 않게 될 것입니다. 오히려 이를 통해 국민의 복지뿐 아니라 지구의 복지에도 기여할 수 있게 될 것입니다. 감사합니다.

**홍종호 교수:** 네, 감사합니다. 지속가능성장을 위한 기후금융 및 상생금융의 혁신을 주제로 한 이번 세션은 지속가능한 성장을 위한 리스크와 수익의 균형의 중요성에 대한 여러 고민과 해결방안을 나누는 매우 유익하고 인사이트 넘치는 시간이었습니다. 앞으로 관련 논의가 더욱 활발하게 이어졌으면 좋겠습니다. 그럼 이것으로 두번째 세션을 마치겠습니다. 경청해 주신 여러분 감사합니다.

## 세션 III
# 인구위기 극복 전략과 금융의 역할

**좌장**
이인실 한반도미래인구연구원 원장/前 통계청장

**기조발표**
조앤 윌리엄스(Joan Wiliams) 캘리포니아주립대 법대 교수
찰스 유지 호리오카(Charles Yuji Horioka) 고베대 석좌교수, IARIW 회장
/前 日경제학회 회장

**패널**
서정호 한국금융연구원 인구변화대응연구센터장
정신동 KB경영연구소 소장(전무)
김경록 미래에셋자산운용 고문

**이인실 원장:** 안녕하세요. 마지막 세션의 사회를 맡은 이인실 한반도 미래인구연구원 원장입니다. 저는 최근 대학교에서 정년퇴임을 하고, 한국의 심각한 인구 문제를 해결하기 위해 이 연구원을 설립하여 운영하고 있습니다. 오늘 세션의 주제는 '인구 위기 극복 전략과 금융의 역할'입니다. 이번 세션에는 두 명의 해외 학자를 모셨습니다. 한 분은 법률학자이시고, 다른 한 분은 경제학자이십니다. 또한, 세 명의 토론자가 함께해 주십니다. 먼저, 기조연설자들을 간단히 소개드리겠습니다.

첫 번째 연사는 조앤 윌리엄스 교수님입니다. 교수님은 캘리포니아 대학교 샌프란시스코 법학전문대학원 교수이시며, 특히 '대한민국 망했어요'라는 밈(meme)으로 널리 알려지신 분입니다. 교수님께서 한국에 오셨을 때 그것에 대해 여쭤봤더니, 본인도 당시에는 과격한 표현이었음을 인정하시면서도, 현재 한국 상황에 대해 우려의 목소리를 내셨습니다. 교수님은 UN의 다양성과 포용성 관련 부문 전문가이시며, 기업들에 대한 자문을 많이 하시고, 직장 내 편견 문제를 다룬 하버드 비즈니스 리뷰 논문 등으로도 유명하십니다. 최근에는 11편의 논문을 발표하시고, 많은 책을 출판하신 대단한 학자이십니다.

두 번째 연사는 찰스 유지 호리오카 교수님입니다. 교수님은 경제학자로, 현재 고베대학교 석좌 교수로 재직 중이시며, 국제소득분배연구협회 회장을 맡고 계십니다. 교수님은 일본 경제학회에서 주는 '나카하라상'을 수상한 경력이 있으며, 인구 위기와 금융 문제에 대한 깊은 통찰력을 가지고 계신 분입니다.

이제 토론자를 소개해 드리겠습니다. 첫 번째 토론자는 서정호 금융연구원 인구변화대응연구센터장님입니다. 서 센터장님은 한국은행, 금융감독원, 하나은행 등에서 다양한 경험을 쌓으셨으며, 금융산업과 디지털 금융 연구에도 깊은 통찰을 가지고 계십니다. 오늘 세션에서 금융의 역할에 대해 좋은 의견을 나누어 주실 것입니다.

두 번째 토론자는 김경록 미래에셋자산운용 고문님입니다. 김 고문님은 미래에셋에서 채권운용과 자산운용을 담당하며, 은퇴 연구소 소장도 역임하셨고, 인구 문제에 대해 심도 있는 연구를 해오신 분입니다. 그의 인구문제에 대한 견해와 해법에 대해 기대가 큽니다.

세 번째 토론자는 정신동 KB경영연구소 소장님입니다. 정신동 소장님은 경제학 박사로, 금융정책 자문과 연구소 활동을 통해 금융산업과 관련된 중요한 연구를 하셨습니다. 현재는 KB금융지주의 경영연구소 소장으로 인구 위기 대응에 관한 연구와 활동을 이어가고 계십니다.

그럼 이제 조앤 윌리엄스 교수님의 영상을 시청하시겠습니다.

**조앤 윌리엄스 교수:** 안녕하세요, 저는 조앤 윌리엄스입니다. 먼저, 'IGE-KB금융그룹의 2024 지속가능성 글로벌서밋' 개최를 축하드리며, 이렇게 훌륭한 자리에 초대해 주신 것에 진심으로 감사드립니다. 직접 참석하지 못하는 점 양해 부탁드립니다.

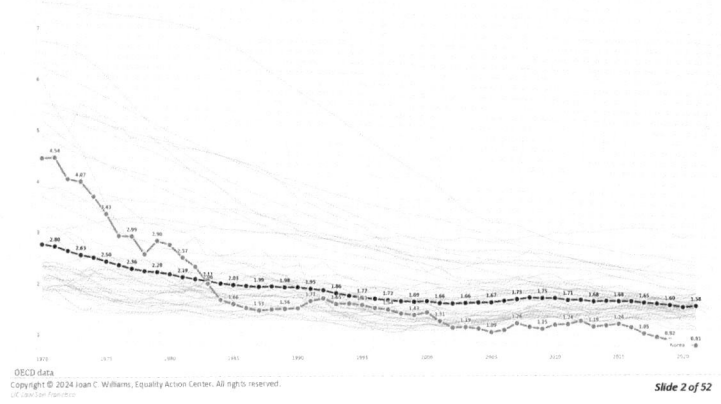

## Why haven't investments paid off?

Korea
- among top OECD countries in childcare & education funding
- greatly ramped up leave
- paying women to have children

Those investments won't solve the problem.

　　오늘은 한국의 출산율과 금융의 연관성에 대해 말씀드리겠습니다. 많은 분들이 제 밈을 보셨을 것입니다. 그 밈은 한국이 OECD 국가들 중에서 출산율이 가장 낮다는 그래프에 대한 제 반응을 담고 있습니다. 그 그래프를 보고 저는 매우 충격을 받았고, 이후로 그 문제에 대해 깊이 생각해 왔습니다. 제가 내린 결론은, 한국의 경제 기적을 가능하게 했던 문화적 가치들이 이제는 이를 누릴 세대를 낳지 못할 위기에 처했다는 것입니다. 이는 매우 아이러니한 상황입니다. 현재 한국은 출산율을 높이기 위해 상당한 투자를 하고 있습니다. 예를 들어, 한국은 육아와 교육에 대한 지원이 OECD 국가들 중 상위권에 속합니다. 또한, 최근 몇 년간 육아휴직 기간을 대폭 연장하고, 여성들에게 아이를 낳도록 유도하는 지원금을 지급하고 있습니다. 그러나 이러한 투자는 높은 비용에도 불구하고, 문제를 해결하는 데 한계가 있다는 점이 안타깝습니다.

## Work system: the ideal worker

- Someone who works 50+ hours a week for forty years straight, taking no time off for childbirth, childcare or anything else
- As compared with OECD average
  - Men are 2x—women 2.5x—as likely to work 50+ hrs/wk

출산율 문제를 주로 여성의 문제로 간주하는 경향이 있지만, 그 문제는 훨씬 더 근본적입니다. 우선, 한국의 노동 시스템을 살펴보겠습니다. 현재 시스템은 주당 50시간 이상 일하며, 거의 40년 동안 쉬지 않고 일하는 노동자를 이상적으로 설정하고 있습니다. 또한, 출산, 육아, 노인 돌봄 등 다른 책임은 아예 고려되지 않은 채 설계된 시스템입니다. 한국 남성은 주당 50시간 이상 일할 가능성이 두 배, 여성은 2.5배 더 높은 상황입니다.

## Work system: work devotion

- Employees are expected *"to demonstrate commitment by making work the central focus of their lives"*
  - Not leaving before your manager
  - Socializing after work

## Work system: parental leave

- Uptake is low
- Only 18% leave takers are men (2019)
- Only 23% of mothers use the leave financed by the National Employment Insurance (2017)

## Work system: discrimination

- Mothers are—and should be—less committed and competent

- *"A good wife should support her husband"*

## Work system: career breaks

- If you take a career break, very hard to get back into "regular work"
  - Mothers: 3x as likely to be in non-regular employment
  - Non-regular employees average 45% less (2019)

이러한 노동 시스템에서 여성들은 '모성 역할'에 대한 편견으로 차별을 받기도 합니다. 저희 연구소는 이 문제를 문서화하는 데 도움을 주었으며, 이 차별은 여성들이 아이를 낳기 전보다 덜 헌신적이고 덜 유능하다는 가정에 근거합니다. 이러한 모성 역할에 대한 편견은 노동 시장에서 큰 영향을 미치며, 여성들이 직장을 그만두고 다시 돌아오는 것 자체가 매우 어려운 현실을 만들어냅니다. 많은 여성들은 출산 후 경력 단절로 인해 평생 직장에서 불이익을 당할 것이라는 우려를 가지고 있습니다.

## Family system: pressure to quit

- 87% of Koreans believe mothers of preschool children should work at most part time...but PT work is rare
- Only 1/3 of mothers stay in the same job (2018)
- One of few OECD countries with "M curve"

또한, 한국 사회에서는 어머니들이 직장을 그만두는 강한 압박을 느끼고 있으며, 한 연구에 따르면 한국인의 87%는 취학 전 아동의 어머니가 파트타임으로 일해야 한다고 생각합니다. 그러나 한국에서 파트타임 근무는 매우 드물고, 그로 인해 많은 어머니들이 출산 후 직장을 떠나게 됩니다. 이런 현상은 OECD 국가들 중에서 한국만의 특징으로, M 곡선이라는 현상을 보여주며, 아이를 낳은 후에는 일을 그만두고, 그 후에는 가정 내 일로 돌아가는 경향이 나타납니다.

### Family system: education system

- Mothers: expected to manage tutoring, cram schools, homework

- Also hard to afford, along with housing, on one income

### Family system: childcare system

- Childcare system: *excellent!* but...

- Childcare and afterschool ends long before parents are home from work

- Again: work system assumes a wife at home

가족 제도의 측면에서도 문제는 여전히 존재합니다. 예를 들어, 어머니들은 과외, 학원 관리, 숙제 등을 맡아야 하며, 이러한 부담은 대부분 한 가정의 수입으로 해결하기 어려운 상황입니다. 그로 인해 많은 가족들이 경제적으로 어려움을 겪고 있습니다. 비록 한국의 보육 시스템은 탁월하지만, 방과 후 돌봄이 부모가 퇴근하기 전에 끝나는 시스템은 여전히 아내가 전일제로 가정을 책임지는 것을 전제로 하고 있습니다.

## Family system: eldercare

- 67% of Koreans rely on "family members" for eldercare (2018)
- Daughters, daughters-in-law

또한, 한국의 노인 돌봄은 가족 구성원, 특히 딸이나 며느리에게 의존하는 경우가 많습니다. 이로 인해 일부 여성들이 결혼을 꺼리는 이유가 되기도 합니다. 결혼과 출산에 대한 부담이 커지면서, 많은 젊은 사람들이 결혼하지 않고 아이를 갖지 않는 방향을 선택하고 있습니다.

## Mismatch of expectations

- Women do 8x more housework
- 6x more child- and elder-care (2019)

*Men's household contributions: 2nd lowest in OECD*

## Divorce rate rises after holidays

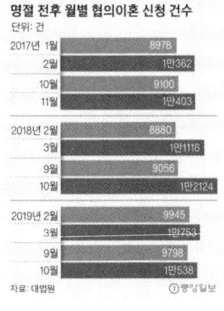

한국에서 여성들이 가사와 자녀 돌봄을 남성보다 8배 더 많이 하며, 이로 인해 가사노동에서 여성의 부담이 상당히 커집니다. 이에 따라 결혼 후 갈등이 발생하거나, 이혼율이 증가하는 경향도 보입니다. 특히 명절과 같은 특정 시기에는 가사 노동의 부담이 더욱 커지며, 아내가 대부분의 일을 맡는 구조로 인해 갈등이 발생하기도 합니다.

## What won't work

- Paying women to have children
  - Would have to pay 15x more than current rates
  - ~75% of births would have happened anyway

Choo and Jales, 2021

결국, 이 문제에 대한 해결책은 무엇일까요? 첫 번째로, 여성을 대상으로 한 단순한 금전적 지원은 큰 효과를 보지 못할 것입니다. 예를 들어, 2021년 연구에 따르면, 한국이 이 문제를 해결하려면 현재의 비용보다 15배 더 많은 비용을 지불해야 한다고 합니다. 그리고 출산율 증가를 위한 여러 정책들은 비효율적이거나 효과가 미미할 가능성이 큽니다.

## Working hard sets us apart!

- Among longest work hours of any country

BUT

- Productivity in Korea is 48% lower than in US
- Need to differentiate between enacting work devotion and working efficiently

두 번째로, 노동 시스템의 근본적인 변화가 필요합니다. 한국의 노동 생산성이 낮은 상황에서 장시간 근무가 낮은 생산성과 연결된다는 사실을 인식하고, 헌신과 효율성의 차이를 구분하는 것이 중요합니다. 이를 통해 일하는 방식의 개선이 이루어져야 합니다.

### 10 steps: redefine the ideal worker

1. Reward managers for productivity, not work devotion
2. Create 30-hour workweek in "regular" jobs with career progression
3. Keep 52-hour limit; "flexibility" proposal
4. Make it easy to return to regular employment after 1-3 years out

### 10 steps: leave

5. Employers need to replace employees on leave – not overwork their colleagues
    Hire a temporary worker

6. Set expectation ***both*** parents will take full leave
    If men don't take leave, women who do will be stigmatized
    Leaves > 1 year discourage ♀'s workforce participation

## 10 steps: end discrimination

7. Enforce prohibitions against discrimination against mothers

> Women with access to leave 3.6x as likely to say they want children—but only if don't report gender discrimination (2024)

8. Heed Korean Supreme Court decision: ERs have a duty of care to accommodate mothers

## 10 steps: resculpt masculinity

9. Address the concerns of Korean youth for good jobs and affordable apartments – rather than encouraging young men to blame young women

## 10 steps: rethink eldercare

10. Do something to provide a workforce to provide eldercare

저출산 문제를 해결하는 데 있어 중요한 방법은 고용 시스템을 유연하게 바꾸는 것입니다. 예를 들어, 여성들이 주당 30시간의 고품질, 장기 파트타임 일자리를 찾을 수 있도록 하고, 경력 단절 후 복귀가 용이한 시스템을 만드는 것이 중요합니다. 또한, 고용주가 휴직 중인 직원을 대체할 수 있는 방안을 마련하고, 휴가를 사용하는 남성들에게도 동일한 기회를 부여하는 등의 조치가 필요합니다.

마지막으로, 여성에 대한 차별을 근본적으로 해결하고, 남성과 여성 모두가 평등한 기회를 가질 수 있는 시스템을 구축해야 합니다. 이러한 변화가 이루어지지 않으면, 한국의 경제와 사회는 지속 가능한 발전을 이루기 어려울 것입니다.

저는 한국 전문가가 아니지만, 미국에서 한국의 중요성을 잘 알고 있습니다. 한국은 우리에게 매우 중요한 파트너이며, 한국의 성공이 우리에게도 중요한 의미를 지닌다고 생각합니다. 그래서 오늘 제가 제시한 생각들이 한국의 미래를 위한 작은 기여가 되기를 바랍니다. 다시 한번, 초대해 주셔서 감사드리며, 직접 참석하지 못해 아쉬운 마음을 전합니다. 여러분의 관심과 참여에 감사드립니다.

**이인실 원장:** 윌리엄스 교수님의 발표를 잘 들었습니다. 다양한 데이터를 활용해서 한국의 저출산과 이에 따른 사회적 문제, 이를 해결할 수 있는 방안 등에 대해 통찰력있는 말씀을 해주셨습니다.

이제 다음으로 호리오카 교수님을 모시겠습니다.

**찰스 유지 호리오카 교수:** 안녕하세요. 저는 일본 고베대학교의 호리오카 찰스입니다. 이렇게 중요한 행사에서 기조 연설자로 참여하게 되어 매우 영광이고 기쁩니다. 이번 행사를 주최하고 후원해주신 세계경제연구원과 KB금융그룹에 깊은 감사의 말씀을 전합니다.

## OBJECTIVE OF THIS TALK

(1) To document trends in population ageing (an increase in the proportion of people who are aged 65 or older)
(2) To explore the challenges posed by population ageing
(3) To explore solutions to these challenges
(4) To explore the role that the financial sector can play to mitigate the demographic crisis

오늘 발표에 앞서, 첫 번째 발표자인 윌리엄스 교수님께서 출산율과 출산율 감소에 대해 다루셨습니다. 이 주제가 제 발표와도 매우 잘 어울려서 기쁘게 생각합니다. 저는 인구의 또 다른 끝, 즉 고령 인구에 대해 이야기하고자 합니다.

오늘 제 발표는 인구 고령화의 추세, 고령화로 인한 도전 과제, 그리고 이를 해결할 수 있는 방안에 대해 다룰 것입니다. 구체적으로, 네 가지 주요 주제를 다루겠습니다. 첫째, 고령화가 진행되고 있는 추세를 문서화할 것입니다. 둘째, 고령화로 인한 문제를 탐구할 것입니다. 셋째, 이러한 문제에 대한 해결책을 제시할 것입니다. 넷째, 금융 부문이 이 인구 문제를 완화하는 데 어떤 역할을 할 수 있는지 살펴보겠습니다.

## MY RESEARCH INTERESTS

I am an economist and my primary field of expertise within economics is **Household Economics**, which is the branch of economics that examines various aspects of the behavior of individuals or households, including:

1. Their consumption behavior
2. Their saving behavior
3. Their borrowing behavior
4. Their housing purchase behavior
5. Their bequest behavior
6. Their caregiving behavior

먼저 제 소개를 드리자면, 저는 경제학자이며 특히 가계 경제학을 전공하고 있습니다. 개인과 가구의 행동에 관한 다양한 측면을 연구하고 있기 때문에, 오늘 발표는 제 연구 분야에 근거한 내용이 될 것입니다.

# TRENDS IN POPULATION AGEING

Population ageing (an increase in the proportion of people aged 65 or older) is occurring throughout the world but its speed and timing varies greatly from country to country and region to region.

It has been especially pronounced in Europe in the past, but it will become especially pronounced in Asia in the future.

Proportion of Population Aged 65 and Older

| Rank | 2020 | | 2030 | | 2050 | |
|---|---|---|---|---|---|---|
| 1 | Japan | 28.40 | Japan | 30.87 | Korea | 38.07 |
| 2 | Italy | 23.30 | Italy | 27.89 | Japan | 37.69 |
| 3 | Portugal | 22.77 | Portugal | 27.05 | Spain | 36.81 |
| 4 | Finland | 22.55 | Greece | 26.51 | Greece | 36.23 |
| 5 | Greece | 22.28 | Lithuania | 26.38 | Italy | 36.01 |
| 6 | Germany | 21.69 | Germany | 26.18 | Taiwan | 34.99 |
| 7 | Bulgaria | 21.47 | Finland | 25.99 | Portugal | 34.81 |
| 8 | Malta | 21.32 | Hong Kong | 25.84 | Hong Kong | 34.68 |
| 9 | Croatia | 21.25 | Slovenia | 25.46 | Singapore | 33.27 |
| 10 | Puerto Rico | 20.83 | Malta | 25.32 | Puerto Rico | 32.65 |
| 11 | France | 20.75 | Puerto Rico | 25.16 | Slovenia | 32.14 |
| 12 | Slovenia | 20.74 | Croatia | 25.08 | Poland | 31.13 |
|  | Korea (42) | 15.79 | Korea (15) | 24.75 |  |  |

Source: United Nations, World Population Prospects

그럼 첫 번째 주제로 넘어가겠습니다. 바로 고령화의 추세에 대한 이야기입니다. 고령화는 전 세계에서 일어나고 있지만, 그 속도와 시기는 국가와 지역마다 큰 차이를 보입니다. 이를 보여주는 자료를 하나 준비했습니다. 이 표는 2020년, 2030년, 2050년 세 시점에서 65세 이상 인구 비율을 보여줍니다. 2020년 수치는 실제 데이터이며, 2030년과 2050년은 유엔의 추정치입니다.

2020년을 보면, 일본은 65세 이상 인구 비율이 28.4%로 전 세계에서 가장 고령화된 사회였으며, 이는 거의 30%에 달합니다. 일본을 제외하고는 매우 작은 국가들만이 그 비율이 높았고, 다른 고령화 국가들은 대부분 유럽에 위치해 있습니다. 이를 통해 고령화는 유럽에서 가장 먼저 시작된 경향을 보입니다. 반면, 한국은 42위에 해당하는 16%로 상대적으로 낮은 수치를 기록하고 있었습니다.

2030년으로 넘어가면 일본은 여전히 1위로, 고령자 비율이 31%에 가까워졌습니다. 유럽 국가들이 상위권에 여전히 많이 자리잡고 있지만, 홍콩이 유일한 아시아 국가로 상위 10위에 들어갑니다. 한국은 42위에서 15위로 급상승했지만, 아직 10위권에는 들지 않았습니다.

2050년으로 가면, 한국은 일본을 제치고 1위에 올라 65세 이상 인구 비율이 38%에 달하게 됩니다. 일본은 37.7%로 약간 뒤처져 있습니다. 또 다른 특징은 상위 10개국 중 유럽 국가들이 대부분 빠지고, 대만, 홍콩, 싱가포르 등 아시아 국가들이 추가되었다는 점입니다. 이를 통해 고령화가 유럽에서 시작된 뒤 아시아로 빠르게 확산되고 있으며, 특히 일본과 한국이 그 중심에 있음을 알 수 있습니다.

# ECONOMIC IMPLICATIONS OF POPULATION AGEING

Population ageing will present at least 3 challenges:

(1) It may lead to a **labor shortage** as the ratio of the working-age population to the retirement-age population declines.

(2) It may lead to a **deterioration of government finances** since expenditures for social safety nets (e.g., public pensions, long-term care insurance, health insurance, etc.) are heavily biased toward the elderly.

(3) It may lead to changes in **consumption** and **saving**.

이제 고령화가 어떻게 진행되는지에 대한 첫 번째 주제를 마쳤습니다. 두 번째와 세 번째 주제인 고령화가 초래하는 도전 과제와 이를 해결할 수 있는 방안에 대해 이야기하겠습니다. 고령화로 인한 문제는 많지만, 저는 경제학자로서 세 가지 경제적 측면에 대해 집중하고자 합니다. 첫 번째는 노동력 부족 가능성, 두 번째는 정부 재정의 악화, 세 번째는 가계의 소비 및 저축 행태의 변화입니다.

## (1) LABOR SHORTAGE

It is true that population ageing may lead to a **labor shortage** as the ratio of the working-age population to the retirement-age population declines, but there are at least three ways to avoid potential labor shortages.

First, we can delay retirement and encourage the **elderly** to work longer. People are not only living longer but also remaining healthy for longer so it is quite possible for them to work longer, and moreover, many people want to continue working because it gives more meaning to their lives.

먼저 노동력 부족에 대해 말씀드리겠습니다. 고령화로 인해 노동 연령 인구와 은퇴 연령 인구의 비율이 줄어들면, 노동력 부족이 발생할 수 있습니다. 하지만 이 문제를 해결할 수 있는 몇 가지 방법이 있습니다.

첫째, 은퇴 연령을 늦추고 고령자들이 더 오래 일할 수 있도록 장려하는 것입니다. 앞서 한 발표에서도 언급되었듯이, 사람들은 더 오래 살고 건강을 유지하고 있습니다. 건강한 사람들은 계속해서 일을 할 수 있습니다. 또한 많은 고령자들이 일을 계속하고 싶어 합니다. 이는 경제적인 이유뿐만 아니라 삶에 의미를 부여하기 위한 측면도 있습니다.

## (1) LABOR SHORTAGE (cont'd)

Second, in many, if not most, countries, **females** are not able to realize their full potential in the labor market and enabling them to do so would also help to alleviate any potential labor shortages.

Third, allowing more **foreign workers** into the country is yet another way of alleviating potential labor shortages.

둘째, 여성들이 노동 시장에서 그들의 잠재력을 충분히 발휘할 수 있도록 도와주는 것입니다. 많은 나라에서 여성들이 노동 시장에서 충분한 기회를 가지지 못하고 있는데, 이들을 적극적으로 노동 시장에 참여시킬 수 있다면 노동력 부족 문제를 완화하는 데 도움이 될 것입니다.

셋째, 외국인 근로자를 더 많이 받아들이는 것도 노동력 부족 문제를 해결하는 방법 중 하나입니다.

## (2) DETERIORATION OF GOVERNMENT FINANCES

It is true that population ageing may lead to a **deterioration of government finances** since expenditures for social safety nets (e.g., public pensions, long-term care insurance, health insurance, etc.) are heavily biased toward the elderly.

To put it another way, government finances will be strained because population ageing will lead to an increase in the number of retired people that each worker needs to support.

다음으로, 고령화가 정부 재정에 미치는 영향에 대해 이야기하겠습니다. 고령화는 공적 연금, 건강 보험, 장기 요양 보험 등 사회 안전망 지출을 증가시키기 때문에 정부 재정에 큰 부담을 주게 됩니다. 간단히 말해, 고령화는 노동 연령 인구가 은퇴한 사람들을 부양해야 하는 부담을 증가시키기 때문에, 정부 재정이 악화될 위험이 있습니다.

## (2) DETERIORATION OF GOVERNMENT FINANCES (cont'd)

The most obvious solution to this problem is to reduce benefits, increase contributions, and/or to delay the age at which people can start collecting public pensions, long-term care benefits, etc., but this will threaten the retirement security of the elderly.

Another possible solution is to shift from a **pay-as-you-go** system to a **fully funded** system so it will not be affect by demographic trends.

이를 해결하는 가장 일반적인 방법은 연금 수급 연령을 늦추거나, 기여금을 늘리거나, 혜택을 줄이는 것입니다. 하지만 이는 고령자의 은퇴 후 안정적인 삶을 위협할 수 있습니다.

## (2) DETERIORATION OF GOVERNMENT FINANCES (cont'd)

A third possible solution is to switch from a **defined benefit** system to a **defined contribution** system.

A fourth possible solution is to increase the role for **private pensions**—company pensions, individual pensions, etc.—as a way of supplementing public pensions.

In my opinion, **extending the retirement age** is the best solution not only to the first challenge but also to the second challenge because it would simultaneously alleviate potential labor shortages and improve the finances of the public pension system.

또 다른 방법으로는 '지급 준비금 시스템'으로 전환하는 것입니다. 이 방식은 인구 고령화와 같은 인구 구조 변화에 영향을 받지 않는 장점이 있습니다. 하지만 제 생각에는 가장 좋은 해결책은 은퇴 연령을 연장하는 것입니다. 이렇게 하면 기여금을 납부하는 사람들이 늘어나고, 혜택을 받는 사람들은 줄어들어 노동 시장과 정부 재정 모두에 긍정적인 영향을 미칠 수 있습니다.

## (3) SAVING AND CONSUMPTION

Population ageing will have various impacts of the saving and consumption behavior of households so its net impact is ambiguous.

Looking first at theoretical considerations, …

## SAVING AND CONSUMPTION (cont'd)

- The **life-cycle hypothesis or model**, the workhorse model of household behavior, assumes that, when individuals are young, they work, earn income, and save part of their income to prepare for their living expenses during retirement, and that, when they are old, they retire and finance their living expenses using the wealth they accumulated during their working years.
- Thus, this model predicts that elderly individuals (at least those who are retired) should be dissaving or decumulating their wealth and that the aggregate household saving rate will be lower the higher is the ratio of the retirement-age population to the working-age population.

## SAVING AND CONSUMPTION (cont'd)

- This implies that population ageing will lead to a decline in the aggregate household saving rate.
- Saving is important because it provides the funds needed to finance investment, and household saving plays the important role of providing the funds needed to finance household investment in housing, corporate investment in plant and equipment, government investment in social infrastructure, and saving shortages abroad, so there is a danger that a decline in the aggregate household saving rate will lead to a saving shortage in the economy (or the world) as a whole.
- However, this is not necessarily the case because many of the countries experiencing population ageing will simultaneously show absolute declines in population, which will reduce the need to expand the productive capacity of the economy and therefore reduce the need to engage in corporate investment in plant and equipment.

## SAVING AND CONSUMPTION (cont'd)

- Furthermore, there is always the option of borrowing from countries with saving surpluses to meet domestic saving shortages.
- Thus, declines in the aggregate household saving rate will not necessarily cause any problems in the economy as a whole.

마지막으로 고령화가 가계의 저축 및 소비 행동에 미치는 영향에 대해 말씀드리겠습니다. 가장 일반적인 가계 행동 이론인 '생애 주기 가설'에 따르면, 사람들은 젊을 때 일하며 저축하고, 노후에는 그동안 모은 저축을 소비하며 살게 됩니다. 이 이론에 따르면, 고령화가 진행되면 가계 전체의 저축률이 낮아지고, 소비가 늘어날 것으로 예측됩니다. 그러나 제가 일본과 유럽에서 연구한 결과에 따르면, 은퇴한 고령자들이 여전히 저축을 계속하거나 저축을 아주 천천히 사용하고 있어 '저축 과다'와 '소비 부족' 문제가 발생하고 있다는 것을 알 수 있었습니다.

## SAVING AND CONSUMPTION (cont'd)

- I have been assuming until now that elderly individuals dissave (decumulate their wealth) after they retire, but my extensive research about the saving behavior of the elderly in Japan and European countries has found that the even the retired elderly in these countries are either continue to accumulate wealth or that they are decumulating their wealth only very slowly and that they can be expected to leave large bequests when they pass away.
- In other words, the problem is not that the retired elderly are dissaving too much (saving too little) but that they are not dissaving too little (saving too much). Since saving and consumption are two sides of the same coin, this implies that the retired elderly in these countries are not consuming enough.

## SAVING AND CONSUMPTION (cont'd)

- This will lower the quality of life of the retired elderly and prevent them from enjoying the fruits of their many years of hard work.
- Moreover, it will also lower aggregate consumption in the household sector as a whole and may cause the economy as a whole to fall into recession.
- In other words, there is a real possibility that population ageing will lead to too much saving and too little consumption not only by the retired elderly but also in the household sector as a whole.

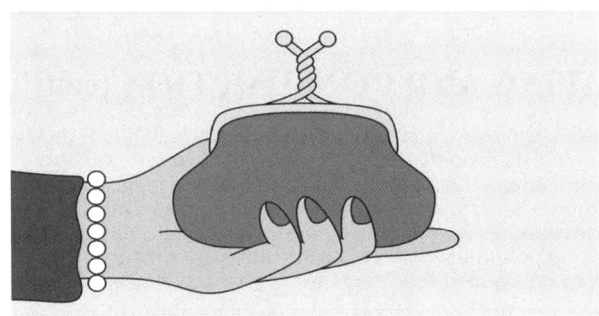

The Economist, June 1, 2024, issue
Finance and economics | Live a little
**Baby-boomers are loaded. Why are they so stingy?**
The mystery matters for global economic growth

# SAVING AND CONSUMPTION (cont'd)

Possible reasons for the excessive saving and inadequate consumption of the retired elderly:

**(1) Bequest motives**

**(2) Precautionary saving** arising from lifespan uncertainty (longevity risk) and/or future uncertain medical and long-term care expenses.

이 문제는 두 가지 이유로 설명될 수 있습니다. 첫째, 고령자들이 자녀에게 남기기 위해 저축을 많이 하고 있다는 점입니다. 둘째, 고령자들이 미래의 건강 문제나 장기 요양 비용 등에 대한 불확실성 때문에 '예비저축'을 하고 있다는 점입니다.

## SAVING AND CONSUMPTION: SOLUTION

Possible solutions to the problem of excessive saving and inadequate consumption:

(If bequest motives are the reason)

(1) Raise **inheritance taxes** and **gift taxes** to encourage the elderly from leaving bequests and *inter vivos* transfers to their children.


## SAVING AND CONSUMPTION: SOLUTION

Possible solutions to the problem of excessive saving and inadequate consumption:

(If precautionary saving is the reason)

(2) Maintain or expand public or private **pension** systems, **health insurance** systems, and **long-term care insurance** systems to help reduce the various risks that the elderly face, which, in turn, induce them to reduce their precautionary saving and increase their consumption.

## SAVING AND CONSUMPTION: SOLUTION

Both of the policies that I am recommending would encourage the elderly to decumulate their considerable wealth holdings more rapidly and to use this wealth for consumption, which would be good for elderly individuals themselves as well as for the economy as a whole.

Moreover, all of my proposals have the added advantage of discouraging bequests and *inter vivos* transfers, thereby alleviating the extent to which wealth disparities are passed on from generation to generation and leading to a more equitable society.

이 문제를 해결하기 위한 방법은 두 가지가 있습니다. 첫째, 상속세와 증여세를 인상하여 고령자들이 더 많이 소비하고 자녀에게 남기는 재산을 줄이도록 유도하는 것입니다. 둘째, 사회 안전망을 확대하여 고령자들이 미래에 대한 불안을 덜 느끼고 더 많은 소비를 하게 만드는 것입니다.

## SAVING AND CONSUMPTION: THE ROLE OF THE FINANCIAL SECTOR

What can the financial sector do to alleviate the problem of excess saving and inadequate consumption by the elderly?

(1) Offer the elderly a variety of private pension, health insurance, and long-term case insurance system that will help reduce the various risks that they face and that, in turn, will induce them to reduce their precautionary saving and increase their consumption. Since public systems will almost definitely have to be scaled back due to the deterioration of government finances caused by population ageing, there will be an increased market for private systems.

(2) In particular, offer the elderly a variety of innovative financial products that make it easier for them to use their wealth on their own consumption such as reverse mortgages.

# SAVING AND CONSUMPTION: THE ROLE OF THE FINANCIAL SECTOR

(3)Help the elderly **manage their assets** wisely, whether they are holding them to leave to their children or to use it themselves.

(4)Provide seminars, training, etc., to increase the **financial literacy** of the elderly, which is often not very high.

마지막으로, 금융 부문이 고령화 문제 해결에 어떻게 기여할 수 있는지 말씀드리겠습니다. 금융 부문은 다양한 방법으로 고령자들을 지원할 수 있습니다. 예를 들어, 개인 연금, 건강 보험, 장기 요양 보험과 같은 상품을 제공함으로써 고령자들이 직면한 다양한 위험을 줄이고, 그들이 저축을 덜 하게 만들어 소비를 증가시킬 수 있습니다.

또한 금융 부문은 고령자들이 자산을 보다 잘 관리할 수 있도록 돕고, '역모기지'와 같은 새로운 금융 상품을 통해 고령자들이 자택을 담보로 평생 연금을 받을 수 있도록 지원할 수 있습니다.

# SAVING AND CONSUMPTION: THE ROLE OF THE FINANCIAL SECTOR

All of these policies would help the elderly to make more optimal consumption and bequest decisions and will, at the same time, help to increase consumption in the household sector as a whole, causing the elderly as well as society as a whole to be better off.

Thus, the financial sector can play an important role in meeting the challenges of population ageing and the demographic crisis.

마지막으로, 금융 부문은 고령자들의 금융 문해력을 높이기 위한 세미나나 교육 프로그램을 제공할 수 있습니다. 고령자들이 보다 나은 재정적 결정을 내릴 수 있도록 돕는 것이 매우 중요합니다.

결론적으로, 금융 부문은 고령화 문제를 해결하는 데 중요한 역할을 할 수 있습니다. 다양한 금융 상품을 제공하고, 고령자들이 더 나은 소비와 상속 결정을 내리도록 돕는 것이 그들의 삶의 질을 높일 뿐만 아니라, 전체 경제에도 긍정적인 영향을 미칠 것입니다.

경청해 주서서 대단히 감사합니다.

**이인실 원장:** 호리오카 교수님, 한국 고령화에 대한 주요 현안과 대응방안 등에 대한 심도있는 발표 잘 들었습니다. 감사합니다.

다음으로 서정호 박사님을 모시겠습니다. 오늘은 줌으로 연결하겠습니다. 박사님?

**서정호 센터장:** 안녕하세요. 저는 한국금융연구원 인구변화대응연구센터장 서정호입니다. 세계경제연구원과 KB금융그룹이 주최하는 '2024 지속가능성 글로벌 서밋'에 초대해 주셔서 진심으로 감사드립니다. 저출산과 고령화 문제는 현재 국가적으로 중요한 화두가 되고 있습니다. 이에 저희 연구원도 인구변화대응연구센터를 새롭게 설립해 체계적인 연구를 진행하고 있습니다. 오늘 이렇게 귀한 자리에 초대되어 너무 감사한데, 불가피하게 현장에 참석하지 못해 죄송한 마음도 전하며 양해를 부탁드립니다.

오늘 두 명의 저명한 학자분들의 발표를 들을 수 있어 매우 영광이었습니다. 윌리엄스 교수님께서는 저출산 문제에 대해 많은 말씀을 해주셨고, 호리오카 교수님께서는 일본의 고령화 경험을 통해 한국이 직면한 문제들에 대해 중요한 인사이트를 주셨습니다. 제 발표는 주로 한국의 상황과 문제에 집중하지만, 두 교수님의 발표와 겹치는 부분이 많아 아마도 서로 비교하면서 들으시면 더 흥미로울 것입니다.

먼저, 오늘 제가 말씀드리고자 하는 주제는 세 가지입니다. 첫째, 한국이 겪고 있는 인구 변화를 살펴보겠습니다. 둘째, 이러한 인구 변화가 한국의 금융 부문에 미치는 영향을 생각해보겠습니다. 셋째, 금융이 이러한 문제들에 어떻게 대응할 수 있을지에 대해 간략하게 언급하겠습니다.

**급격한 출생률 저하 → 총인구 감소**

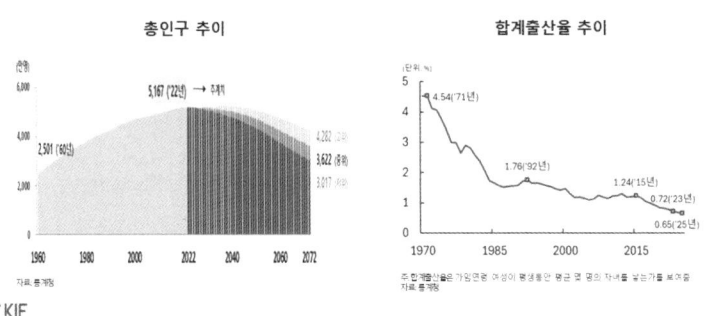

먼저, 한국의 인구 변화를 보겠습니다. 2020년 기준으로 한국의 총인구는 약 5200만 명이었으나, 현재는 감소세로 전환되었습니다. 수명 연장에도 불구하고 출생률이 너무 낮아서 인구가 감소하는 상황입니다. 한국은 OECD 국가들 중에서도 저출산율이 최하위를 기록하고 있으며, 내년에는 출산율이 0.6명대로 떨어질 것으로 예상됩니다. 이러한 출산율 수준은 초저출산 국가라고 할 수 있습니다.

**유소년인구 감소, 생산연령인구 감소, 고령인구 증가**
**→ 노동공급 감소, 급격한 고령화**

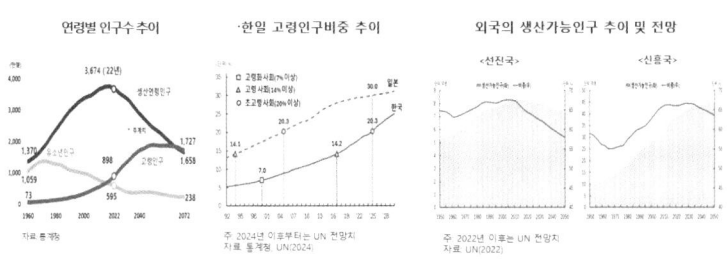

다음으로, 한국의 인구 구조가 급격히 변화하고 있다는 점을 주목해야 합니다. 65세 이상의 인구는 증가하고, 65세 미만 인구는 급격히 줄어들고 있습니다. 이로 인해 한국의 인구 피라미드는 빠르게 역삼각형 형태로 변하고 있으며, 이 속도는 일본보다 훨씬 빠릅니다. 현재로서는 2045년경 한국의 고령 인구 비중이 일본을 초과할 것으로 예상됩니다.

또한, 한국은 고령화가 빠르게 진행되는 동시에 글로벌 고령화도 함께 겪고 있다는 점이 중요합니다. 전 세계적으로 생산 가능 인구 비중이 감소하고 있으며, 이는 한국에 추가적인 도전 과제가 될 것입니다.

### 인구변화 요인들은 다양한 경로로 금융부문에 영향을 미침

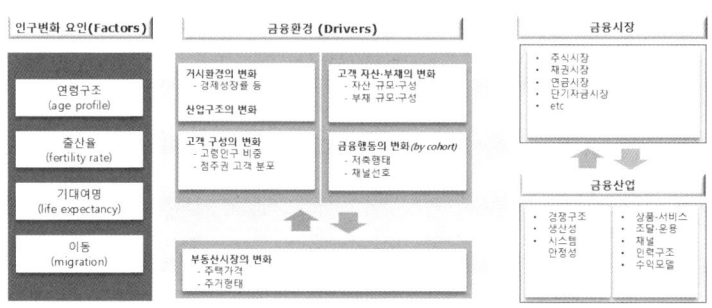

### 고령화가 금융시스템에 미치는 파급경로

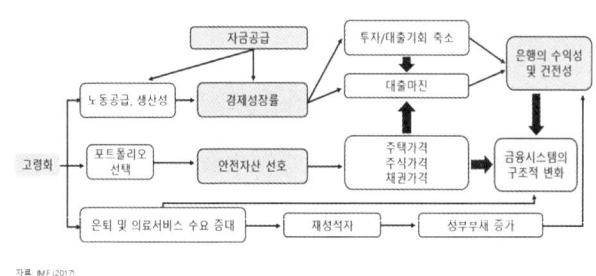

자료: IMF (2017)

　인구 변화는 금융 부문에 직접적으로 영향을 미칩니다. 예를 들어, 고령화로 인해 경제 성장률이 떨어지고, 자금 운용 기회가 축소되며, 금융기관의 수익성이나 건전성도 악화될 수 있습니다. 또한, 고령화가 경제 주체들의 자산 선호에 영향을 미쳐, 금융 시장의 변화가 예상됩니다.

### 금융이 할 수 있는 두가지 역할

**완화적 역할**
- 금융산업이 저출생 문제 완화에 어떤 도움을 줄 수 있을까?
- 금융산업이 고령층의 어려움 해소에 어떤 도움을 줄 수 있을까?

**적응적 역할**
- 이러한 변화에 직면해 국내 금융산업이 어떻게 경쟁력을 유지해 나갈까?
- 이러한 변화에 직면해 어떻게 금융시스템의 안정을 강화해 나갈까?
- 인구변화를 어떻게 성장의 기회로 활용할 것인가?

∷ KIF

이러한 인구 변화에 대응하기 위해 금융 부문은 두 가지 관점에서 접근할 수 있습니다. 첫째, 저출산과 고령화 문제를 완화하는 방안을 고민해야 하고, 둘째, 금융 산업이 급격히 변하는 환경에 어떻게 적응하고 경쟁력을 유지할 수 있을지에 대한 고민이 필요합니다.

### 완화적 역할 예시 (금융당국)

- 국민들의 체계적인 재산형성 및 부(wealth)의 세대간 이전을 촉진하기 위해 세제혜택 등 충분한 유인책을 부여해야 함
  - 이는 정부가 미리 마중물을 부여줌으로써 미래에 국가가 짊어져야 할 재정적 부담을 사전에 국민 스스로 준비하도록 하는 효과
  - 부의 세대간 불균형이 심화되는 현상을 완화하기 위해 상속 및 증여 관련 세제개편 논의도 본격화

- 금융시장에서 모험자본이 축소되지 않도록 하고, 금융부문의 부동산 의존도를 축소해 나가야 함

- 고령화에 대응하기 위해 신탁제도를 과감하게 개선하고 세제지원도 확대
  - 종합재산신탁이 활성화될 수 있도록 수탁가능재산의 범위 확대
  - 다양한 비금융서비스와 연계할 수 있도록 위수탁 혹은 재신탁 등을 유연하게 허용

- 출산율 제고를 위해서는 주거비용 절감에 초점을 맞추고 제도 개선
  - 출산가구가 가입·투자하는 금융상품(모기지 포함)에 대해 세제지원 확대 및 한도산정 시 유리한 조건제공

∷ KIF

완화적 측면에서, 정부는 청년층에게 강력한 유인책을 제공하여 체계

적이고 안정적인 재산 형성을 촉진할 필요가 있습니다. 또한, 고령화가 진행됨에 따라 안전 자산에 돈이 몰리는 현상을 관리해야 하며, 과도한 부동산 의존도를 줄여야 합니다.

**적응적 역할 예시** (금융회사)

- 대출 및 투자수요 축소에 따라 금융의 새로운 역할 모색
- 보유 부동산의 소득화가 점진적으로 진행될 수 있도록 상품 및 서비스 개발
- 부동산 리스크 관리 강화
- 의료·요양·상속 등 고령층의 니즈와 금융서비스 간의 연계성 강화
- 일과 가정이 양립할 수 있는 근무환경 및 기업문화 조성하고 양질의 일자리를 창출
- 고령층의 금융접근성 제고

KIF

금융 부문에서는 고령화로 인한 대출 및 투자 수요 감소를 대비하여 신규 수익원을 발굴하고, 고령화된 인구 비중이 높은 국가로 진출하는 전략도 고려해야 합니다. 또한, 부동산의 유동화 문제를 해결하기 위해 역모기지 상품 등을 개발해야 할 필요가 있습니다.

마지막으로, 금융권이 지속 가능성 문제에 적극적으로 대응해야 한다는 점에서, 저출산과 고령화 문제를 해결하는 것이 한국 사회의 지속 가능성을 높이는 중요한 과제가 될 것입니다. 이상으로 제 발표를 마치겠습니다. 감사합니다.

**이인실 원장:** 서정호 박사님, 훌륭한 발표 감사드립니다. 이제 김경록 고문님께서 말씀해주시겠습니다.

**김경록 고문:** 앞서 두 분 연사님의 발표 잘 들었습니다. 인구 고령화와 과소 소비(under consumption)에 대해 언급해 주셨습니다. 저는 이 부분에 대해 한국의 상황을 중심으로 어떻게 대응할 수 있을지에 대해 말씀드리겠습니다.

일본은 이미 우리보다 훨씬 고령화가 진행된 국가로, 축적된 자산을 어떻게 소비로 이끌어낼 수 있을지에 대한 논의가 매우 중요한 이슈가 되고 있습니다. 그러나 한국은 아직 그 정도의 상황에까지 이르지 않았습니다. 그렇기 때문에 한국은 우선 자산 축적 문제부터 해결해야 하는 상황입니다. 그와 함께, 한국에서는 향후 고령층의 소비를 어떻게 활성화할 것인가가 중요한 과제가 될 것입니다. 이 부분에 대해 좀 더 구체적으로 다뤄보겠습니다.

먼저, 일본을 비롯한 고령화가 이미 진행된 나라들의 발표를 참고하면서 우리나라와의 차이점을 인식할 필요가 있습니다. 일본은 2007년 이미 초고령 사회에 진입했으며, 독일은 2010년 우리보다 15년 앞서 초고령 사회에 접어들었습니다. 반면 우리나라는 내년 정도에 초고령 사회에 진입할 예정입니다. 이처럼 초고령 사회 진입 시점에서 다른 선진국들과 차이가 나기 때문에, 한국은 현재 상황에서 맞춤형 해결책을 모색해야 한다는 점이 첫 번째로 중요한 부분입니다.

두 번째 큰 차이점은, 다른 OECD 국가들과 한국의 청년 연령 차이입니다. 한국의 정년 연령은 60세이고, 대부분의 OECD 국가들은 65세 이상 또는 정년 연령이 없는 경우가 많습니다. 또한 한국의 실질적인 퇴직 연령은 대개 55세 전후로, 이는 다른 선진국들과 큰 차이를 보입니다. 이로 인해 한국은 55세에서 65세 사이의 재취업 시장이라는 독특한 노동시장이 형성되어 있습니다. 이 특수한 노동시장을 어떻게 발전시킬 것인가가 한국만의 과제입니다.

또한, 한국의 인구 구조는 매우 특이한데, 1955년부터 1995년까지 약 40년 동안 출생한 '베이비 붐' 세대가 경제에 미치는 영향이 크다는 점에서 다른 선진국들과는 다릅니다. 이러한 점들을 고려하여 해결책을 마련해야 합니다.

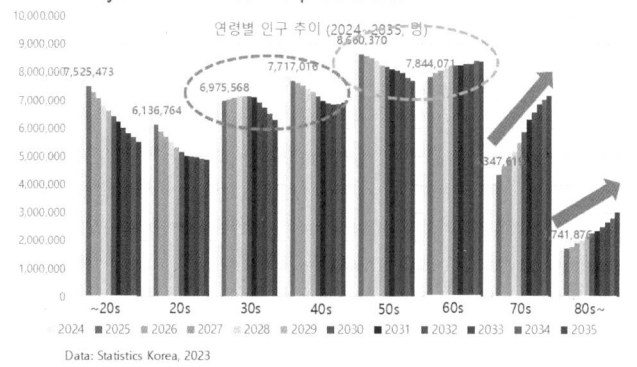

또한, 우리나라의 향후 10년간의 연령대별 인구 구조를 보면, 50대와 60대 인구가 여전히 주축을 이루고 있으며, 30대와 40대의 인구도 여전히 일정 부분 존재하고 있습니다. 이는 다른 선진국들과 큰 차이를 보이는 점입니다. 따라서 향후 10년 동안 한국 사회는 50대와 60대 인구를 어떻게 관리하고, 70대 이상의 고령층 시장에 대응할 것인가가 중요한 포인트가 될 것입니다.

## Conditions for alleviating excessive savings (under-consumption) among the elderly

- Need a stable income in old age. Conditions for securing a stable income
  ① A well-organized re-employment market for those in their 50s and 60s
  ② Enhancing the liquidity of illiquid assets – reverse mortgage (housing pension)
  ③ Securing stable retirement income through systematic withdrawals
  ④ Accumulating financial assets through private pension

## Labor market for those in their 50s and 60s

- The reemployment market is a kind of lemon market (used car market) : information asymmetry.
- Matching jobs that fit one's abilities is necessary.
- Data organization and accumulation are necessary.

| | | KOREA | OECD | G7 | EU27 | 일본 |
|---|---|---|---|---|---|---|
| Employment ratio | 15~24세 고용률 | 27.6% | 42.8% | 34.8% | 47.3% | 46.7% |
| | 55~64세 고용률 | 68.8% | 62.9% | 65.8% | 62.3% | 78.1% |
| Temporary Employment Ratio | 55~64세 임시직 | 34.4% | 8.6% | 6.9% | 6.2% | 22.5% |
| | 65세~ 임시직 | 70.0% | 17.1% | 14.9% | 17.4% | 39.2% |

International comparison of employment ratios and temporary employment ratios by age (2022)

자료: OECD, http://data.oecd.org/emp/
주: 고용률: 취업자/해당 연령 그룹 인구

이제 한국에서 '과소 소비' 문제나 노후에 안정적인 소득을 마련하기 위한 방법에 대해 네 가지 해결책을 제시하고자 합니다. 첫째, 50대와

60대의 재취업 시장을 잘 정비하는 것이 매우 중요합니다. 현재 한국의 노동 시장에서 55세 이상의 고용률은 높지만, 비정규직 비율이 OECD 국가들에 비해 매우 높습니다. 이로 인해 소득 안정성이 떨어지고, 결국 과소 소비가 발생할 수 있습니다. 따라서 고용 안정성을 높이는 것이 가장 시급한 과제입니다.

**Expanding and activating housing pension**

- House rich, Cash poor
- Currently, up to 1.2 billion won worth of housing is covered by the housing pension
  ① For houses worth 1.2 billion won more, private housing pensions need to be activated.
  ② Linking housing pensions and basic pensions

둘째, 한국에서는 주택 부분의 비중이 매우 크기 때문에, 이를 어떻게 소득흐름으로 연결할 것인가가 중요한 문제입니다. 주택연금은 이미 도입되었지만 여전히 사용 비율이 낮기 때문에, 이를 어떻게 활성화할 수 있을지에 대한 논의가 필요합니다. 특히 저소득층을 대상으로 주택연금과 기초연금을 연계해 소비를 촉진할 수 있는 방법을 모색해야 합니다.

### Securing retirement income through systematic withdrawals

- 3 risks when withdrawing
  - Longevity, Investment return sequence, Inflation
- For securing retirement income,
  ① Diversification of fixed income products for retirees through introduction of pension bonds and retirement bonds
  ② Activation of insurance companies' longevity pension and guaranteed dividend products
  ③ Personalized withdrawal system based on big data and AI

셋째, 안정적인 인출 상품에 대한 고민이 필요합니다. 은퇴 후 안정적인 소득을 위한 다양한 인출 시스템이 마련되어야 합니다. 현재 한국은 장수연금이나 연금채권 같은 상품이 부족한 상황인데, 이를 통해 사람들이 안정적으로 소비할 수 있도록 해야 합니다.

**Accumulating retirement assets through private pensions**

- Two puzzles of lifetime asset management
  - Stock market participation puzzle, Annuity puzzle
- In Korea, two puzzles stand out in extremes. In particular, retirement pension assets are extremely biased towards principal and interest guaranteed products
  - Improving retirement pension performance
  - Excluding principal and interest guaranteed products from default options
  - Activating TDFs and qualified default products

넷째, 자산 축적 문제입니다. 한국에서는 많은 사람들이 아직 자산 축적을 해야 하는 연령층에 속해 있습니다. 현재 한국의 연금 자산에서 주식 자산의 비중은 매우 낮습니다. 이는 매우 중요한 문제로, 더 나은 자산 축적을 위해 주식 자산 비중을 높이고, 다양한 재정적 제도들이 활성화되어야 합니다.

마지막으로, 중소기업 퇴직연금과 같은 제도들이 실제로 활성화되지 않고 있는 문제도 해결해야 합니다. 특히 30인 이하의 중소기업 퇴직연금 기금은 저소득층을 위한 노후 소득 보장에 중요한 역할을 할 수 있습니다. 따라서 이 부분을 더 잘 보완하여 노후 소득을 보장할 수 있는 시스템을 만들어야 합니다. 이상으로 제 코멘트를 마치겠습니다. 감사합니다.

**이인실 원장:** 굉장히 중요한 지적을 해주셨습니다. 감사합니다. 이제 마지막으로 정신동 소장님께서 말씀해주시겠습니다.

**정신동 소장:** 안녕하세요. KB경영연구소 정신동 소장입니다. 오늘 발표와 토론을 잘 들었습니다. 특히 조앤 윌리엄스 교수님께서 한국의 실태에 대해 실감 나게 말씀해 주셔서 많은 공감을 느꼈고, 호리오카 교수님께서 제시하신 고령화 대응책에 대해서도 저희가 생각하고 있는 바와 유사한 점들이 있어 공감이 되었습니다. 저희 연구소도 인구 문제에 대해 큰 관심을 가지고 연구하고 있으며, 이를 지속적으로 지켜보고 있습니다.

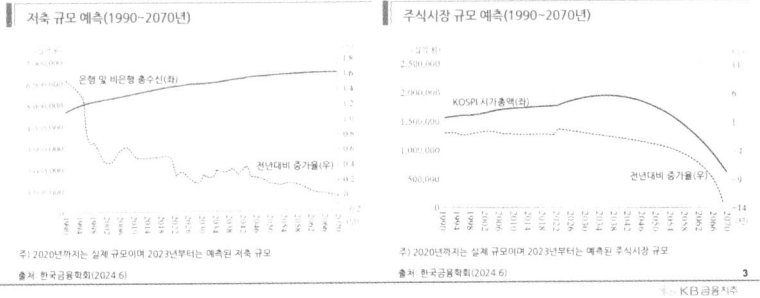

오늘 제가 말씀드리고자 하는 부분은 개인적으로 금융의 역할에 대한 생각입니다. 우선, 인구 현황에 대해서는 앞서 발표자들께서 잘 다뤄주셨기 때문에 별도로 언급하지 않겠습니다. 또한, 인구 구조 변화의 영향에 대해서도 이미 충분히 설명되었으므로 생략하도록 하겠습니다. 대신, 금융학회에서 발표된 연구 결과를 잠깐 소개드리겠습니다. 주식시장은 1950년대 이후 급락 현상이 나타난다는 '멜트다운(Meltdown)' 이론이 있으며, 왼쪽 표에서 보듯이 저축은행, 4금융권을 중심으로 구조조정이 이루어질 수 있다는 내용을 제시하고 있습니다.

### ① 저출생 극복

### Ⅲ. 금융의 역할

- **(저출생의 근본 원인)** 여성 의식과 권리가 향상됨에 따라 출산과 육아를 스스로 결정하고 선택
  - 가부장제 및 남성 중심 사회는 여성으로 하여금 결혼과 출산에 부정적 인식을 야기 → 여성 미혼율은 약 33%까지 상승
  - **여성과 육아에 대해 사랑과 존중, 지원을 아끼지 않는 풍토 마련 필요**
- **(금융지원)** 해외 사례 참조 및 일·가정 양립의 사각지대 개선
  - (헝가리) 상환 유예 및 원금 감면 등 파격적 주거지원 정책 / (미국, 프랑스) 일·가정 양립 등 양질의 보육환경 확보
- **(금융회사)** 조직문화의 모범사례 구축 및 컨설팅 등을 통해 거래 중소기업에 전파
  - 청년 및 신혼부부의 자산형성과 주택자금을 지원하기 위한 다양한 상품·서비스를 개발

**헝가리의 가족 주택 지원금 제도**

| 구분 | 주요내용 | 비고 |
|---|---|---|
| 대상 | • 만 41세 미만 기혼 여성 가정 | |
| 대출금액 | • 1자녀: 1,500만 포린트<br>• 2자녀: 3,000만 포린트<br>• 3자녀 이상: 5,000만 포린트 | 1포린트 = 3.73원 |
| 금리 | • 연 5% 이하 | 기준금리 6.75% |
| 대출기간 | • 10년 ~ 25년 | |
| 추가 출산 혜택 | • 1자녀: 1년 상환 유예<br>• 2자녀: 1,000만 포린트 원금 감면<br>• 3자녀: 1,000만 포린트 원금 추가 감면 | |

출처: 2024 세계지식포럼 '헝가리 인구대역전 비결' 및 언론보도 정리(2024.9)

**저출생 극복 관련 상품 예시**

| 구분 | 주요 내용 |
|---|---|
| 예적금 | 어린이 고객, 다자녀 양육 부모 등에게 수신금리 우대 |
| 대출 | 신혼부부, 다자녀, 난임부부에 대한 금리 및 한도 우대 |
| 신탁 | 증여신탁 등 신탁 다양화 및 활성화 |
| 금융투자 | 저출생 대응펀드 및 관련 기업 ETF 출시 |
| 자산관리 | 자산형성을 지원하기 위한 금융서비스 강화 |
| 보험 | 태아보험, 어린이보험, 자녀 관련 특약 등에 대한 상품성 개선 및 보험료 인하 검토 |
| 카드 | 카드 포인트 확대, 유아·아동 용품 구매시 할인, 바우처 사업 활성화 등을 통한 실생활 혜택 증대 |
| 주거안정 | 주택구매를 위한 장기 적금 또는 연금 출시 검토 |
| 사회공헌 | 저출생 극복을 위한 사회공헌 사업 확대 |

출처: KB경영연구소

저출생 문제를 극복하기 위한 금융의 역할에 대해 간단히 말씀드리겠습니다. 금융의 역할을 논의하기에 앞서, 저출생 현상이 왜 발생했는지에 대한 근본적인 성찰이 필요하다고 생각합니다. 여러 요인이 있겠지만, 가장 중요한 원인은 출산의 주체인 여성들의 권리와 의식의 변화입니다. 예전에는 출산과 육아가 당연한 것으로 여겨졌으나, 이제는 스스로 결정하고 선택할 문제로 인식되기 시작한 것입니다. 저도 두 딸을 두고 30년간 가정생활을 해본 결과, 가장 큰 갈등의 원인은 바로 여성을 어떻게 배려할 것인가 하는 문제였습니다.

우리 사회는 여전히 가부장적인 남성 중심의 구조가 강하게 남아 있어서, 많은 여성들이 결혼과 출산에 대해 부정적인 생각을 갖게 됩니다.

현재 이혼율이 33%에 달하며, 이는 초저출산의 주요 원인으로 작용하고 있습니다. 이를 해결하기 위해서는 여성과 육아에 대한 사회적 사랑과 존중, 그리고 적극적인 지원이 필요하다고 생각합니다.

이와 관련하여 헝가리의 사례를 참고할 수 있습니다. 헝가리는 자녀 수에 따라 대출 상환을 유예하는 등의 금융적 지원을 아끼지 않고 있으며, 이러한 사례는 우리에게 큰 시사점을 줍니다. 또한, 미국과 프랑스와 같은 선진국들은 일과 가정의 양립과 출산 후 양질의 보육 환경을 확보하는 데 중점을 두고 있는 만큼, 그들의 사례도 참고할 필요가 있다고 생각합니다. 우리나라는 일과 가정 양립 정책 면에서 선진국에 뒤지지 않지만, 여전히 사각지대가 존재하는 점이 문제입니다. 따라서, 이러한 부분에서 조직 문화의 모범 사례를 구축하고 이를 중소기업 등으로 확산시키는 것이 금융기관의 역할 중 하나일 것입니다.

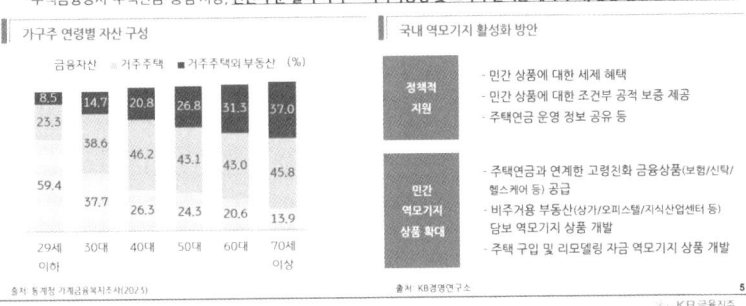

고령화 문제에 대해서는 앞서 많은 분들이 언급해 주셨으므로 간략히

말씀드리겠습니다. 현재 고령층의 부동산 자산 비중이 약 70-80%에 달하는데, 이 자산을 어떻게 현금 흐름으로 전환할 것인지가 금융의 중요한 역할이라고 생각합니다. 또한, 일본의 역모기지 사례를 참고할 필요가 있습니다. 우리 연구소에서도 이와 관련한 조사를 진행했으나, 일본에서는 다양한 상품이 존재하는 반면, 우리나라에서는 그 활성화가 미비합니다. 따라서 민간 차원에서의 지속적인 정책적 지원과 노력이 필요하다고 생각합니다.

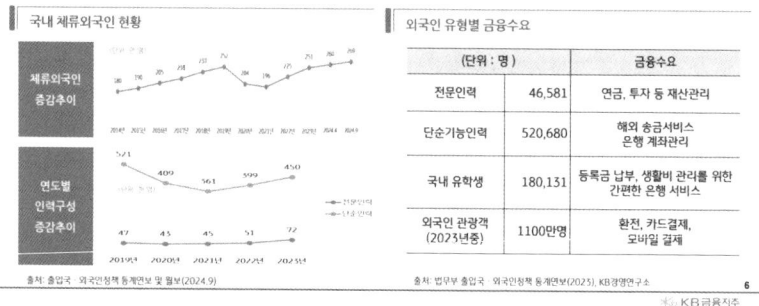

다음으로, 외국인 근로자 문제에 대해 간단히 말씀드리겠습니다. 지난 4월, 우리나라 외국인 근로자 비율이 5%를 초과하면서 다문화 국가로의 진입을 선언하게 되었습니다. 앞으로도 전문 인력을 계속해서 확충할 계획이므로, 외국인 비율은 지속적으로 증가할 것으로 보입니다. 이에 따라, 외국인을 포용하고 금융 서비스를 제공하는 것은 중요한 과제이며, 아직 초기 단계에 있는 외국인 대상 금융시장이 크게 성장할 가능성이 있다는 점에서 금융기관이 적극적으로 나서야 한다고 생각합니다.

# III. 금융의 역할

④ (제언) 교육 집중 및 인재 육성

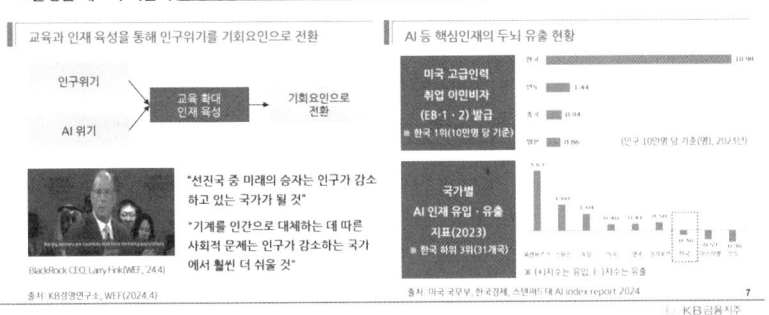

마지막으로, 교육과 인재의 중요성에 대해 말씀드리겠습니다. 21세기는 단순히 교육 경쟁을 넘어서 교육의 전쟁 시대라고 할 수 있습니다. 특히, 인공지능(AI)의 등장으로, 미래 사회는 AI를 잘 다룰 줄 아는 사람과 그렇지 못한 사람으로 계급화될 가능성이 크다고 전망되고 있습니다. 이러한 점에서 저출산이 오히려 한국의 축복이 될 수 있다는 외신의 보도가 있었습니다. 소수의 자녀에게 교육을 집중 투자함으로써 글로벌 경쟁력을 갖춘 인재를 양성할 수 있다는 주장입니다. 그러나 최근 한국의 우수 인재들이 해외로 이탈하고 있다는 보도가 있어 우려스럽습니다. 오른쪽 그래프에서 보시듯, 10만 명당 인구 유출 비율이 우리나라가 다른 국가들에 비해 매우 높습니다. 이는 우수 인재들이 충분한 대우를 받지 못하거나 근무 환경이 조성되지 않아서 해외로 유출되고 있다는 문제를 보여줍니다. 따라서 인구 위기를 극복하기 위해서는 출산율 증가뿐만 아니라 우수 인재를 어떻게 육성하고, 그들이 역량을 발휘할 수 있는 환경을 어떻게 조성할 것인지도 중요한 과제입니다.

## IV. KB의 추진현황

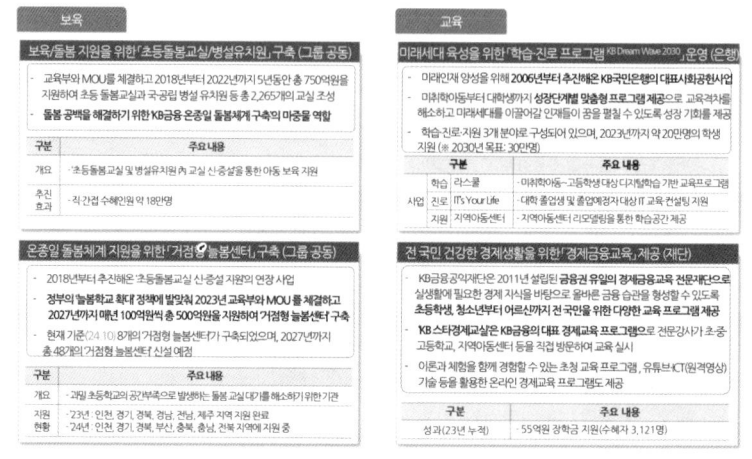

끝으로, KB의 추진 현황에 대해 간단히 말씀드리겠습니다. 저희도 조직 문화 조성 및 보육 교육 등 다양한 사회 공헌 활동을 활발히 진행하고 있습니다. 2018년부터 교육부와 협력하여 750억 원을 지원, 전국에 2265개의 초등 돌봄교실을 만들었고, 2023년부터는 추가로 500억 원을 투자하여 거점 센터를 신설하고 있습니다. 오늘 논의를 바탕으로 한국의 인구 위기 대응이 성공적인 사례로 자리 잡기를 기대하며, 제 발언을 마치겠습니다. 감사합니다.

**이인실 원장:** 훌륭한 말씀 감사합니다. 마칠 시간이 다 되어, 호리오카 교수님께 마무리 발언 부탁드리겠습니다.

**찰스 유지 호리오카 교수:** 마무리 코멘트를 할 수 있는 기회를 주셔서 감사합니다. 한국에 대한 지식이 부족했던 저에게 이번 발표들을 듣는 것은 매우 유익한 시간이었습니다. 한국의 출산율에 관련한 윌리엄스 교수님의 발제와 다른 훌륭한 연사님들의 한국의 여러 측면에 대한 자세한 논의를 통해 많은 것을 배울 수 있었습니다. 일본과 한국 사이의 유사점 뿐만 아니라 차이점에 대해서도 많은 것을 알게 되었으며, 두 나라가 서로 배우며 우리가 직면한 공통의 도전 과제들을 함께 해결할 수 있기를 바랍니다. 앞으로도 이와 같은 논의의 장이 계속될 수 있기를 기대합니다. 다시 한번 감사드립니다.

**이인실 원장:** 말씀 감사합니다. 시간 관계상 이번 세션은 여기에서 마치겠습니다. 앞으로 한국경제의 지속가능한 발전을 위한 이러한 다양한 논의가 좀 더 적극적으로 확대될 수 있기를 희망합니다. 오늘 회의 주제에 대해 앞으로 더 의미있고 진전된 논의가 펼쳐질 것이라 믿습니다. 오늘 끝까지 자리해 주신 여러분 진심으로 감사드립니다.

# 영문 번역본

# Contents

Foreword .................................................................. *201*

Program .................................................................. *203*

Opening Ceremony ................................................... *205*

      [Opening Address]
      **Jun Kwang-woo** Chairman, Institute for Global Economics (IGE)

      [Congratulatory Address]
      **Na Kyung-won** Member of the 22nd National Assembly/
      President of Population and Climate, Tomorrow (PACT)
      **Joo Hyung-hwan** Vice Chairman, Deputy Prime Minister Level,
      Presidential Committee on Ageing Society and Population Policy(PCASPP)
      **Kim Byoung Hwan** Chairman, Financial Services Commission(FSC)

      [Special Address]
      **Chung Un-chan** Chairman, Korea Institute for Shared Growth
      /Fmr. Prime Minister of the Republic of Korea & President, SNU

      [Special Conversation]
      **Joseph Stiglitz** Nobel Laureate in Economics/Chair Prof., Columbia Univ.
      Fmr. Senior Vice President, World Bank

Session 1 | Navigating Post-US Election Geopolitical and Global Economic Shifts ................................ *245*

[Moderator]
**Shin Sung-hwan** Member of Monetary Policy Board, Bank of Korea (BOK)/ Prof., Hongik Univ.

[Keynote Speaker]
**Nicholas Lardy** Senior Fellow, Peterson Institute for International Economics(PIIE)

[Panelists]
**Fukagawa Yukiko** Professor, Waseda Univ.
**William Pesek** Nikkei/Forbes, Award Winning Columnist
**Lee Jong-Wha** Prof., Korea Univ./Fmr. President, Korea Economic Association/Fmr. Chief economist, ADB
**Choi Byung-il** Prof. Emeritus, Ewha Womans Univ

Session 2 | Innovating Climate and Inclusive Finance
for Sustainable Growth ........................... *273*

[Moderator]
**Hong Jong-ho** Prof., Graduate School of Environmental Studies at SNU

[Keynote Speakers]
**Vinod Thomas** Senior Fellow, Institute of Southeast Asian Studies, Singapore
Fmr. Senior VP, World Bank
**Sanjay Patnaik** Director of the Center on Regulation and Markets, The Brookings Institution
**Koo Bonjay** Partner, Deloitte Consulting

[Panelists]
**Lee Hyung-hee** President, Communication Committee, SK SUPEX Council
**Lee Jin** Director General, Financial Supervisory Service(FSS)

Session 3 | The Role of Finance in Mitigating and Overcoming the Demographic Crisis ........................... *305.*

[Moderator]
**Yi Insil** President, Korean Peninsula Population Institute for Future Fmr. Commissioner, Statistics Korea

[Keynote Speakers]
**Joan Wiliams** Sullivan Professor of Law and Founding Director of the Equality Action Center, UC San Francisco
**Charles Yuji Horioka** Prof., Kobe Univ., President, International Association for Research on Income and Wealth(IARIW)/Fmr. President, Japanese Economic Association

[Panelists]
**Suh Jeong Ho** Head of Demographic Change Research, Korea Institute of Finance(KIF)
**Kim Gyungrok** President & head of retirement research institute, Mirae Asset Global Investments
**Jeung Shin Dong** Head of KB Research, KB Financial Group

# Foreword

The world is navigating a turbulent era of transformation—shaped by the aftermath of the U.S. presidential election, mounting geopolitical tensions, shifts in global monetary policies, and rapid advancements in artificial intelligence and technology. These dynamics are further compounded by structural challenges such as the climate crisis and demographic changes, demanding new approaches to ensure resilient and sustainable growth.

In response to these evolving global realities, the Institute for Global Economics (IGE), in collaboration with KB Financial Group, hosted the international conference titled "Navigating the New Waves of Global Transformation and Policy Pivot: Towards a More Resilient and Sustainable Future." This summit served as a meaningful platform for in-depth discussions on how finance can play a pivotal role in addressing interlinked issues across geopolitics, macroeconomics, climate action, inclusive growth, and demographic sustainability.

This publication compiles the conference's key presentations and discussions, offering valuable insights and practical strategies for those committed to navigating today's challenges and shaping a more sustainable future.

We would like to express our sincere gratitude to all the distinguished speakers and participants who enriched the conference with their insights, and to KB Financial Group for its steadfast partnership and support in making this event a success.

Thank you.

Jun Kwang-woo
Chairman & CEO, Institute for Global Economics (IGE)

# IGE – KB Financial Group
# 2024 Sustainability Global Summit

Navigating the New Waves of Global Transformation and Policy Pivot:
Towards a More Resilient and Sustainable Future

Dates | November 21, 2024
Venue | Conrad Seoul, Korea

| Time | Session | Role | Speaker |
|---|---|---|---|
| 09:00 ~ 10:20 | Opening Ceremony | Opening Address | **Jun Kwang-woo** Chairman, Institute for Global Economics(IGE) |
| | | Congratulatory Address | **Na Kyung-won** Member of the 22nd National Assembly / President of Population and Climate, Tomorrow (PACT) |
| | | | **Joo Hyung-hwan** Vice Chairman, Deputy Prime Minister Level, Presidential Committee on Ageing Society and Population Policy(PCASPP) |
| | | | **Kim Byoung Hwan** Chairman, Financial Services Commission(FSC) |
| | | Conference Keynote Speech | **Seike Atsushi** Chairman, Policy Studies Group for an Aged Society (Japanese Government) / President, Japanese Red Cross Society/Fmr. President, Keio Univ. |
| | | Special Address | **Chung Un-chan** Chairman, Korea Institute for Shared Growth / Fmr. Prime Minister of the Republic of Korea & President, SNU |
| 10:30 ~ 10:50 | | Special Conversation | **Joseph Stiglitz** Nobel Laureate in Economics/Chair Prof., Columbia Univ. / Fmr. Senior Vice President, World Bank |
| 10:50 ~ 12:30 | Session 1 Navigating Post-US Election Geopolitical and Global Economic Shifts | Moderator | **Shin Sung-hwan** Member of Monetary Policy Board, Bank of Korea (BOK) |
| | | Keynote Speakers | **Nicholas Lardy** Senior Fellow, Peterson Institute for International Economics(PIIE) |
| | | | **Cho Dong Chul** President, Korea Development Institute(KDI) |
| | | Panelists | **Fukagawa Yukiko** Professor, Waseda Univ. |
| | | | **William Pesek** Nikkei/Forbes, Award Winning Columnist |
| | | | **Lee Jong-Wha** Prof., Korea Univ./Fmr. President, Korea Economic Association / Fmr. Chief economist, ADB |
| | | | **Choi Byung-il** Prof. Emeritus, Ewha Womans Univ. |
| 12:30 ~ 13:40 | Luncheon | | |
| 13:50 ~ 15:40 | Session 2 Innovating Climate and Inclusive Finance for Sustainable Growth | Moderator | **Hong Jong-ho** Prof., Graduate School of Environmental Studies at SNU |
| | | Keynote Speakers | **Vinod Thomas** Senior Fellow, Institute of Southeast Asian Studies, Singapore / Fmr. Senior VP, World Bank |
| | | | **Sanjay Patnaik** Director of the Center on Regulation and Markets, The Brookings Institution |
| | | | **Koo Bonjay** Partner, Deloitte Consulting |
| | | Panelists | **Lee Hyung-hee** President, Communication Committee, SK SUPEX Council |
| | | | **Lee Jin** Director General, Financial Supervisory Service(FSS) |
| | | | **Kim Hye-sung** Attorney of Kim & Chang |
| 15:50 ~ 17:00 | Session 3 The Role of Finance in Mitigating and Overcoming the Demographic Crisis | Moderator | **Yi Insil** President, Korean Peninsula Population Institute for Future / Fmr. Commissioner, Statistics Korea |
| | | Keynote Speakers | **Joan Wiliams** Sullivan Professor of Law and Founding Director of the Equality Action Center, UC San Francisco |
| | | | **Charles Yuji Horioka** Prof., Kobe Univ., President, International Association for Research on Income and Wealth(IARIW) / Fmr. President, Japanese Economic Association |
| | | Panelists | **Suh Jeong Ho** Head of Demographic Change Research, Korea Institute of Finance(KIF) |
| | | | **Kim Gyungrok** President & head of retirement research institute, Mirae Asset Global Investments |
| | | | **Jeung Shin Dong** Head of KB Research, KB Financial Group |

# Opening Ceremony

**Opening Address**
**Jun Kwang-woo** Chairman, Institute for Global Economics (IGE)

**Congratulatory Address**
**Na Kyung-won** Member of the 22nd National Assembly/
President of Population and Climate, Tomorrow (PACT)
**Joo Hyung-hwan** Vice Chairman, Deputy Prime Minister Level,
Presidential Committee on Ageing Society and Population Policy(PCASPP)
**Kim Byoung Hwan** Chairman, Financial Services Commission(FSC)

**Special Address**
**Chung Un-chan** Chairman, Korea Institute for Shared Growth
/Fmr. Prime Minister of the Republic of Korea & President, SNU

**Special Conversation**
**Joseph Stiglitz** Nobel Laureate in Economics/Chair Prof., Columbia Univ.
Fmr. Senior Vice President, World Bank

# Opening Address

## Jun Kwang-woo

Good morning, distinguished guests, ladies and gentlemen.

It is a great honor to open the IGE-KB Financial Group International Conference on behalf of our organizers and supporting institutions. I warmly welcome each of you, especially our international participants.

We gather at a pivotal moment marked by shifts in global political leadership, along with geopolitical tensions, macroeconomic uncertainties, and technological innovations. These challenges are further complicated by the escalating climate changes and demographic pressures, testing our pursuit of resilient and sustainable growth. In this era of unprecedented global transformation, our conference aims to address critical challenges and opportunities in management strategies and policy-making. This event serves as a crucial platform for discussing the recent and prospective developments in sustainable finance and fostering solution-driven collaborations for a more innovative future.

The conference will explore a broad spectrum of issues under our main theme, including the evolving global economic landscape post-U.S. election, climate and inclusive finance innovations for sustainable development, and the special focus this year—strategies and policies addressing the demographic crisis.

I am deeply grateful to be joined by nearly 30 esteemed scholars, industry leaders, and senior public officials. Although time prevents me from recognizing each participant individually, I would like to extend our deep appreciation to Dr. Chung Un-chan, former Prime Minister of Korea and former President of Seoul National University, for his special address; Dr. Seike Atsushi, Chairman of Japan's Policy Group for an Aged Society and President of the Japanese Red Cross Society, for the keynote speech; Ms. Na Kyung-won, Member of the National Assembly and President of Population and Climate, Tomorrow (PACT); Dr. Joo Hyung-hwan, Vice Chairman of the Presidential Committee on Aging Society and Population Policy; Mr. Kim Byoung Hwan, Chairman of the Financial Services Commission.

I also wish to acknowledge our distinguished speakers, including Nobel Laureate Prof. Joseph Stiglitz; Dr. Nicholas Lardy from the Peterson Institute; Dr. Vinod Thomas, former World Bank Senior Vice President; Prof. Fukagawa Yukiko of Waseda University; Mr. William Pesek, the renowned columnist; and all other prominent speakers on our program. We are most privileged to have such a wealth of expertise.

Special thanks must go to Dr. SaKong Il, founder of IGE, for his vision spanning over 30 years; Mr. Sung Ki-hak, Chairman & CEO of Young-one Corporation, for his exceptional patronage for IGE activities; and Mr. Yang Jong Hee, Chairman & CEO of KB Financial Group, for his invaluable support of this event.

I trust that this conference will be both productive and inspiring, contributing to a better future for Korea and the world.

I wish you all the best and thank you very much.

# Congratulatory Address

## Na Kyung-won

Distinguished guests, ladies and gentlemen,

Good morning. It is a pleasure to meet you all. My name is Na Kyung-won.

First and foremost, I would like to extend my sincere gratitude to Chairman Jun Kwang-woo of the Institute for Global Economics, as well as Chairman Yang Jong-hee of KB Financial Group, for organizing this highly meaningful event.

I believe the theme of today's conference is especially timely and relevant. In particular, we are gathered here to discuss strategies to overcome the demographic crisis—an issue of great importance. As some of you may know, I recently established a forum in the National Assembly titled "Demographics, Climate, and Tomorrow." I firmly believe that how we respond to demographic and climate challenges will determine not only the future of the Republic of Korea but also the sustainable growth of the global community. The effective use of science and technology in this context is also critical, which is why I have been actively engaged in this forum's activities within the National Assembly.

In the aftermath of the recent U.S. presidential election, there appears to be considerable confusion and uncertainty. However, I do not view President Trump's election as a crisis for Korea, but rather as an opportunity. Given President Trump's emphasis on "America First," I believe that in efforts such as reshoring U.S. manufacturing and stabilizing global supply chains, Korea stands out as a uniquely valuable and reliable partner.

I returned just a few days ago from the COP 29 summit, where I held extensive discussions with the U.S. delegation. Although the U.S. may appear to be taking a different stance on climate issues on the surface, I was reassured during bilateral discussions that Korean businesses need not be concerned. The U.S. delegation even went so far as to calm my own concerns. It reaffirmed for me that the United States continues to see Korea as a trusted and strategic partner. Thus, I believe the changes following President Trump's election represent both a challenge and an opportunity for Korea.

This year's COP 29 placed a major focus on climate finance. Not only were there discussions on securing financial resources for climate response, but also in-depth conversations on the structuring of climate-related finance. Ultimately, overcoming the climate crisis hinges on the effective implementation of carbon neutrality goals, and constructing a future-oriented financial framework to support these goals is of paramount importance. I hope today's conference will include a robust and comprehensive discussion on these financial structures.

The issue of low birth rates and an aging population is not only a domestic challenge but also a fundamental and structural problem affecting the sustainable growth of both Korea and the global economy. Given the profound economic ripple effects and implications for the future of the financial industry, I believe it is imperative that we accurately diagnose the low birth rate crisis and devise strategic, policy-oriented financial solutions. The financial sector, in particular, must take a proactive role.

During my tenure as Vice Chair of the Presidential Committee on Aging Society and Population Policy, I introduced Hungary's response to declining birth rates as a potential model. At the core of that solution was housing finance policy—offering long-term, ultra-low interest loans at around 1% to newlyweds as a financial incentive to encourage marriage and childbirth. This initiative provided housing stability through these loans and was complemented by policies offering interest and principal forgiveness. Though aggressive in nature, I believe such measures could serve as valuable references in addressing Korea's demographic challenges.

Finally, I would like to express my hope that today's conference, with the participation of senior government officials, renowned global scholars, leading business figures, and members of the press and expert community, will serve as a platform for generating practical solutions to ensure Korea's sustainable development. I assure you that the National Assembly stands ready to provide full policy support for the meaningful discussions held here today.

Once again, I extend my deepest appreciation to the Institute for Global Economics and KB Financial Group for making this event possible.

Thank you.

# Congratulatory Address

## Joo Hyung-hwan

First, I would like to extend my sincere congratulations to you on the launch of the 2024 Sustainability Global Summit today. I would like to express my deepest gratitude to Dr. Kwangwoo Jeon, President of the World Economic Institute, and all the organizers for organizing such a meaningful event.

Would also like to thank all the participants for joining us, including National Assembly Member Na Kyung-won, Chairman of the National Assembly for National Unity, Jung Un-chan, Chairman of the Korea Institute for Shared Growth, Kim Byung-hwan, Chairman of the Financial Services Commission, Joseph Stiglitz, Distinguished Professor at Columbia University, and Atsushi Seike, Chairman of the National Council on Aging.

Ladies and gentlemen,

Today, I'd like to talk about the population crisis, which has emerged as one of the most serious of the many challenges that threaten Korea's sustainable growth. Korea currently facing a demographic crisis, which is characterized by the so-called triple bottom line of ultra-low birthrate, ultra-elderly society, and demographic cliff.

For starters, South Korea's fertility rate is not only the lowest in the world in absolute terms, it is also the fastest deteriorating in relative terms. From a total fertility rate of 6.0 in 1960 to less than one in 1984 (1.74) in just 20 years, the rate has fallen to a shocking 0.72 in 2023.

The world is aging at an unprecedented rate. Next year, South Korea will become an ultra-elderly society after 25 years as an aging society and seven years as an older society. This trend is expected as the second baby, the largest population group, retires. The proportion of people aged 80 and over has increased nearly fivefold over the past years, and the growth of the late-age, which carries a heavy medical and care burden, has been steep. If birthrate and ultra-aging, Korea will lose about 360,000 people every year, or about the size of Sejong City today, and by 2100, the total population will be less than half of what it is today.

This demographic shift far-reaching implications across all areas of the economy, society, and security, including weakening potential due to a shrinking force, the sustainability of national finances due to soaring pension and welfare expenditures, military, and increasing intergenerational conflict.

Various problems are expected to arise, which will lead to a major crisis in the national system itself. Based on this dire realization, the government declared a "population national emergency" in June this year and announced "measures to reverse the declining birthrate trend".

We also hold monthly meetings to review the implementation of the policy and continuously prepare new measures.

First, to address the current ultra-low birthrate, we are working at the national level, centering on two pillars: policy responses and social attitude change. When we analyzed the direct causes of the decline, we found that people are marrying less or later, fewer or later children, and choosing not to have children at all.

The main reason for this phenomenon is the increasing burden and opportunity cost of having and raising children, as well as changing values. The heavy burden of childcare and housing costs, unstable jobs, and poor work-family balance making young people hesitate and avoid marriage and childbirth. In response, the government focusing its policy capabilities on three core areas, including "support for work-family balance", "childcare burden reduction", and "housing support", centered on the needs of the people through selection and focus.

More fundamentally, low birthrates are a product of structural problems. Good jobs are scarce and concentrated in the metropolitan areas, and to get into the few good jobs available, students to go to good schools, and the competition to get into those schools has caused the cost of private education to skyrocket. The concentration of the population in the metropolitan area has led to rising housing prices and intense physical and mental competitionmaking marriage and childbirth more difficult.

Going forward, we will continue to respond to structural issues such as these from the perspective of the population crisis with a long breath. Alongside these policy responses, we also working to change social perceptions. Based on the importance of family and bonding with the community

We will continue to mobilize the capabilities of the broadcasting and media industries, as well as the business, religious, and civil societies, to ensure that the answer to the question of "why have children" is "happiness." Fortunately, there signs of a rebound in the long decline in the fertility rate, with the number of marriages increasing for five consecutive months and the number of births increasing for two consecutive months, and positive attitudes toward marriage and childbirth spreading.

The government will continue to implement the previously announced measures smoothly and consistently to further solidify this trend, while constantly communicating with the field and complementing policies. Along with measures to reduce the birthrate, we also preparing to deal with the rapidly aging population. Currently, Korea is experiencing an ultra-low birthrate trend.

The world is aging at an unprecedented rate, life expectancy increasing by 11 years over the past 30 years and the largest demographic cohort, the baby boomers, entering their senior years.

At the current pace and pattern of change, the next decade, as the second wave of baby boomers retire, will be the last golden time for aging policy responses.

In responding to these policies, three aspects in particular should be considered. First, the senior population is heterogeneous. The elderly can be divided into two age groups: the early elderly, aged 65 to 74, and the late elderly, aged 75 and older. The early elderly, especially the baby who are just entering their senior years, have higher levels of, and assets, are healthier, and have greater ability and willingness to work the late elderly. Second, the and pattern of varies region. Currently, the national median age is 46, but in 24 counties, the median age is already over 60. Jobs and living conditions also vary by region. Finally, as technologies such as AI, IoT, and robots are rapidly advancing, smart care and personalized medicine using these technologies are emerging as new policy instruments.

Based on these considerations, the government will prioritize continued employment, retirement income security, and health, care, and support, we are preparing an Society Response Plan," which centers on age-friendly housing, industry, and social participation, and plan to have measures in place by early next year.

First, we will create conditions for continued employment so that seniors can work if they want to and strengthen the multi-layered old-age income security system. With regard to healthcare, nursing care, and care, we will shift to community-centered policies so seniors can receive the services they need in their preferred places of residence. With regard to housing, we will create conditions for seniors to live safely and independently for as long as possible.

In addition, we will expand senior-friendly cultural and sports facilities and revitalize lifelong education and social contribution activities so that many seniors can enjoy a vibrant retirement.

Even with these ultra-low birthrate and ultra-aging efforts, adaptation efforts must also be driven by the fact the productive population will continue to decline for the foreseeable future.

Basically, the government aims to compensate for the decline in the productive population by actively engaging various groups that still have room for improvement, such as 700,000 NEETs, women in their 30s and 40s who have lower economic participation rates than those in developed countries, and elderly workers who want to work even after retiring from their main jobs, and by making better use of foreign workers by reforming immigration policies.

In addition, we will reorganize the industrial structure centered on high-tech industries such as AI, bio, and green through drastic and increased investment in R&D and education, and work to increase the productivity of the economy as a whole.

Ladies and gentlemen, declining birthrate and aging population is a global phenomenon, beyond individual national responses, more practical solutions be found by sharing experiences and working together. In particular, South Korea and Japan have a lot in common not only in terms of demographics, but also in terms of corporate culture, such as long working hours and gender discrimination in the workplace.

Two countries have agreed to engage governments as well as the private sector, particularly business and academia, to share best practices and find solutions on topics of common interest, such as long working hours, addressing gender discrimination, and supporting work-family balance.

In a similar vein, the presentations and proposals of the international and national luminaries who are here today provide new perspectives and insights into the challenges we face, and will help us find solutions.

Once again, we would like to extend our sincere congratulations to you on the 2024 Sustainability Global Summit.

Thank you.

# Congratulatory Address

## Kim Byoung Hwan

Hello, I'm Byung-Hwan Kim, Chairman of the Financial Services Committee.

Today, I am delighted to join you at the 2024 Sustainability Global Summit, co-hosted by the World Economic Institute and KB Financial Group. I would like to express my sincere gratitude to Chairman Jun Kwang-woo and Chairman Yang Jong-hee for inviting me to participate in this event. I would also like to thank Representative Na Kyung-won and Vice Chairman Hyung-hwan Joo for taking time out of their busy schedules to deliver congratulatory remarks, as well as Mr. Atsushi Seike, Chairman of the National Council on Aging, and Mr. Un-chan Chung, Chairman of the Board of Directors, for delivering today's keynote address.

Today's topic will discuss the key challenges for sustainable growth on critical global issues such as the "Global Economy in the Trump Era," "Geopolitical Change," "Combating Climate Change," "Overcoming the Population Crisis," and more. With a mix of short-term changes and mid- to long-term structural topics, we expect this to be a very meaningful discussion.

As I attend this event, I've been thinking about what the common keywords are that can connect these three topics, and I'd like to suggest the theme of cooperation and solidarity.

Since the inauguration of President Trump, there is a high likelihood of increased protectionism, supply chain fragmentation, and a more "America First" mentality. In this situation, I believe that cooperation and solidarity are even more important, especially in a country with an open, export-oriented economy like ours. Cooperation with other countries, as well as cooperation with governments, businesses, and the private sector, will help us diversify our economic structure and counter protectionism.

We are also already seeing that climate change and the population crisis cannot be solved without cooperation between countries. International solidarity and cooperation are essential to tackling the climate crisis, and there can be many disagreements domestically on how to achieve and implement climate goals. In times like these, we need to have in-depth discussions and solidarity on how to collaborate and work towards the same goals.

The population challenge is one that requires broader cooperation and solidarity. Without cooperation between regions, individuals, governments, and businesses, as well as solidarity between metropolitan areas, provinces, and generations, it will be difficult to solve this problem.

I think the very fact that we are here today, with scholars and experts from all over the world, can be a starting point for cooperation and solidarity.

In April of this year, we launched the Future Finance Response Task Force to bring together experts to discuss how finance should respond to population, climate, and digital environmental change. As part of this, we announced a target of KRW 420 trillion in policy finance by 2030 for climate finance, which we will work to fulfill.

I look forward to meaningful discussions and policy recommendations here today, and I would like to emphasize once again the importance of cooperation and solidarity.

Again, congratulations on this event and thank you for your interest and participation.

# Special Address

## Chung Un-Chan

Good afternoon, and thank you to the World Economic Institute and KB Financial Group for inviting me to join you today. Let's get right down to business.

South Korea has become a big country, one of only seven countries in the world with a population of over 50 million and a per capita income of over $30,000. The other six are the United States, Japan, Germany, the United Kingdom, France, and Italy. Despite this remarkable achievement, South Korea is facing a crisis of low growth and polarization.

Since the IMF crisis in 1997 and the global financial crisis in 2008, South Korea's economic vitality has declined and low growth has become entrenched. The average annual economic growth rate was over 10% in the 1960s and 1970s, and was in the 8% range until the 1980s, but since the Kim Young-sam government (1993-), the long-term growth rate (10-year moving average) has fallen by 1% with each change of government and is currently in the 2% range. The imitative education of the industrialization era has not led to the accumulation of creative human resources, the spirit of community has weakened, and hope for the future has faded. Income distribution shows that the top 1% take 15% of all income, and the top 10% take 47%. Furthermore, the concentration of economic power in the hands of large corporations, especially the Big Four, is unparalleled in any other country in the world.

Where did this situation come from? South Korea's economic policy is based on a "chaebol-centered, export-led, first-growth, second-distribution" strategy. It has relied on the so-called trickle-down model, whereby certain sectors, such as exports and heavy chemicals, are fostered first and their performance is expected to ripple through the economy as a whole. Maximizing growth and efficiency is the overarching goal, while distribution and equity are secondary considerations. The result of this unbalanced growth has been an industrial structure that is heavily concentrated in the hands of a few large companies, while small and medium-sized enterprises, which provide employment and income for the majority of the population, have been relegated to an unfair position in vertical relationships with large companies.

The polarization of enterprises has inevitably led to polarization of income and wealth and stagnant growth. The stellar performance of exporting conglomerates hasn't helped either, because the rapid opening up and informatization of the global economy over the past quarter century (i.e., 25 years), coupled with the culture of kleptocracy unique to Korean society, has severed the linkages between domestic industries and, as a result, greatly weakened the virtuous cycle that generates employment and income between exports and domestic demand, and between large and small enterprises.

I have been arguing for the past decade that shared growth is the best alternative to resolve economic polarization while bringing about a renaissance of the Korean economy. However, economic polarization, which started with corporate polarization, has led to a number of other problems, one of which is population decline due to declining birth rates.

South Korea's total fertility rate (the average number of births a woman can expect to have in her lifetime) began falling below the population replacement level of 2.1 in 1983 and reached an all-time low of 0.72 in 2023 last year. While fertility rates in well-off countries have been declining, South Korea is currently the only country with a fertility rate below 1.

The causes of low fertility can be categorized into four main groups. First, the income factor due to the instability of future income, second, the child factor due to the benefits and costs of children, third, the value factor due to changes in lifestyle, and fourth, the social factor due to gender inequality. In South Korea, the declining birthrate started in the early 2000s after the IMF bailout and is believed to be mainly due to income or employment insecurity, or economic polarization.

'Shared Growth' is a social philosophy of 'growing together and living well together'. The idea is to create a 'partnership' between individuals, groups, and nations that make up a social community, so that the community can operate sustainably. If Korean society had actively promoted shared growth a decade ago, and SMEs working with large corporations had better working conditions and could afford to live more comfortably, the majority of people working in SMEs would have found a partner, married, and had children. Or, if older people had actively invested their pension funds in the youth venture startup ecosystem, the economic situation of young people would have improved, which would have naturally led to marriage and childbirth. However, we ignored polarization, which led to a very low birthrate.

Many rural cities are now facing the risk of disappearing, and there are 1,587 elementary schools in the country that will have fewer than 10 new students in 2023 due to the declining school-age population. It goes without saying how much of a security threat this poses to South Korea, the world's only divided country, with half of its citizens over the age of 50 by 2031, and by 2044, the country will have 10 million fewer people of working age, the key foundation for economic growth, according to the 2024 Population Report by the Korea Future Population Institute (founded by Hanmi Global Chairman Kim Jong-hoon). Inevitably, the government must actively support and develop budgets and policies for the declining birthrate.

According to the National Council on Aging and Social Affairs and the National Assembly Budget and Policy Office, over the past 17 years, from 2006 to 2023, the total amount of projects announced by the government as a low-birthrate budget amounted to 379.8 trillion won in national expenditures. The budget has increased 22.9 times, from 2.1 trillion won in 2006, when the measures were first announced, to 48 trillion won in 2023. However, the fertility rate has steadily declined during this period. We have to admit that the government's fertility policy has failed.

For example, building a foundation for tourism revitalization, strengthening domestic tourism capacity, fostering the gaming industry, strengthening the capacity of AI convergence technicians, fostering the manga industry, fostering new marine and fisheries industries, and supporting companies to attract investment - all of these projects were included in the budget to address the declining birthrate. There are too many projects that are not directly related to solving the birthrate problem.

The easiest way to reduce the birthrate is to follow the lead of France, Sweden, and Japan and provide direct cash transfers to families with children. However, pouring money into the budget without evaluating the effectiveness of each program is just pouring water on the poison. Going forward, we need to develop a system to measure and evaluate the effectiveness of each program, but it is difficult to solve the birthrate problem through government efforts and budgets alone. The political, business, academic, and religious communities need to pool their wisdom and strength to solve the problem. One of the key causes of the declining birthrate is the burden of childcare and education on mothers, fathers, and parents. Let's take a look at some examples of how recognizing this reality has improved the birthrate problem.

When a child is born, it's usually hard for mom or dad to leave their child's side for the first two years. At age 2, children can be dropped off at daycare centers so that mom and dad can return to work. From the first grade, the child has to go to and from school by himself, and the school is not involved in the work before and after school. Parents cannot leave the child unattended after school until it's time to go home from work, so they tutor English, math, national language, and even physical education. This is to ease the hard work of working parents and to survive the fierce competition in Korean society. As a result, 'hagwon' has dramatically increased the cost of childcare and the emotional burden on parents, with the average monthly cost of private education per student reaching 27 trillion won in 2023, and the average monthly cost of private education per student reaching 434,000 won.

It is difficult for a child who is left at a school to grow up with proper character. A child who grows up playing only with friends of the same age may not respect adults and may be disrespectful to parents. When parents see such a child, it is not easy for them to decide to have a second child. As a result, "schooling for the sake of convenience and the child's future" has become a major cause of hesitation to have a second child.

In a Korean society where people are afraid to have children, the case of Dangjin Dongil Church (Pastor Lee Soo-hoon) in Chungnam province has become an inspiring example of how to overcome the declining birthrate and grow together. Dangjin Dongil Church runs the Visionary Christian Academy (VCA) Vision School, an after-school care program for elementary school students. For a monthly membership fee of 400,000 won, the program provides holistic care for about six hours during the week, from 14:00 to 20:00. Preschoolers can be entrusted to 'Salem Children's Home' for up to 12 hours from 7:30am to 7:30pm.

At VCA Vision School, church buses drive around the surrounding area elementary schools to pick up children and bring them to the church, where the church provides dinner and snacks and runs programs in English, math, physical education, and character education. The English program is taught by foreign university students who live with the children for a month during their summer vacation. Some parents volunteer, and the children are cared for in an emotionally stable environment. Students do not need to be Christian to enroll. As a result, in 2020, the fertility rate in Dangjin, a city of 170,000 people, was 1.25 children (0.84 nationwide in the same year), the highest in the country, and more than 150 of the newborns born in the area (about 12.4%) were the children of church members. The average number of children per household in Dangjin Dongil Church is three, and the church is now organizing a "five-child" childbirth campaign. It is important to note that customized infant and elementary school care is directly related to the birth rate.

Traditionally, after-school care for elementary school students has been centered around schools and local governments. However, there are limitations to school and local government-run after-school care. Schools already have the space and staff needed for childcare. The Ministry of Education has declared that it will start operating free "always-care schools" for first graders nationwide from 2024 and expand to sixth graders in 2026. This will inject a huge amount of financial resources into elementary schools nationwide.

However, elementary schools and teachers' unions are opposed to the operation of after-school care, saying that elementary school children are not listening to school teachers and are growing up differently. This is because our society and families have failed to educate children in social skills, resulting in the collapse of the school system. From the children's point of view, there is also a problem with after-school care in elementary schools. School is a place to study, so they want to get out as soon as possible, but if they are told to get out after dark, they want to rebel.

Local government and private after-school programs require significant facility and human investment, but society has already experienced the limitations of local government and private after-school programs. A typical example is private daycare facilities called nursery schools. Since the enactment of the Infant Childcare Act in 1991, close to 43,000 nursery schools have been established, and the infrastructure for leaving children after the age of two has been put in place. However, the birth rate in our society has continued to decline, and more than 14,000 nursery schools have disappeared. I don't think it would make much of a difference if the state directly operated daycare centers, and even if they had the space and staff, the labor intensity and working conditions would limit them to 7 p.m. However, young parents sometimes want affordable care for their children until later, such as 9 or 10 p.m.

When a mother sees her child running from school to school, grabbing a bite to eat at a convenience store, and then falling asleep waiting for her at home, she feels sorry for her child. When a mother feels sorry for her child, she doesn't want to have a second child. But when a mother has raised her first child safely and satisfactorily, she doesn't feel overwhelmed by the prospect of having two or three more. When a child is safely cared for at a religious facility, with English, math, Korean, and holistic education, plus dinner and snacks, her heart doesn't break when she returns from work, and she feels secure and determined to have another child.

Children's changes lead to fathers' decision to have children again. At Dangjin Dongil Church, the children experience a small social life. In institutionalized schools, children usually have relationships centered around their classmates and grade level. In contrast, in the church after-school care, children are cared for in the same space from the first grade to the sixth grade, so they experience a wider variety of relationships, such as seniors, peers from other schools, and parents, and thus receive social education. This is similar to the family or village community of the extended family era in the past, creating a typical environment for mutual growth. Children who have learned a variety of social skills may even greet their dads when they come home and say, "Good job, Dad!" After hearing that, won't they decide to have another child? The decision of moms and dads to have children is directly related to the birth rate. The belief that the community take care of their children safely is becoming a key factor in the decision to have a second and third child.

It is also interesting to note that Mr. Jeon's proposal to reduce the birthrate is a businessman who has been working on brown rice research for a long time and believes that changes in food culture are deeply related to changes in the birthrate of human societies. In the UK, Dr. Anakaming and Dr. FR Inz conducted a clinical trial in which delinquents in prison were fed whole wheat, unrefined oat porridge, and vegetable salad. As a result, the delinquents became milder and had a healthier mindset. In this way, food changes people.

Brown rice is rich in minerals, including manganese (Mn) and B vitamins. Manganese is a mineral necessary for affection, and if you eat only white rice or white flour, you're less likely to feel affection for the opposite sex, which inevitably leads to lower fertility. The vitamin E in grainy seeds also promotes vasodilation and blood circulation, and along with the B vitamins, it's a good source of sex hormones. Above all, seed eyes are full of factors that make plants reproduce themselves, so if humans eat seed eyes, they will become more affectionate, have a clearer brain, and reproduce more. Therefore, it is said that if you eat a lot of brown rice, whole wheat, vegetables, and fruits, you will not get modern diseases, become more emotional, and miss the opposite sex.

Therefore, Jeon suggests that if all Koreans ate whole grains such as brown rice as their staple food, they would naturally develop more affection for the opposite sex, have more healthy relationships and marriages, and inevitably have more children, thus solving the current low birthrate problem.

In Korea, where working couples are the norm, low-cost, safe childcare and holistic education is a key infrastructure that society must have. Currently, most churches in Korea have vacant church spaces on weekdays and are fully staffed. If we utilize them and operate them as 'infant and toddler kindergartens' and 'elementary care schools', I think we can solve many of our society's childcare problems. In a society with a declining birthrate, churches and other religious communities need to consider their role to grow together with the community.

Governments need to create an environment where parents who have had one child will naturally decide to have another, and they need to give clear signals through laws and institutions as soon as possible to instill in people the belief that if they have a child, the state and community will nurture it. And if people improve their diets, eating brown rice and whole grains to promote health and love, that's icing on the cake.

# Conference Keynote Speech

## Seike Atsushi

Thank you very much for your kind introduction. This morning, I would like to talk about the meanings of a Lifelong Active Society. This is a society in which the will and ability of older people can be fully utilized regardless of their age.

I believe that both Korea and Japan need to establish the Lifelong Active Society. The reason is very clear because both countries are facing tremendous ageing population. Please share Fig.1 which shows the trend of the proportion of the older people aged 65 and over in Japan and Korea. In Japan, the proportion of older people aged 65 and over is already very close to 30%, marking it the world's highest level.

In Korea, it is about 19 % which is still lower than that of Japan, but it is projected to exceed that of Japan in the first half of the 2040s. By the way hereafter, in addition with this Figure, I will show some Korean statistics. Taking this opportunity, I would like to express my gratitude to Dr. Kim Myung Jun from NLI Research Institute in Tokyo for helping me in searching Korean statistics.

In this Figure, you can also see that the inclination of the line graphs is much steeper in Korea and in Japan than in European Countries such as France and Germany. Thus, this Figure shows that Korea and Japan are experiencing globally unprecedented aging population both in the level and the speed of an aging.

Furthermore, an aging population is accompanied by several waves of baby boomers. In the case of Japan, the large waves have been created by the first baby boomers who were born between 1947 and 1949 when 2.7 million babies were born every year, and by their children, namely the second baby boomers who were born between 1971 and 1974 when 2 million babies were born every year.

Unlike Korea and the U.S. of which baby booms lasted for a long period of time, the Japanese baby booms were concentrated in a short period of time. Please share Figure 2. This Figure shows Japan's population pyramids in 2025 and 2040.

All of the first baby boomers will reach age 75 until 2025, and the population pyramid of 2025 will have a noticeable wave at this age group. After the age 75, the likelihood of having disease and the need for long term care increases significantly. This is one of the reasons behind Japan has gradually raised the consumption tax rate from 5% to 10%. Then all of the second baby boomers will reach aged 65 in 2040, and because of this the absolute number of older people aged 65 and over in Japan will peak out in the first half of the 2040s.

The aging population will cause many difficult problems. But I'd like to tell you at first that an aging population itself is the result of increase in per capita income by economic development. First of all, the longevity which brings about an aging would not have been realized without increase in per capita income.

Another factor that brings about an aging is the declining birthrate. In the process of shifting from a developing country to a developed country, any society experiences so-called a Demographic Transition from the society of high births and high deaths to the society of low births and low deaths. Please share Figure 3. This figure shows that Japan and Korea are typical examples which experienced very rapid Demographic Transitions.

Of course, recent decline in birthrate in Korea and in Japan are excessive, but one of the reasons of this is the increased opportunity cost to women of raising children. This is also the result of wage increase of women due to the economic development, and ironically it brings about an excessive decline in the birthrate which have negative impact on economy. So, in order to reverse this declining trend of the birthrate, it is necessary to reduce the opportunity cost of women by improving childcare services, and by reforming working styles to allow men to have more time to participate in childcare.

As you can imagine, the most significant result of this aging is a decline in number of work force. If I am allowed to use the case of the labor force projections of Japan as an example, please share Figure 4. At first, please look at the Case A in the Figure, and you can see that the total size of labor force in Japan is projected to decrease by 9 million from about 69 million in 2023 to about 60 million in 2040 if labor force participation rates of people would remain. It may have a serious negative impact on Economy and Society.

With such a drastic decline in labor force, the Domestic Production may decrease unless there is substantial improvement in the productivity per worker to make up for the decline in labor force. It also leads to lower total earnings from work and therefore decreasing consumption, unless there is a substantial increase in earnings per worker to make up for the decline in number of wage earners. Thus, declining labor force may have serious negative impact both on the supply side and the demand side of Macro Economy. And it will also reduce the sustainability of social security system.

In order to cope with these problems, one of the most important solutions is to promote the labor force participation of older people. In other word, we need to establish a Life-long Active Society in which the will and ability of older people can be fully realized.

The increase in number of active workers and consumers in their older age are the driving forces of economic growth both in the supply side and demand side of Macro Economy. And if more numbers of older people continue working beyond the current retirement age, per capita burden of social security system including the burden of younger people could be reduced.

So, please look at the Case B in Figure 4 which shows the case of increasing labor force participation in the future. If we could increase the labor force participation of older people as well as that of women, it is projected that we will be able to maintain lacor force as much as about 68 million, which is a decline by just above 1 million. If the magnitude of decline in labor force would be that extent, we will be able to maintain both domestic production and consumption as well as the sustainability of social security system by steadily increasing productivity and wages to the practically feasible extent.

Of course, you should not force people to work against their will. But in this respect, there is an advantage in Korea and Japan. Please share Figure 5 and you can see the labor force participation rates of older people are significantly higher in Korea and in Japan in comparison with European countries. Because by definition, the labor force participation rate is the proportion of people who have the will to work, this means that older people of Korea and Japan still maintain a strong motivation to continue working.

So, though both Korea and Japan are facing Globally unprecedented aging population, we are also having a favorable condition to cope with it. By taking advantage of this strong motivation among older people to continue working, we will be able to establish the Life-long Active Society. So, in what way we can do that?

First, we have to recognize that in the matter of fact, the older labor force has already been an indispensable part of labor force in Japan and Korea. More than past 2 decades, the older labor force has been keep increasing in both countries. Please share Figure 6 and you can see that in Japan, the labor force aged 65 and over was slightly less than 5 million in 2000, but in 2023, it exceeded 9 million which is nearly 1 in 7 of the total labor force in Japan in 2023. And you can see that in Korea, the labor force aged 65 and over was about 1 million in 2000, but in 2023 it became about 3.6 million which is about 1 in 8 of the total labor force in Korea in 2023.

So, what is needed to continue this trend? I think there are three important things. First of all, the most important thing is health conditions of older people.

Our econometric analysis shows that the health condition is the largest and the most significant variable to explain the labor force participation behavior of older people. In this respect the most important things for us to do is to extend so-called the healthy lifespan. Please share Figure 7 and you can see the trend of healthy lifespan by which I mean the average lifespan that people can be active without health problems. Although the healthy lifespan has been increasing in Japan, there is still a gap between the average lifespan and healthy lifespan by about 8 years for men and about 12 years for women.

In order to extend the healthy lifespan, preventive medicine plays the key role. It has been found that regular health checkups, prevention of lifestyle-related diseases, various vaccinations, and more recently, such as improved oral hygiene and so on are all highly effective in extending healthy lifespan. So, expenditures on such preventive medicine can be regarded as a good investment that brings about high returns as promoting labor force participation of older people that increases the sustainability of economy and society.

The second thing is the retirement practice. In Japan, employers are legally allowed to set up a mandatory retirement aged 60 and over, and many of them apply this practice for regular employees who usually are paid seniority-based wages. But the law also requires to employers to provide workers with job continuation plans up to age 65 even if these plans are not regular job. By taking this plan, older workers are able to continue working at the same company, and some workers change jobs and continue working at the so-called secondly workplaces.

However, the problem is that your wages usually fall substantially whether it is in job continuation at the same company or in the secondly workplace. Please share Figure 8 and it shows that wages are falling after aged 60. Discouraged by this wage fall, some workers completely retire from the labor market when they reach the age of mandatory retirement. In order to solve this problem, I think substantial reforms of the mandatory retirement practice and the seniority- based wage system are necessary.

The third problem is relating to the public pension system. Particularly in Japanese employee pension system, if you continue to work after pension eligible age, the amount of your pension benefit is reduced dependent on the earnings you are making from work. Therefore, pension eligible workers tend to reduce their working hours or even in some cases completely stop working to avoid this pension benefit reduction. In order to solve these problems, it is also important to reform the public pension system so as not to discourage older people continue working.

By the way, there are concerns that extending the retirement age and encouraging older people to continue working will take away employment opportunities for younger people. But now as younger population is shrinking, such an opinion is becoming less prevalent at least in Japan. Please share Figure 9 and as you can see in the Figure, the job openings over job applicant ratio for younger people has always been higher than that of older people throughout the 2010s. The job market of younger people has become a sellers' market as the job openings over job applicant ratio has been far above 1.

Employers are finding it difficult to hire young people, rather than it being difficult for young people to find work. In addition, promoting the employment of older people is effective in shortening the working hours of younger workers up to the adequate level. And increase in number of older workers who continue paying social security premiums and income taxes reduce the per capita burden of social security including that of younger people.

And in respect for improving the lives of younger people, the most important things for us to do is to make further enhancement of social security benefits for the younger people especially who are raising children. I used to be a Chair of the National Council on Social Security System Reform, and we submitted a recommendation report to the Japanese government in 2013. It stated that the most important aspect of future social security reforms was measures to cope with the declining birthrate, especially promoting support for childcare substantially.

Since then, support for childcare has been improved in line with this recommendation in a past decade, but it is still not enough. So, the Japanese government created the Council for the Construction of an All-Generation Social Security System to further enhancement of support for childcare.

Measures to cope with the declining birthrate are the most important policies for Japan now on, and I believe that this is also the case for Korea.

Korea is an important neighboring country for Japan, and I believe this is also the case for Korea as well. Our economies are closely related and we are facing the same challenge of Globally unprecedented aging population.

As I told you so far, the necessary measures to cope with an aging population for Japan and Korea are almost the same though the stage of aging is a slightly different. There are many rooms for Japan and Korea to promote further mutual learnings and make further collaborations in research to find the best solutions to cope with an aging population. And if the two countries can share their wisdom and build a model of the Life-long Active Society, it will be of great reference for other countries and regions that will be aging in the future.

In this respect, this conference is an extremely important opportunity to foster such momentum. Therefore, I would like to close my speech by expressing my deepest gratitude to all the people who made this Conference possible. Thank you all very much.

# Special Conversation
## Joseph Stiglitz

**Jun Kwang-woo:** Dr. Stiglitz, it's great to see you again. And thank you very much for joining us at this very late hour in New York.

Now, we are bracing for greater geopolitical tensions and economic challenges as we anticipate Trump 2.0 in a couple of months. So at this critical time, we are very fortunate to have Dr. Stiglitz as our special keynote speaker today.

Dr. Stiglitz is one of the most influential economists of our time—a Nobel Laureate in Economic Sciences, whose scholarly work and public service have shaped both academic discourse and global policy. Dr. Stiglitz served as Chief Economist and Senior Vice President of the World Bank, and as Chair of the U.S. Council of Economic Advisers under President Bill Clinton. Notably, more than two decades ago, Dr. Stiglitz was awarded the Order of Civil Merit—Mokryun Medal—by the Korean government, in recognition of his contributions to Korea's successful recovery from the Asian financial crisis.

Without further ado, let's welcome Dr. Stiglitz. Thank you for your special address today.

**Joseph Stiglitz:** Well, thank you very much for that very kind introduction. And I really do wish I could have been there with you in person. But as you know, this has been a very busy time in the United States with the elections and so much going on. So next time, hopefully.

The subject of my talk, centering around the tidal shifts in globalization, couldn't be more appropriate. We've just gone through an American election in which Donald Trump was the victor. That comes on top of the pandemic, the Russian invasion of Ukraine, the slaughtering of Gaza and Lebanon, and the inability of the international community to do anything about it.

Not surprisingly, questions are being raised about democracy, about the rule of law, both domestically and internationally, and about multilateralism. But I should probably preface these remarks by saying my concerns, my deepest concerns are about the future of democracy and the future of multilateralism.

Let me begin in the United States. It is still the largest economy. What happens in the United States will have global consequences. I want to divide my remarks about the future, the immediate and long-term future, in two parts. The first focuses on what happens if Trump goes through with his promises, if he's successful in convincing Congress to adopt them, if they pass legal muster. And the second part will look more carefully about what might actually happen.

We have to go back and remember that in his first term, much of what he promised, much of what he aspired to do, he failed at. So beginning with what he has promised, what he has articulated during the campaign, what he wants to do, it's very clear that it would be very bad for the U.S. economy, and I think very bad for the international economy. It will have repercussions in almost every aspect of what is going on.

So let me sort of try to be a little bit systematic about this. The economic issue that probably bothered voters the most has been inflation. The result of supply chain interruptions associated with the COVID-19, the pandemic, exacerbated then by the Russian invasion of Ukraine. These supply side interruptions led in turn to demand shifts, and all of this led to inflation of the kind that we had not seen in almost half a century.

I believe that Trump's policies, if they were implemented, would have been a risk, leading to another bout of inflation, particularly problematic, as I said, because we're just getting over the current one.

The rate of inflation came down remarkably rapidly. Inflation is down to the levels that most central banks, bankers, feel very comfortable with. But just as we've gotten inflation under control, Trump promises to get it up again. There are several of his policies that are highly inflationary. Perhaps of the most concern are his high tariffs—100% on goods from China. And America, like much of the world, depends very heavily on China for apparel, for appliances, for computers, for our iPhones, for our telephones, for so much. And tariffs of that magnitude would be devastating.

Of course, some companies would be able to shift their production from China to other countries, but that would be disruptive and costly. And it's hard to see how that would not lead to inflation. The reason countries have chosen to produce in China is because it is the place where production occurs at the least cost. That's the nature of capitalism. So by imposing these large tariffs, which are just another name for taxes on imports, it would be inflationary. In fact, most economists think, except particularly inflationary form of taxation.

Moreover, it's a form of taxation that hurts those at the middle and the bottom more than any other group. They depend more on these kinds of imported goods as a larger fraction of their consumption basket. So most economists agree that these tariffs would be highly regressive, i.e. hurt those at the bottom disproportionately.

There are further effects that we will experience because it is possible, some say likely, that other countries will retaliate. They will impose taxes, the tariffs on our goods. They will do it strategically. And if that happens, then of course, we will be in the worst of all possible world—demand for our goods will go down, and at the same time, prices will be going up.

We will face a bout of stagflation.

My own view is that, looking at his record, the transactional perspective is likely to dominate. If that is the case, we may be able to muddle our way through the next four years like we did the four years of Trump between 2017 and 2020. But we have to recognize, this time, the risks are greater. This time, there are likely to be multiple scars resulting from Trump's presidency. There are enormous challenges facing Korea, facing all the countries of the world, as the United States has made a historic election. Thank you.

**Jun Kwang-woo:** Thank you very much for your inspiring and thought-provoking remarks. I would now like to move on to a few questions, beginning with one on tariffs.

For many countries that export to the United States—including Korea—the word "tariffs" evokes significant concern. However, listening to your remarks today, I was struck by your insight that Mr. Trump tends to approach many issues from a transactional perspective. That raises the possibility that, in practice, the tariff measures may not be as severe as some of the campaign rhetoric suggests.

What is your assessment on this? Do you believe there is reason for cautious optimism?

**Joseph Stiglitz:** Yes, in two ways. First, I believe that many American businesses and political donors who supported Mr. Trump are likely to push back strongly against his tariff policies—and in many cases, they may succeed in doing so. This suggests that the actual impact of a potential Trump administration's tariff agenda may not be as severe as some fear.

And the other side is countries—Korea, even China—will say, "If you lower your tariff, we won't impose tariffs on your goods." So there'll be a negotiation. He loves negotiations.

And we saw from the first term that his announcements are the beginning of a negotiation. And so where this will lead, one doesn't know. But I think, in the end, it won't be as bad as his campaign says.

But it will still be much worse than we are now, and the international rules-based trading order will be in shambles. And I think that's a very important point to realize—what's happened to multilateralism and the rules-based system. You weren't supposed to have to negotiate every transaction, and we had what was called the most favored nation principle in trade. That's being put aside. That's being destroyed. So the whole architecture of trade of the last 70 years is being destroyed. People aren't talking about it, but it's being destroyed and going back to a world before the most favored nation principle—not only before WTO, but before GATT. So this is a big deal.

Let me mention one more thing, which is part of the bind that he's in. He wants to finance the tax cuts for the billionaires and the corporations through the tariffs. And if he does run the tariffs, the deficits soar. But I said before, those $7 trillion—if he doesn't get the tariff revenue, that goes up even more. So he's sort of caught, and then his deficit hawks get either even louder or look more foolish. And they will appeal to what is called dynamic scoring—"It's all going to lead to more growth." But you can only do a limited amount of hocus pocus.

**Jun Kwang-woo:** Thank you once again for your insightful response. If I may, I would like to turn to another area of concern—namely, two hallmark initiatives of the Biden administration: the Inflation Reduction Act (IRA) and the CHIPS and Science Act.

These landmark pieces of legislation have catalyzed substantial investment commitments from governments and major multinational corporations around the world, including Korea. Many of these investments are already being implemented, based on the assumption of a stable and predictable U.S. policy environment.

In light of this, there is growing unease that a second Trump administration—if it adheres strictly to its campaign rhetoric—might seek to repeal or significantly scale back these initiatives. This prospect is generating considerable anxiety not only in Korea, but also among many of the United States' closest allies who have made long-term strategic decisions based on these frameworks.

Given the scale and scope of these programs, how likely do you think such a reversal would be? And what implications might this have for global partners who have aligned themselves with these policies in good faith?

**Joseph Stiglitz:** Much of the discussion of IRA is that it was designed—or in effect was—Trump-proof. Much of the benefits went to red states, and it has been remarkably effective in generating investment and jobs in the red states.

Now here we have another conflict between venom on the one hand and politics on the other. The politics is very much. You would be foolish to get rid of a bill that affects your workers so much.

But you have to remember the level of venom that Trump has against Biden.

So it is conceivable that he will push for, as he said in the campaign, getting rid of IRA. I don't know which of these two will dominate. I think any reasonable politics would say politics wins—jobs win. But you're dealing now not with a reasonable person. So I can't reason about what an unreasonable person is going to do. I can say there are many cases where he does something that is politically unreasonable. So I think your companies should continue to be worried.

I should mention one more element of that that I didn't highlight. I talked about inflation. The IRA has the name Inflation Reduction Act because it was intended to reduce inflation. It reduced inflation in two ways. One, by enhancing the supply of low-cost renewables, it will get our energy prices down. The IRA would let those prices go up and would again be inflationary. So another dimension that worries me about the repeal is the inflationary consequences.

Finally, if there were a repeal, it would be such a major step back from it was the only step forward that America was really doing in addressing climate change. Korea has been really one of the leaders in climate change you have a hydrogen policy; you've actually been trying to deal with climate change. The U.S. had not been doing very much because of our fossil fuel lobby. So IRA is really important for the U.S. And a repeal would be such a setback it would be heartbreaking. And when I say heartbreaking, it would be heartbreaking not only for me as an economist, as somebody involved in the climate battle, but for our young people who see this as one of the key areas. And they are very unhappy that they're inheriting an earth that is burning up.

**Jun Kwang-woo:** That's great. You have shared invaluable insights into the key challenges and outlook for the U.S. and global economy as we approach the potential start of a second Trump administration. It has been a truly enlightening keynote and discussion. We are deeply grateful for your time and generosity in joining us this evening, especially at such a late hour in NYC.

We very much hope to have the opportunity to welcome you in person at a future occasion. Thank you once again.

**Joseph Stiglitz:** It has been a great honor to join you today. Thank you for having me.

# SESSION 1

# Navigating Post-US Election Geopolitical and Global Economic Shifts

**Moderator**
**Shin Sung-hwan** Member of Monetary Policy Board, Bank of Korea (BOK)

**Keynote Speaker**
**Nicholas Lardy** Senior Fellow, Peterson Institute for International Economics(PIIE)

**Panelists**
**Fukagawa Yukiko** Professor, Waseda Univ.
**William Pesek** Nikkei/Forbes, Award Winning Columnist
**Lee Jong-Wha** Prof., Korea Univ./Fmr. President, Korea Economic Association/Fmr. Chief economist, ADB
**Choi Byung-il** Prof. Emeritus, Ewha Womans Univ

# Shin Sung-hwan

Good morning, my dear guests.

Winston Churchill, the legendary UK Prime Minister and an icon of wartime courage, said a pessimist sees the difficulty in every opportunity, and an optimist sees the opportunity in every difficulty. We gather today at a pivotal moment of global economic war. The aftermath of the U.S. presidential election coupled with U.S.'s number one rival China's ongoing economic challenges. Actually, it foretells huge changes in global economic landscape toward the rather extreme version of capitalism and mercantilism world.

Now is the time for us to figure out how we navigate through the restriping global economic landscape and create opportunities. The changes we are facing are substantial, the U.S.-China decoupling could disrupt global supply chains significantly and make our non-U.S. export markets crowded with flooding Chinese products excluded from the U.S. market. The possibility of terminating IRA subsidies and imposing tariffs may create difficulties for our corporate sectors. On top of that, the strong dollar driven by high market yields and a resilient U.S. economy may constrain our economic policies On the diplomatic side, global geopolitical conflicts and dynamics may dramatically change and the Korea-U.S.

defense version sharing rules may reset Korea is a small open economy where exports account for more than 40 of our GDP. For your information, U.S. less than 10%, Japan less than 20%, and China less than 25%. How we adapt ourselves to this changing external environment is crucial for continuing our prosperity. In this session, I hope that we can have some insights on the following questions. as Dr. Nicholas lardy, senior fellow at the Peterson Institute and former Yale University professor argues, is Chinese economy really fine now? despite the sluggish domestic demand and the tough trade environment.

Would China be able to transform its economy from investment-driven to consumption-driven economy by successfully managing its substantial non-performing asset problem?

As the KDI president Cho Dong-chul will show, the downtrend in long-term productivity is a strong headwind us which policies or policy making framework should we introduce to improve the productivity of our economy and how we can leverage the current external environment as professor Yukiko Fukagawa of Waseda University will discuss establishing cooperation frameworks with allies is very important especially in the current environment of economic and geopolitical conflicts. However, full-scale economic integration is practically not very feasible so many countries try to start from specific sectors Which sectors are feasible for the global cooperation frameworks between Korea and Japan and among our allies? as Mr. William Pesek, award-winning columnist for Nikkei and Forbes, will address, would the tensions between U.S. and China and U.S. and the rest could really be ratcheted up to the extreme level with high probability. as professor Lee Jong-hwa of Korea University will present, would any alternative regime emerge that can replace the current dollar dominance regime in the near future, say, within our lifetime? Last but not the least, I hope that Professor Choi Byung-il, Professor Emeritus of Ewha Women's University, gives us some insights on which policies or policymaking framework we should introduce to successfully reposition ourselves in the new supply and economic security chains and to strengthen our comparative edge in key technology and industrial sectors.

In this session, I hope that audiences keep those questions in mind and listen to the presentations of our distinguished speakers and panelists. The session will proceed as follows. First, we will have two keynote presentations. Dr. Nicholas Lardy will begin, followed by President Cho Dong-chul. Each speaker will give a presentation for 15 to 20 minutes. Then we will move on to panel discussions in the following order professor Yukiko Fukagawa, Mr. William Pesek, professor Lee Jong-hwa, and professor Choi Byung-il each panelist will discuss or may make a presentation for 10 minutes for the remaining 20 minutes, we will have some interactive discussions with the speakers and panelists. If time permits, I will get some comments or questions from the floor. Thank you for your attention. Now I invite our first speaker, Dr. Nicholas Lardy.

## Nicholas Lardy

I would like to begin by thanking the organizers for inviting me to participate in this incredibly timely and fascinating conference. My remarks today will be divided into two parts. First, I will discuss the shift in global geopolitics following the U.S. election. Then, I will focus on what I believe are some misconceptions about the Chinese economy.

Regarding the president-elect, it's nearly impossible to predict with certainty what his policies will be. He often makes inconsistent statements and frequently changes his mind. As a result, it will be very challenging for countries in Asia to anticipate the direction in which he will move.

The president-elect has outlined three main themes that he has been consistent about: tariffs, tax cuts, and the deportation of immigrants. The first thing to note is that he claims the revenue from tariffs will fund his tax cuts. However, this is highly unlikely. According to estimates from the Peterson Institute, if he imposes a 60% tariff on imports from China, the import volume will decline by 75%, meaning no additional revenue will be generated. This will ultimately lead to a higher budget deficit and, over time, more inflation. This inflationary pressure will be exacerbated by policies that result in the deportation of a large number of workers, especially in industries like construction and food processing. This will further drive up prices.

With inflation on the rise, the Federal Reserve is likely to raise interest rates. This, in turn, will attract more capital inflows into the U.S., causing the dollar to appreciate. Despite high tariffs, the trade deficit is unlikely to shrink significantly. As a result, my conclusion is that if the president-elect's policies unfold as proposed, we can expect higher inflation in the United States, a continuing large global trade deficit, and significantly higher interest rates. These higher rates could have two major consequences. First, there is an increased likelihood of a major stock market correction. The stock market has boomed largely due to the expectation of falling interest rates, but with rates rising, this perception may change. Second, higher interest rates will likely lead to lower U.S. growth, as businesses will invest less and the housing market will weaken.

Given these inconsistencies, it is important to watch how they play out in the coming months and years.

Now, I would like to turn to China. It is well-known that China faces substantial economic headwinds. These include geopolitical tensions, the trend towards deglobalization, the prospect of higher tariffs from the U.S., demographics, a shrinking workforce, and a decline in factor productivity. While these are major challenges, they are widely understood, and I will not delve into them today. Instead, I will address some common misconceptions about the Chinese economy.

The first misconception is that China's convergence toward the economic levels of advanced economies has stalled, or what some call "Peak China." For example, The Economist published articles both last spring and again a couple of weeks ago arguing that China is falling behind, citing a relative decline in China's GDP compared to that of the United States. I believe this is a complete misconception. The reason U.S. GDP is rising relative to China is largely due to the very high inflation in the United States over the past few years. From 2021 to 2023, U.S. inflation, as measured by the GDP deflator, was about 16%, while China's inflation was under 6%. This means U.S. nominal GDP appears higher because inflation has been roughly three times higher. If we look at real growth rates, the picture is quite different. As shown in this slide, most of Europe and Japan have had very little growth over the past five years. The U.S. has performed relatively well, by the standards of other advanced industrial economies. However, China has outpaced the U.S., growing at more than twice the rate.

Therefore, the idea that China has reached "Peak China" and that convergence has stopped does not seem to be supported by the evidence, at least so far.

The second misconception is that there is weak consumer demand in China since the end of the COVID-19 pandemic. However, the evidence does not fully support this claim. In 2023, disposable income grew by just over 6%, but household consumption in real terms rose by 9%. This implies that the savings rate must have declined. If consumption is growing faster than disposable income, the savings rate naturally decreases. If consumers had truly lost confidence, their savings rate would have risen, as they would be more concerned about the future. However, the data suggests the opposite.

Similarly, in the first three quarters of 2024, disposable income grew by about 5%, but real household consumption increased by 6%. This again shows a decline in the savings rate, indicating that consumption is making a substantial contribution to economic growth. As illustrated, final consumption contributed significantly to the economy's expansion in 2023.

The third misconception concerns deflation. Some argue that China is following the same path as Japan in the 1990s, experiencing deflation and low growth. This theory, known as a balance sheet recession, suggests that businesses and households pay down debt, reduce borrowing, and lower aggregate demand, which slows economic growth. While China does have low inflation, as shown on the left-hand side of the slide, the situation does not appear to be spiraling downward like Japan's deflationary period. The core CPI has been running below 1% for a few years, but it remains relatively stable. The PPI is declining slightly, but it is not causing a drastic reduction in economic activity. As previously mentioned, household consumption is rising, and the savings rate is falling, indicating that debt repayment is not the driving force behind the economy's challenges.

The fourth misconception involves the property sector. While it's true that property investment has declined, it is important to note that the decline in investment has not been as steep as the drop-in housing starts. For example, housing starts declined sharply in 2021 and continued to fall in 2022. However, completions have been increasing. In 2023, completions exceeded new housing starts for the first time. This shift is crucial for stabilizing the property market and for maintaining Chinese households' perceptions of property as an asset class. It is vital that pre-purchased homes are delivered to consumers, as failure to do so would tarnish the housing market for a long time.

The government is moving in the right direction by focusing on completing these ongoing projects. The creation of a "white list" indicates which projects banks should continue to lend to, based on their progress toward completion. This should help stabilize the property sector and ensure that consumers receive the properties they have paid for.

The final misconception is about the role of the private sector in China. Over the years, I have researched the importance of the private sector in China's economic growth. While private investment has indeed declined recently, this decline is largely due to the property sector's correction. As shown on the left-hand side of the slide, private investment in the property sector has fallen significantly since the government implemented the "three red lines" policy. However, outside the property sector, private investment actually grew by over 9% in 2023. This demonstrates that the private sector remains robust and continues to contribute significantly to China's GDP. Contrary to the perception that government policies have stifled the private sector, the evidence shows that private firms are still a major driver of innovation and economic growth in China.

In summary, while China does face significant headwinds, such as demographic challenges and geopolitical tensions, many of the negative perceptions about the Chinese economy are overstated. The idea that China has reached its peak, that household consumption is weak, and that the country is heading for a Japanese-style balance sheet recession are not supported by the data. Likewise, the decline in property investment is largely due to a shift in focus towards completing existing projects rather than starting new ones. Finally, the misconception that government policies have depressed the private sector overlooks the continued growth and dynamism in non-property sectors. Overall, I am more optimistic about China's prospects than what is often portrayed in Western financial media.

Thank you.

## Fukagawa Yukiko

First of all, I would like to express my heartfelt gratitude for the invitation to this meaningful event. I would also like to extend my sincere thanks to Dr. Jun Kwang-woo and the IGE staff. As a quasi-member of the IGE family, I am truly pleased to be back in this arena.

Today, I have been asked to speak about Japan-Korea relations, which I believe have emerged as one of the key assets in the past year or two. My talk will focus on the potential of Japan-Korea cooperation.

Globally, the challenges we face are increasingly similar. Japan, once a major global economic force and a key player in the tripartite trade power alongside the U.S. and Europe, is now facing a gradual decline. Similarly, Korea is facing shared challenges, particularly with an increasing reliance on exports, although the pace of this change has been relatively slow. We are both navigating through negative cycles in the global economy, including the rise of protectionist measures, economic security concerns, geopolitical tensions, and dysfunctions in the world trade system, particularly as represented by the WTO.

Given these challenges, it is imperative that we find reliable counterparts to collaborate with in order to create a consensus-based global order. One potential path forward is regional trade agreements, which have historically been common for economies like Europe and Korea. However, Japan and Korea have been exceptional in that they do not have an official, institutionalized regional trade agreement (RTA) between them, despite being members of the OECD.

Therefore, the question is: How can we establish a framework to foster better cooperation? Japan and Korea both participate in plurilateral frameworks, such as the CPTPP (Comprehensive and Progressive Agreement for Trans-Pacific Partnership). Although the U.S. has withdrawn from TPP, there are ongoing efforts to enhance this network. Moreover, we share another common regional network, the Regional Comprehensive Economic Partnership (RCEP), which includes China. This partnership represents a form of trilateral cooperation between Japan, Korea, and China, and the basic structure is quite similar to TPP. Given that China has already expressed its intention to join TPP, the challenge now is deciding whether Korea, Taiwan, or China should be prioritized in these discussions.

As globalization evolves, so too do the external conditions that Japan and Korea face. For Japan, deeper integration with regional partners like Korea is crucial. In return, Korea could find an opportunity for integration, especially in sectors like entertainment, content, and service industries, which are becoming increasingly important for economic growth. Japan, in turn, could benefit from positive competitive pressure, ideally coming from neighboring countries.

Another area for collaboration is technology. As Dr. Cho rightly pointed out, the U.S. economy can no longer solely rely on its vast domestic market. Innovation in domestic markets often leads to global success, and this is equally true for China. The question, then, is how Japan and Korea, both limited by the size of their domestic economies, can boost innovation. Moreover, we face significant demographic challenges in human capital, particularly in science and engineering. However, if Japan and Korea integrate their human capital, we could combine our strengths to realize new potentials.

While Japan and Korea have much in common, there are also substantial differences, particularly at the microeconomic level. Therefore, I believe our strategy should be to combine these differences and similarities to enhance market-driven integration, which would benefit both nations. For example,

Korea's largest companies are still predominantly manufacturing and export-driven, while Japan's largest companies are mostly service-oriented (with the notable exception of the automobile industry). Japan's economy is increasingly service-based, but it faces innovation challenges, which is where Korea could potentially offer valuable expertise.

Historically, Korea's rapid catch-up with wealthier economies was driven by manufacturing, with Japan as a key target in this process. However, that era of competition has largely ended. The rise of the Korean industry, particularly in sectors like entertainment and cultural exports, has been noteworthy. Korea now plays a leading role in global content exports, contributing to 15% of the global content market, second only to China at 40%.

This shift highlights the power of soft power and cultural influence, which Japan can learn from. The presence of Korean content and the influx of Korean inbound tourism have become significant drivers of growth for Japan as well. As we move into a new phase of cooperation, the focus is no longer purely on competition but on addressing shared sustainability challenges. For example, both countries face environmental issues and the pressures of rapid aging populations. Japan's experience in dealing with an aging society could offer valuable insights for Korea, especially in areas like medical reform and local development.

In addition, bilateral cooperation between Japan and Korea may shift from global competition to more localized, mutually beneficial partnerships. By cooperating on global issues, such as promoting professional exchanges and representing our views in international organizations, we can enhance our collective influence. Additionally, Korea's extensive official development assistance (ODA) to developing countries could align with Japan's own international strategies, providing another avenue for collaboration.

In summary, Japan and Korea have much to offer each other in terms of cooperation. While we share many challenges, our differences also provide an opportunity for complementary growth. Whether it's through regional trade agreements, technological collaboration, or addressing demographic and environmental issues, there is a strong foundation for a deeper partnership between our nations.

Thank you.

**William Pesek**

It's a great pleasure to be here.

This morning, while I was listening to the presentations, I was looking across the table, looking at Mr. Lardy, and I realized that the last time that I saw him was in 2015. We were in Azerbaijan at the ADB meeting. I was moderating a panel. He was speaking. And it had me thinking about the last decade.

We all maybe know the story of Rip Van Winkle. at least Americans do, Westerners do. It's a Washington Irving's short story about a man who basically goes to sleep for a long time. and he wakes up and he's shocked by the world around him. And I wrote down spontaneously this morning 10 things that might have surprised Mr. Lardy back in 2015 when we were in Azerbaijan.

Number one, China, its top export might now be deflation. Japan, 10 years later, It's on its fourth prime minister, and the Bank of Japan is still struggling to get interest rates above 0.2%. India's population is now bigger than China's. A giant pandemic shut down the global economy for almost two years. AI, artificial intelligence, is the new dot-com, changing everything apparently. Bitcoin, apparently, isn't a scam after all. K-pop is the new Motown, taking the world by storm. The Marcos family is back in power in the Philippines. A general is once again leading Indonesia.

And number 10, Donald Trump, a reality TV star, married three times, bankrupt six times, has been elected US president twice. This is the most shocking thing for me of all.

I wrote down my top ten list of the ten reasons why the second Trump presidency will not go well for Asia.

Number one, Donald Trump is angry and his revenge tour will begin in Asia. Donald Trump is just an angry guy. He's angry about losing the 2020 election. He's angry about being impeached. He's angry about being indicted. He is angry that his first trade war with China didn't work. He is angry that China's trajectory hasn't really changed the way he expected. He is angry that Japan and South Korea are actually talking.

He is annoyed that China is investing more than the US in semiconductors, renewable energy, electric vehicles, aerospace, biotechnology, AI, robotics, green infrastructure. Trump is angry that Vietnam won all the jobs that he thought would come back to the US. He is also angry that his trade war did not drag Asia back 10 years. Now, Trump is angry and he has no guardrails. The Supreme Court has basically said he's immune from committing crimes in the Oval Office, which scares me. The Republican Party in the US is acting like Russian Duma members. The media is scared. Victor Orban style. So Trump is super angry and Asia will be his first port of call.

Number two, Trump's only real economic plan is eating Asia's lunch. Now, Trump talks about tax cuts, nice. He talks about deregulation, great. He talks about destroying different departments of the government. At the end of the day, Trump has what I call a 1985 problem. His policies are stuck in 1985. Tariffs would have worked back then, maybe. Trade wars, maybe. Another Plaza Accord that weakens the dollar, it might have worked back then. Trickle-down economics. Maybe. But the game now is wrestling jobs from Asia and pulling them back to Trump districts and states. Trump thinks this will be very easy. He's wrong.

Number three, the idea of transactional Trump is a fantasy. I know we all think that Trump's tariffs are a negotiating tactic and that his real game is a grand bargain with China that creates this incredible trade deal, the kind of which the world has never seen. There are a variety of problems with this idea: One is that Donald Trump doesn't negotiate. He takes. Is China going to give? I have my doubts. Will Donald Trump use Taiwan? protection of Taiwan as a bargaining chip. Should Taiwan be looking at Ukraine thinking, are we next? We've all seen movies. Koreans, of course, love movies. And we all know that the sequel is usually worse than the original. And that's Trump to me.

Number four, I'll accelerate here because my time is running out. Number four, Trump's 60% tariff is just the beginning. He'll add more. He wants to put a 100% tariff on all cars made in Mexico. Does Japan and South Korea really think that Trump will not start threatening to do the same here? Maybe.

Number five, Trump will make bilateral trade deals great again. He will force Japan, South Korea, other countries to engage in bilateral trade deals where Trump will take and not give.

Number six, Japan and South Korea should be prepared for the next great military shakedown. Last time around, Trump, basically like a mob boss, went to Seoul, went to Tokyo, and said "Pay us billions of dollars to maintain U.S. troops". Expect that to happen all over again.

Number seven, Trump wants control of the Federal Reserve. Not good for the dollar. Trump wants to devalue the dollar. Not necessarily good. Number nine,

Trump even wants to make default great again. Donald Trump has talked about making a deal when US debt gets too much. US debt is now 36 trillion dollars, double the size of China's economy. Most of the US, well a lot of the US budget at this point is interest payments. So will Trump default? Maybe.

And finally, Will Trump invite Kim Jong-un to the Oval Office? Anyone who thinks this won't happen has been paying attention. Will Donald Trump visit Pyongyang? I don't know. But I think that in many ways, when you look at the idea, I mentioned Rip Van Winkle and things that might surprise you 10 years on. Did anyone think that North Korea's biggest export in 2024 would be soldiers? I don't think I saw that coming. It was not on my bingo card. Anyway, I hope I'm wrong. I want to be here a year from now so you can all laugh at me. But I'm deeply worried, and I think that Asia has a target on its back.

And it's best that governments here adjust, prepare, and batten down the hatches, because I really do see this as a buckle-the-seatbelts moment. I really, again, I want to be wrong, but we will see. On that note, I think we should be serving whiskey along with our coffee, but I'll turn it back to the moderator. Thank you.

### Lee Jong-wha

Good morning, Chairman Jun, and honored guests. Ladies and gentlemen, it's a great honor to speak before you today. I will be discussing the significant developments in the global economy following the recent U.S. election.

There are both optimists and pessimists, and while I may lean toward realism, my goal is to provide an objective analysis of the current state of the world economy. Let me begin by reviewing the global economic outlook based on the latest IMF projections from October. As you know, the global economy experienced a strong recovery following the COVID-19 pandemic, but the pace of recovery has since slowed.

The IMF's projections indicate that global economic growth will decelerate in 2025, particularly in the U.S. Despite the ongoing robust growth, the expansion is expected to slow down in the coming year. China's growth is also anticipated to moderate in 2025. On the other hand, inflation, as we heard from earlier presentations, has been decreasing globally, primarily due to lower energy costs and the impact of tighter monetary policies. In the U.S., the labor market has been a key driver of inflation. However, this has been partially offset by the decline in energy prices.

Looking ahead, as the output gap closes and the labor market stabilizes, wage growth is expected to moderate, and U.S. inflation is likely to decline. In summary, the IMF's October projections suggested a soft landing for both the U.S. and global economies. However, these projections were made before the recent developments that have caused significant disruption, particularly with Donald Trump's victory in the U.S. presidential election.

President-elect Trump has pledged to implement policies such as higher tariffs, tax cuts, deregulation, and lower interest rates. As you can see from the chart on the left, his victory had a considerable impact on financial markets. U.S. stock prices reached record highs, the U.S. dollar surged, bond prices fell, and Bitcoin reached new peaks. These movements were driven by expectations of economic growth under the Trump administration, fueled by tariffs, tax cuts, and deregulation. This has boosted optimism about U.S. economic growth but has also raised concerns about inflation, which became evident in the bond markets.

One of the key issues we must address is the potential spillover effects of

Trump's policies on the global economy. As seen in the currency fluctuations, uncertainty and risks are likely to increase in the global markets over the next year. What should we watch for? While there are many factors to consider, I will focus on U.S. monetary policy, as it will be a key factor in the coming year. In Korea, we understand well how U.S. policy rates can have a significant impact on both Korea's monetary policy and financial markets.

A second Trump administration is expected to focus initially on tariffs and tax reforms, which could drive inflation higher. As a result, the Federal Reserve may be hesitant to implement the rate cuts it had previously announced for next year. Many predictions about future monetary policy have emerged, with some forecasts suggesting that the Fed may be reluctant to lower rates in 2025 until it sees concrete evidence of how Trump's economic policies impact inflation.

At this moment, it is difficult to predict the precise effects of Trump's policies on the global economy, as well as on the U.S. and Korean economies. However, I'd like to share one simulation by the IMF, which highlights potential downside risks to both the U.S. and global economies. The IMF's simulation considers key shocks such as a blanket tariff on U.S. imports followed by retaliatory tariffs from the Euro area and China, uncertainty over trade policies, a 10-year extension of business income tax cuts, a reduction in migration flows to the U.S. and Europe, and tighter global financial conditions.

The chart on the right illustrates the simulated impact of these anticipated policies. A 10% tariff could reduce U.S. GDP by about 0.4% in 2025 and 2026, which is not a negligible impact. China's GDP is expected to decline by 0.2-0.3%. If all these shocks occur, U.S. GDP could decline by about 1%, and China's GDP by the same amount. This would represent a significant shock to both economies.

However, the magnitude of the shocks would depend on the extent of tariff increases and retaliations. On the positive side, the large tax cuts in the U.S. economy could have a countervailing effect.

Looking beyond short-term projections, we must also consider long-term issues such as protectionism, economic fragmentation, and the use of economic tools for geopolitical purposes. These trends will likely continue, with reshoring, plundering, and the shifting of trade and financial flows toward allied nations. The U.S.-China trade and technology tensions are likely to escalate further. China's response will likely focus on revitalizing its domestic economy and building technological independence.

China's economic growth is expected to decline gradually due to factors such as population decline, slower technological growth, and reduced investment. Even with reforms, China's growth rate is projected to decline to between 1% and 2% over the next two decades. However, China's GDP in real terms has converged to that of advanced economies, and its growth rate will likely remain higher than the U.S. for the foreseeable future.

Regarding technological advancements, China has seen success in areas like AI, where it has surpassed the U.S. in the number of patent applications. Yet, in the long term, the key question remains: how will China manage its trade, financial, and technological relationships with the United States?

One important question to consider is whether the U.S. dollar will maintain its status as the key global currency over time. Although demand for U.S. dollars remains strong, China and BRICS nations are working closely to reduce their reliance on the U.S. dollar and promote local currencies for trade and financial transactions. Under a second Trump administration, known as "Trumponomics," U.S. dollar assets could become less secure, potentially undermining confidence in the dollar's status.

As shown in the chart on the right, the U.S. dollar remains dominant in global reserves, but its share has been declining. If it falls below 50%, we could see significant changes in the global economic system, though this shift will likely take a few decades. Nonetheless, the gradual decline of the dollar's dominance as a key currency seems increasingly likely.

In conclusion, the policies under "Trumpomics" will have a significant impact on the global economy. We must watch closely for the effects of high tariffs, tax cuts, and trade tensions, particularly between the U.S. and China. These factors will have far-reaching implications for global markets, including Korea's economy. It would not be surprising to see a further decline in the dominance of the U.S. dollar under a second Trump administration.

Thank you.

## Choi Byung-il

If we take a step back and consider the broader context, we can observe a significant global contest between globalists and populists. In this critical struggle, populism appears to be gaining ground, with a ratio of two to one. This phenomenon is closely tied to the events of the summer of 2016, notably the Brexit referendum. If we reflect on the significance of Brexit and the election of Donald Trump in 2016, it is clear that these events marked a profound transformation in global politics and political economy. Many analysts rushed to label this as a transformation of the "zeitgeist."

However, despite extensive analysis, President Trump's economic policies—particularly his trade policies—do not entirely align with the stated objectives. His rhetoric of universal tariffs, including the imposition of a 60% tariff on

China, was intended to stimulate investment and create jobs in the United States. Nevertheless, our analysis suggests that the results do not fully support this approach.

Despite these challenges, I remain confident that Trump will continue to press forward with his strategy, particularly in terms of strengthening U.S. borders. I believe two key aspects stand out in his trade policy. First, he sought to revive the U.S. manufacturing sector, especially the automobile industry, which is crucial for winning elections in the United States. Second, he pursued a policy of complete decoupling from China. As we know, during his first term, he employed tariffs as a tool to exert pressure on China. However, the results were mixed, and we cannot predict the full outcome as the COVID-19 pandemic struck just as his term came to an end.

As a result, Trump left behind a "Phase One" trade deal with China, leaving more complex issues unresolved for future negotiations. My intuition tells me that a second-phase negotiation will not take place. Rather, Trump is more likely to push China further out of the U.S. market. From this perspective, I would like to offer four policy proposals for Korean policymakers, politicians, and corporate leaders.

First, develop a Comprehensive Negotiation Strategy: during his campaign, Trump emphasized the need for a significantly higher defense budget and pointed to the trade deficit as a major concern. He argued that exports are beneficial, while imports should be reduced. In this regard, countries like Mexico, Korea, Germany, and Japan, which have substantial trade deficits with the U.S. in sectors like automobiles, are prime targets. If we attempt to engage with each of these issues individually, we risk missing the bigger picture. Therefore, it may be wise to develop a more comprehensive negotiation strategy that links defense and trade issues. While we are willing to make concessions, it is essential that we secure some benefits in return. For instance, Korea's nuclear cooperation treaty with the U.S. is not as advantageous as Japan's, particularly in terms of spent fuel reprocessing. This is an important consideration in our negotiations.

Second, adopt a Sustainable Investment Strategy: Korean companies making substantial investments in the U.S. need to adopt a more sustainable investment strategy that extends beyond the period of Trump's presidency, from 2025 through 2028. Many of these investments, particularly in sectors such as batteries, semiconductors, and electric vehicles, are concentrated in so-called "red" Republican states like Tennessee, Ohio, and North Carolina. Even if the federal government attempts to revoke agreements made during the Trump administration, it is crucial to engage with grassroots politics at the state level. This will be essential for securing long-term investments and fostering a positive business environment in these regions.

Third, enhance Workforce Development and Skills: Many global CEOs who are establishing manufacturing facilities in the U.S. have expressed concerns about the challenge of securing a skilled workforce. For years, the U.S. decided to relocate many of its manufacturing operations to Southeast Asia. Now, even as companies invest in factories within the U.S., it remains difficult to retain high-skilled workers with the necessary expertise. This is an issue that Korean companies and policymakers must address by demanding that state lawmakers improve workforce development. If we are to succeed in these markets, it is essential that we work collaboratively to strengthen the local labor force.

Forth, rebuilding Global Trade Institutions: As we all recognize, the existing global trade institutions—such as the WTO—are no longer functioning effectively, particularly in terms of trade. The G20, which was established in the aftermath of the 2008 global financial crisis to bridge the gap between advanced and emerging economies, has failed to live up to its promise and has become little more than a forum for photo opportunities. For years, I have argued that we need to rebuild the G7. While the G7 is a legacy of the past, it is no longer effective in its current form. We must reinvent the G7 by inviting countries like Korea, Australia, and India to provide a more balanced representation of global economic interests and enhance its role in shaping global policy.

In light of these considerations, we must look beyond the immediate challenges and focus on the longer-term future. There are significant opportunities in the midst of crises, and history has shown that those with the courage and ability to implement change are the ones who seize those opportunities. In the first term of Trump's presidency, he focused on countering the rise of China in high-tech sectors. From Korea's perspective, this presents a unique opportunity to further strengthen our edge over China, particularly in semiconductors, and to overcome recent challenges in electric vehicle and battery technologies.

The paradigm that once saw Korea relying on the U.S. for security and China for economic growth is no longer viable. In response, Korea must build more effective alliances and strengthen cooperation with like-minded countries. This includes revising institutions such as the G10. By doing so, Korea can navigate through the turbulence of these changing times and remain competitive on the global stage. Thank you very much.

## Shin Sung-hwan

Thank you very much. Now, I would like to ask a quick question to our speakers and panelists.

My question is related to Korea. Economic theories suggest that capital tends to flow from low-growth countries to high-growth countries. So, if our productivity is lower than that of, for example, the U.S., capital will move from Korea to the U.S., making the U.S. dollar stronger and the Korean won weaker. This, in turn, should lead to an increase in our exports, which ultimately boosts domestic production due to the rise in export activity. However, in reality, this mechanism does not seem to work as expected. For instance, when we look at Japan, its potential growth rate has been lower than that of the U.S. for the past 30 years, and it remains low, which weakens the Japanese yen. This is because the Bank of Japan has been unable to raise interest rates despite the sluggish domestic economy.

In this context, I strongly agree that improving productivity should be our number one economic policy objective—not only for this government, but for the next government and possibly beyond, for a very long time. However, achieving this is not easy, and one of the key factors for enhancing productivity is deregulation. Deregulation is a central component of Trump's economic policies as well.

I would like to hear your views on how we can push for deregulation and accelerate the speed of deregulation in Korea. We have been talking about deregulation for a long time, but the conversation has not yet led to significant action. Can anyone share their thoughts on how we can push forward with deregulation?

## Choi Byung-il

Well, perhaps I can answer the question because I served as the president of the Korea Research Institute 10 years ago, and we faced the same questions. The same old questions continue to persist with us. I believe, as President Cho Dong-chul mentioned during his talk, that somehow, the Korean government—since the administrations of Lee Myung-bak, Park Geun-hye,

Moon Jae-in, and now President Yoon—has failed to recognize that without a strong and resilient economy, we do not have a strong future. This, I think, is truly related to political courage. In this regard, some of my friends told me that the election of Trump might provide a boost, because Korea has had to prove, time and again, that when faced with a severe exogenous shock, we can suddenly overcome all our divisions and differences and rise again. I hope this happens this time.

**Shin Sung-hwan**

Thank you. The question I would like to ask as our final inquiry is whether China will be able to handle the non-performing asset (NPA) or bad asset problem going forward. One of the reasons why China is following the path of Japan is that, unlike the U.S., where balance sheets are marked to market almost immediately, Japan actually spread out the pain over time. In contrast, the U.S. tackled the problem and absorbed the pain in a relatively short period. Politically, it is not easy to impose such pain on their citizens.

So, this is the question many investors have: is China both willing and able to tackle this bad asset issue and clean up all the bad assets in a short period of time?

**Nicholas Lardy**

Well, I think this is a very, very good question. The first problem in answering it is that we don't really have a very good estimate of the bad assets in the system. China was very successful, almost two decades ago, in dealing with bad assets in the banking system. However, the bad assets now are primarily in local government financing vehicles and some of the smaller banks that have lent to them. There are uncertainties about how large this series of assets is, and there is not very much information about the quality of the assets. I think the quality varies enormously—some are fine, while others are not earning enough money to cover the interest on the debt.

The government has recently announced a small step to try to address this issue, issuing new bonds that can be used to redeem existing bonds. The new bonds have a lower interest rate and a longer maturity, which should somewhat reduce the debt burden of these local government financing vehicles, which primarily involve provincial and local governments. However, I think the preliminary assessment is that the magnitude of relief from this new program will actually be quite small. It's a small bite of a big problem, and much greater effort will be needed to deal with it.

Again, this is a political economy issue, and the central government does not want to assume responsibility for the outstanding liabilities of local governments. Local governments have been more or less forced to undertake significant borrowing to finance various programs, both social and investment programs, due to the limited fiscal resources they have, stemming from the fiscal system reforms made in 1994. Therefore, there is a significant conflict between the central government and the local governments. The local governments believe that, ultimately, the central government will have to assume responsibility for these debts, but the central government is resisting that idea. This is a situation that is likely to take a long time to resolve.

If growth returns to a higher level and if more economic reforms are implemented, it will be possible to absorb these bad assets. However, if growth continues to decline due to decreasing total factor productivity and the increasing role of the state and the party, it will become much more difficult, and possibly impossible, to resolve the issue.

## William Pesek

I'll just add something briefly to that. You know, since last Friday, President Xi Jinping has been positioning China once again as the protector of globalization in the Trump 2.0 era, as he did back in 2017. And it's great that China is stepping up to become a stakeholder in the global financial system, not just a shareholder. But I wonder if President Xi understands the cost of becoming a stakeholder in the global economy.

Does President Xi, now in his third term, the strongest Chinese leader since Mao Zedong, have enough time to come up with a viable plan to address the property crisis? Shouldn't that be enough time to create a policy proposal to combat deflation? Shouldn't it also be enough time to deal with these local government financing vehicles, which are now twice the size of Japan's annual GDP in 2020 in terms of debt? Shouldn't it be enough time to come up with a solid plan to reduce youth unemployment and address the aging population?

It should be enough time to stop announcing annual GDP targets, which warp incentives and create arbitrary goals. It makes President Xi Jinping, like the CEO of a Silicon Valley company, try to meet his numbers every year. This just distorts incentives.

Is there a plan to stop subsidizing SOEs, to stop exporting excess goods and capacity? Is there a plan for China to become a more confident leader and step away from censorship?

How is China going to become a leader in artificial intelligence when its best innovators are afraid of doing anything that might cause them to flee the country, or when the best innovators in China cannot interact with the global community online to brainstorm?

Finally, does President Xi Jinping, now in his third term, have enough time to come up with a viable system of safety nets to encourage Chinese consumers to spend more and save less? I mean, to become a global stakeholder, China has to at least begin importing something closer to what it's exporting.

And again, Xi Jinping is a very, very smart man, a very strong leader. Donald Trump calls him "out of central casting," loves the guy. But again, we're into his third term. Shouldn't that be enough time to come up with a strategy to put China on more stable footing? And once again, I hope I'm wrong here too, but we'll see.

## Shin Sung-hwan

Okay, thank you very much, my dear speakers and panelists. I think time is up, and thank you very much for listening to our presentations throughout the session. Thank you very much.

# SESSION 2

# Innovating Climate and Inclusive Finance for Sustainable Growth

**Moderator**
**Hong Jong-ho** Prof., Graduate School of Environmental Studies at SNU

**Keynote Speakers**
**Vinod Thomas** Senior Fellow, Institute of Southeast Asian Studies, Singapore
Fmr. Senior VP, World Bank
**Sanjay Patnaik** Director of the Center on Regulation and Markets, The Brookings Institution
**Koo Bonjay** Partner, Deloitte Consulting

**Panelists**
**Lee Hyung-hee** President, Communication Committee, SK SUPEX Council
**Lee Jin** Director General, Financial Supervisory Service(FSS)

## Hong Jong-ho

Welcome to Session Two of this conference. The focus of this session is on climate finance, inclusive finance, and sustainable growth. Finance is an integral part of a sustainable economy. Without effective and timely finance, there will be no innovation or investment, and without these, sustainable growth is not achievable. Therefore, the topic of this session is both timely and critical.

We are fortunate to have three distinguished speakers, as well as three panel discussants, with us today.

Our first speaker is Dr. Vinod Thomas, a Senior Fellow at the Institute of Southeast Asian Studies in Singapore. He is also the former Senior Vice President of the World Bank Group. Dr. Thomas, are you ready? Let's welcome him with a round of applause.

## Vinod Thomas

Great pleasure to see you again, and also a big thank you to Dr. Jun for inviting us.

I'll switch to the PowerPoint to be efficient today.

There are four big topics and much of it is familiar to us because climate change is headline news all over the world, including Korea.

The first, the state of play it's important to recognize. We may be focused on the fine details of climate finance—each of which matters—but all of this risks being overshadowed by the likely direction of U.S. climate policy. According to the Project 2025 blueprint, policies already proposed could lead to an annual increase in U.S. carbon emissions equivalent to the total emissions of the EU and Japan combined. So if that happens, it doesn't mean the other policies by Korea and everybody else is not important, but you won't see the effect because the atmosphere only cares about emissions. And that going up could be disastrous for the global natural disaster scenarios.

The one other thing I want to mention here is the third bullet on the slide. There is a tendency to think that tariffs increased by one country can be insulated and it is good for domestic industry, but in a highly globalized setting-that means that India surely will also increase emissions. Russia will surely will increase emissions, so will Indonesia, Brazil, and across the world that could be what might be called the co- fallacy of composition. One organizer, one country raising emissions and tariffs, leading to a global problem.

I don't mean to bring this up so much in the beginning to discourage our discussion, but just to give a realistic picture of what we need to be keeping in mind as we go along. This is a very familiar picture but interestingly, the global emissions, which is on the right, it's very steadily going up. If we had another picture of the warming, it would go exactly in the same direction, exactly in the same rate of increase, they fit like a glove.

In the case of Korea, that has been the story for 20 to 30 years. However, in the last few years, there is a dip in the Carbon emissions, nevertheless Korea is the thirteenth largest emitter in the world. And so everything we say today is of acute relevance to the policy making in Korea.

This picture may surprise us in a way that the red bar which is Asia and the Pacific does not look great compared to the others on environmental protection, not on economic growth, absolutely no. But if you think about the East Asian miracle, we celebrate that as a great achievement and right, it is rightly so. However, if you had done a one that was based on environmental protection, it would look more like this. So we need to qualify because now, as time is running out, environmental protection is becoming inimical or a problem for even economic growth.

Now South Korea's climate profile. This is well-known to this group, but I could just emphasize that action needs to take care of the second bullet: that is 40% power, industry 26%, and transport 18%. And you know that the constraints for reducing $CO_2$ from each of those are quite distinct. And they really enter the political economy and even cultural aspects. So, they have challenges that are different. Having said that, I ask as an outsider if the priority might indeed be to tax coal and sharply increase renewables which would be, in this case, wind, solar, for which Korea has excellent possibilities, plus hydrogen down the road.

Just to move quickly, the session is about financing, so I want to make one point: why financing is very, very important and so is technology. We can be rest assured that financing will come if people believe that this is a top priority. Just remember COVID-19. The world raised $19 trillion within a matter of a year because people felt that this is a top priority.

So financing is very important, so is technology, and the techniques of doing that is critical. However, unless people's mindset gives a priority to climate financing, that assumption may not hold. In the U.S elections, this was not an issue at all. Even for young people.

So with that, I would say one revelation is that it's very important to note that bottoms-up and top-down financing are both critical. We may be discussing a lot of the bottoms-up, which is the COVID-19 model. But the top-down is equally important because when we think of the digital revolution into which trillions of dollars went up—there were no meetings like this to say we need to increase digital financing or expand the internet.

Many of the innovations have been financed by people just either crowdsourcing or putting their money in to earn a dividend, et cetera, et cetera. So that comes from the world of technology, which is spurred by people believing that this is consistent with economic growth and not inimical to economic growth.

Climate change, unfortunately, falls on the wrong side of that spectrum. Wrongly, people think that it is inimical to sustainable development.

So while this session is on finance, I would say that dissemination and changing people's mindsets is probably the most important issue that we face.

Now, in the case of South Korea—again, just to emphasize—the key takeaway may well be the story of expanding renewables. It's not that we're unfamiliar with this, but the developments in offshore wind turbines, and the ambitious—very ambitious, even super ambitious—plans for solar energy and possibly green hydrogen, deserve renewed attention. These could very well save the day.

I think of Singapore's plan, which is extraordinarily ambitious: despite the fact that 96 percent of its energy currently comes from fossil fuels, the country is nonetheless committed to achieving net zero by 2050. One might ask—how on earth is that possible? Well, the answer—at least in Singapore's case—is hydrogen. The hope is pinned on hydrogen.

So the question becomes: could that also be a possible scenario for Korea?

So on renewables, I won't spend time on it. This picture just makes the point that going in, we have a problem—and that is, the risk of investment is too high if it is solar, wind, and so on, and the returns, on the other axis, are too low, right? So you need to raise the returns and reduce the risk. Typically, that is good economics—not bad economics—if we are talking about the so-called negative externalities. It's not wrong to subsidize renewables if the society gains more than the private individuals combined.

So here the question would be: can we reintroduce feed-in tariffs in Korea? Why not? It's good economics. But there may be issues—there may be financial issues, even of balancing the budget. But this picture, again and again, is making the point that we need a two-pronged action on renewables for this to happen.

Again, since we are talking about inclusive and sustainable finance, just a global picture—and we go crazy with these numbers. We used to talk in billions with a "B"; now it's trillions with a "T." This is a background paper done for ADB, and in the slides I summarize: it sounds like $5 trillion a year for the next 10 years would be what it takes. The COP29 that's going on in Azerbaijan talks about seven, not five. Okay, I mean, at this stage, I would take five if we can get it—but we are not close. But this goes into quite some detail to see why it is seven, and the question is: is it incremental? Meaning, does a country have to raise savings and investment by that much? If that's the case, it's not going to happen. Very realistically, there are so many other issues—including wars.

But if it is a substitution for fossil fuels, then we're talking. But will we substitute renewables for fossil fuels? I don't see it right now. It's not in the cards right now. Fossil fuels are going up, not down—as Azerbaijan is signing off on lots of fossil fuel deals. So we have a problem.

And just to get this out of the way—we're talking about the good financing that we need, but there is also bad financing that we need to avoid. According to the IMF, seven trillion (that was the previous year, and last year was probably five trillion) went into wrong financing—meaning subsidies for fossil fuels. I mean, if you are a very hard-nosed economist, it's like doing the opposite of what we learned in Economics 101. Rather than taxing the bad and subsidizing the good, we are taxing the good and subsidizing the bad. Now, the IMF estimate, just to be clear, includes health effects—so it's social, it's not private. If it were private, it would be probably more than 500 billion, not five trillion.

When you talk of financing, we really have to have a layering approach, whereby various forms of financing—some straightforward debt and equity that don't quite work for renewables—need to be complemented by just-in-time, fit-for-purpose types of financing.

Some examples of that from ADB: there is the energy transition mechanism. Leveraging the balance sheet with guarantees sounds a no-brainer, right? If you have a prosperous balance sheet, why don't we use it to support and guarantee those who are not sure? That's what ADB is trying to do.

World Bank's green bonds are going up. They are still a drop in the bucket in the big scheme of things. And the Climate Funds is right here in Korea based in Songdo has a particular relevance for the Pacific Islands and countries who's going to rely on more grant loans.

Now in the case of Korea important to note that a number of very valuable initiatives are underway. You are familiar with this history, but let me just say that the carbon neutrality of 2050, I wish we could overshoot that and make it 2045. Push for that with renewables, it's good for Korea, and it's good for the world.

Then KDB's effort to raise financing, especially in green energy facilities. And the emission trading system(ETS). I'll spend only a few minutes on come into play ETS, is a complement to finance. Just in a word, it's essentially pricing the bad stuff which is emissions, right?

You can address emissions in three ways. The most straightforward is to tax the emissions directly—I'm somewhat in favor of this approach. Another method is an Emissions Trading System (ETS), which sets a cap on total emissions and allows trading within that limit. Korea is implementing ETS and, in many respects, is ahead of other countries.

The third option is to impose tariffs on imports that are emission-intensive. We could discuss the pros and cons of this at length, but I believe all countries, including Korea, have this option. The ideal scenario would be that no one actually pays the tariff because they are already participating in an ETS or paying a carbon tax. I prefer the carbon tax mainly because it generates revenue more readily—not through auctions—and that revenue can be used to support social security programs related to climate change.

Now, this picture—also taken from the IMF—kind of summarizes the situation. If you look at Korea, represented by the red dot on the lower right, it shows that Korea is a very important country: it is a sizable emitter with good coverage across emission sectors. The nationwide coverage is high, similar to Singapore and Japan.

However, the carbon price in Korea is relatively low compared to New Zealand. You can build many scenarios from this: very good coverage with a very low price is not very effective, and similarly, very low coverage with a very high price is also not very effective. Ideally, you want to be in the upper right quadrant—the northeast.

In my humble opinion, Korea is one country that can achieve this and truly position itself in that favorable quadrant for its own benefit. When comparing New Zealand, Kazakhstan, Korea, and China, Korea stands out quite strongly in a positive direction across several indicators related to emission trading.

Finally, and very importantly, we need to ask: how can the financial sector help beyond what the private sector will do individually? This question is especially relevant because climate change is a negative externality.

This picture shows that when financing is constrained by the risk and reward balance I mentioned—and since financing is an essential part of monetary outcomes—it makes sense for central banks to be more engaged rather than less. The only hesitation would be if such involvement threatens the independence of the central bank.

However, these two are not mutually exclusive. A central bank can be both engaged and independent. With that in mind, a proactive approach would be to support a level playing field for decarbonization.

Defensive measures—such as Korea's current mechanisms for disclosure, oversight, and risk management—are important.

At the end of the day, I close with this picture: we need substantial investments, which require both top-down and bottom-up financing approaches, much like in the case of the digital revolution. Korea is very well-positioned to combine these two approaches, and doing so will benefit not only the welfare of the country but also drive strong economic growth. Thank you very much.

## Hong Jong-ho

Thank you, Dr. Thomas. I have a question for you—please feel free to sit. Two years ago, I gave a lecture to undergraduate students at a university in India. After the lecture, three students asked me the same question. They argued that the climate crisis we are facing isn't India's responsibility, but rather the responsibility of the US and Europe, the developed nations. They emphasized that without financial support and technology transfer from these developed countries, India has no incentive or intention to reduce emissions, as we are currently focused on economic growth.

You mentioned Azerbaijan and COP29, where the topic is climate finance and the establishment of climate funds. Given the current political climate, especially with Mr. Trump in power, what are your prospects for the developed world financing and creating funds that could assist developing countries like India in addressing climate change?

### Vinod Thomas

Should I give a very brief response? This is a huge topic. India, though its per capita income is a fraction of Korea's, has a total income much higher than Korea's, which drives its emissions. India is the third-largest emitter globally—not on a per capita or GDP basis, but in total. So, if India—and China, of course—don't act on mitigation, then all bets are off.

But here's the key distinction for this conversation: there's mitigation and there's adaptation. Mitigation means preventing further damage, while adaptation is about learning to live with it—albeit in a better way. India is largely focused on adaptation, not mitigation, relatively speaking. This tends to come up frequently in the classes I teach: those who support adaptation often don't prioritize mitigation.

The one thing that could have triggered stronger action on mitigation would have been finance. And that's where the Azerbaijan situation becomes critical—because it's largely driven by oil interests, and the US has a stated policy, not just my own view, that in 2025, it won't focus on mitigation but rather the opposite. This provides an ideal excuse for India. If you were to visit Rajasthan a year from now, the conference would likely be even more resistant to mitigation because if the US isn't mitigating, why should India sacrifice its economic growth?

It's a tough situation, but I'm an optimist. I believe the private sector will play a key role. If they push solar and wind energy to scale, they can drive down costs to a level that can overwhelm emissions.

## Hong Jong-ho

Thank you. Let's move on to our second speaker, Sanjay Patnaik, the Director of the Center on Regulation and Markets at the Brookings Institution. Is he online now?

## Sanjay Patnaik

Hello everyone, good afternoon in South Korea, and good evening from Washington, D.C. It's a bit after midnight here. I apologize for not being there in person, but I'm glad to speak with you today.

As you can imagine, with the new administration in the United States, many eyes are on the US and its impact on global climate policy. I want to focus on three areas that I believe will remain relevant, even with the change in leadership, and how we can leverage them to address the climate crisis.

The first area is the intersection of climate and AI. This is becoming an increasingly important topic, both from an innovation standpoint and in terms of energy consumption. We are organizing a virtual event on this at Brookings, scheduled for December 2nd. Climate and AI can be examined in two ways: first, looking at the energy consumption of AI and data centers, and how this will affect decarbonization; and second, examining how AI can help mitigate and adapt to climate change.

On the energy side, the US has seen a strong shift towards decarbonization, particularly under Biden's policies. Many tech companies are investing heavily in renewable energy, and there's a trend towards decarbonizing the electricity grid. This has, however, driven up energy demand, especially for renewables. At the same time, AI data centers are emerging all over the country, particularly near Washington, D.C. In Virginia, for example, there are a lot of new data centers, and they are large consumers of energy. The estimated demand for data center power will grow significantly by 2030.

The issue here is the clash between these two trends—decarbonization and the rapid growth of AI data centers. Without a matching increase in energy supply, this will drive up prices, which could undermine the acceptance of climate policies.

Looking at the demand for renewables, we see tech giants like Amazon, Microsoft, Meta, and Google being major players in the US renewable energy market. These companies have purchased enough energy to match the entire generation capacity of Sweden. They have strong incentives to secure energy: protecting against price fluctuations, reducing their environmental impact, and enhancing their brand reputation. However, they face challenges due to the variability of wind and solar sources, and the fact that the energy supply is struggling to meet growing demand. As an example, Microsoft recently signed an agreement with an energy company to restore the Three Mile Island nuclear plant, the site of a significant nuclear disaster decades ago. This shows just how desperate some of these companies are for reliable energy.

On the flip side, AI has great potential to mitigate and adapt to climate change. I'm genuinely excited about AI's promise in this regard. We are seeing innovative AI applications in sectors like energy, where it's being used to improve grid reliability and efficiency. There are also companies emerging that use AI to predict extreme weather events—some can forecast events up to six months in advance, which is groundbreaking for supply chain and location planning. AI is also being used to tackle deforestation, often combined with satellite imagery. In material science, AI could play a significant role in developing new technologies, such as better batteries. While the fundamental challenges of climate change remain, I believe AI holds tremendous potential.

The second area I want to touch on is carbon pricing and carbon tariffs, a topic already mentioned by Mr. Thomas. This is especially relevant given the European Union's decision to implement a carbon border adjustment mechanism (CBAM) starting in 2026. The EU is already running a pilot program to gather data and refine the methodology. The CBAM means that companies from outside the EU will have to either show that their home country has a carbon price equivalent to the EU's or pay the EU's carbon price at the border. This is causing concern among other nations, including South Korea, as it will affect exports.

Looking at the United States, it remains an outlier among wealthy nations, as we don't have a national carbon tax or cap-and-trade system. While some states, like California, have their own emissions trading programs, there has been little success in passing a national carbon pricing bill. In response to this, President Biden's Inflation Reduction Act (IRA) has focused on subsidies and tax credits to facilitate a low-carbon transition. However, it's still too early to gauge the effects.

The likelihood of President Trump revisiting or altering IRA provisions, even if Congress doesn't fully repeal the law, is significant.

As we move forward, there are additional policies that give me hope for continued progress on climate action, even with a Republican trifecta in the Senate, House, and presidency. As I mentioned earlier, the Inflation Reduction Act (IRA) has already been passed, and many of the investments from the IRA are directed into districts represented by Republican Congress members. Therefore, I find it unlikely that the entire law will be repealed.

While certain provisions may be targeted for repeal by Republicans, it is likely that actions will be taken through the executive branch or government agencies to slow the disbursement of some of these funds. Another bill currently under consideration, which also enjoys bipartisan support, is the "Prove-It Act." This bill, which has not yet passed, is primarily focused on data collection. Specifically, it mandates that the United States study the carbon intensities of certain industrial goods produced domestically or imported. This bill is a direct response to the European Carbon Border Adjustment Mechanism (CBAM). The motivation behind this is that Americans do not want to be excluded as other nations, particularly in Europe, adopt carbon pricing standards and methodologies.

This leads me to my next important point, which is that we are now seeing significant bipartisan support, both from Republicans and Democrats, for some form of carbon border adjustment mechanism. This is particularly unique because, as I have mentioned, the United States has unsuccessfully attempted to pass any form of carbon pricing for over 20 years. The rising interest in this issue is, in itself, a noteworthy development.

What unites both Republicans and Democrats in this approach to a potential carbon tariff is their shared stance on China. Both parties have become increasingly hawkish toward China, viewing a potential carbon tariff as a way to penalize China for its higher carbon intensity. When we compare carbon intensities, the United States actually has relatively favorable numbers, with much lower carbon intensity than both China and India.

Currently, there are two proposed bills being considered in Congress. One is the Clean Competition Act, introduced by Senator Sheldon Whitehouse, a Democrat. This bill aims to establish a carbon border adjustment mechanism and also proposes the implementation of a domestic carbon price. On the Republican side, there is the Foreign Pollution Fee Act, introduced by Senator Cassidy, which seeks to establish a carbon tariff without a domestic carbon price. It will be interesting to observe in the coming year whether a carbon tariff, in some form, could be included in the legislative discussions, particularly as Congress debates the extension of the Trump-era tax cuts. The potential for this happening is significant and should not be underestimated.

I would like to conclude this section by referencing a study conducted by Resources for the Future, a think tank based in Washington, D.C. Their study found that the CBAM could incentivize exporting countries to adopt a domestic carbon price. The rationale is simple: if a country without a carbon price faces costs when exporting to the European Union, instituting a domestic carbon price similar to the EU's would allow the government to raise revenue domestically. Rather than having their companies pay money to the European Union, these countries could keep the revenue within their own borders. I believe this could result in a domino effect globally, as countries realize that instituting a domestic carbon price could be a more beneficial option than paying the EU.

Looking at the growth of carbon pricing worldwide, the World Bank has an excellent dashboard that tracks carbon pricing initiatives. In 2019, there were slightly more than 50 carbon pricing initiatives globally. By 2024, the number has increased to 75 programs, covering about 24% of global emissions. This trend is moving in the right direction, and I do not anticipate that a change in administration in the United States will significantly alter these fundamental dynamics.

The final point I would like to address is climate finance, a topic that was also a key theme in the keynote address and was discussed by the previous speaker. I will focus specifically on the perspective of the United States, as the country has well-developed capital markets but is experiencing underinvestment in both climate mitigation and climate adaptation from the private sector. Recently, I co-authored a paper at Brookings examining the obstacles to increasing climate finance in the United States.

As many of you know, the challenge lies in the clear externality problem when it comes to the intersection of nature and financial markets. Markets fail to recognize the indirect costs borne by society due to greenhouse gas emissions. The damage caused by climate change is not factored into market pricing, and it is difficult for markets alone to price the damage of climate change.

To identify the obstacles, we consulted a broad range of stakeholders in the private sector. These discussions revealed why we are seeing insufficient investment in climate mitigation and adaptation measures. In the United States, adaptation needs are rising due to events like wildfires in California, increased hurricanes in Florida, and flooding in areas like North Carolina, which had never experienced such flooding before. The damages are substantial, and the economic costs are considerable.

When we examine the available instruments for investment—such as sustainable investments, ESG bonds, and green bonds—there is still significant demand in the market. However, there are empirical findings indicating that the track record has been poor. Nature-based credits, such as carbon credits and biodiversity credits, often face credibility challenges. New companies focused on nature preservation, where landowners lease or sell conservation easements to third parties, are emerging. Yet, despite the availability of these instruments, the investments are not reaching the scale necessary to address climate challenges.

Some of the primary obstacles identified in our study include the immature state of climate accounting methods. Many stakeholders indicated that we lack the sophisticated climate accounting methods required for effective investment.

Additionally, the information environment surrounding climate investments tends to disadvantage smaller players, thereby limiting capital mobilization. There is also limited government capacity, particularly at the local and state levels, to facilitate investments or create conditions that would encourage private sector involvement. Furthermore, climate-related benefits and costs are often either underpriced or unpriced, primarily due to the absence of established carbon pricing metrics.

Other challenges identified include financing models that favor greenhouse gas-emitting projects using established technologies rather than new technologies. There is also a misalignment of incentives and potential returns for projects that focus on adaptation, such as raising sea walls or protecting infrastructure from flooding or hurricanes. Private investors are finding it difficult to secure funding for these adaptation efforts. Additionally, fragmented political authority over projects can create uncertainty and delays for private investors, particularly in the renewable energy sector, where coordination between federal, state, and local governments often leads to significant delays in permitting.

Finally, public debates often struggle to balance the need for new climate investments with ongoing demands for funding established economic activities, especially where clean technologies are not yet available. In industrial processes, for example, technology is often not advanced enough to allow for decarbonization. Political timelines also tend to misalign with the long-term nature of many climate projects. Election cycles and changes in administration can lead to significant shifts in climate policy, as seen with President Biden's focus on climate action, followed by the potential de-emphasis under President Trump. This inconsistency is a challenge for the United States, but despite this, I remain optimistic about the positive trends in the marketplace, particularly in areas such as carbon capture and storage and electric vehicles. These trends will continue regardless of changes in administration.

Thank you for your attention.

## Hong Jong-ho

Thank you for your excellent presentation, which covered a wide range of important issues. There are many questions I could ask, but I'll limit myself to one. You discussed the role of AI, and I'd like to ask about its potential impact on energy consumption, electricity demand, and carbon emissions.

As you mentioned, there are offsetting factors to consider. On one hand, AI has the potential to improve efficiency in energy use, which could reduce consumption. On the other hand, as we all know, the increased demand for electricity driven by the growth of data centers and AI applications could lead to higher energy consumption.

What are your thoughts on the future prospects of these offsetting factors? Do you believe that improved energy efficiency through AI will ultimately offset the increased demand for electricity, or do you foresee the opposite scenario?

## Sanjay Patnaik

I haven't seen an empirical study that directly examines the exact figures, but my intuition is that, in the short term, the efficiency gains may not be sufficient to offset the increased demand for electricity. This is largely due to the rapid growth of AI data centers, particularly in the United States. At the same time, electricity demand is also rising due to efforts to electrify and decarbonize various sectors.

From my perspective, this is ultimately a matter of both economic and national security. Companies will want to build data centers, and they will be drawn to countries that can provide relatively cheap and accessible energy to support those facilities. Many countries in the Middle East are already reaching out to big tech companies, offering abundant energy—though often from fossil fuels. If countries like South Korea and the United States are unable to provide adequate energy, we may see a shift of some data centers abroad, which we should try to avoid.

This situation will likely require innovative solutions, such as the development of small-scale nuclear reactors, which are currently being explored in the U.S. In the near future, we may also see a continued reliance on fossil fuel plants to support the growth of AI data centers, as the transition to alternative energy sources will take time. I hope this answers your question.

### Hong Jong-ho

Thank you, Dr. Patnaik. Our next speaker is Koo Bonjay, Vice President of Deloitte Consulting. Please join me in welcoming him.

### Koo Bonjay

Good afternoon, I am Koo Bonjay from Deloitte. Today, I would like to present on a perspective that differs from the climate finance topics previously mentioned, focusing on self-employed individuals and small business owners. The survival and growth of small business owners are closely tied to the sustainable growth of the national economy, and from the viewpoint of financial institutions, financing them is highly relevant to inclusive financing, making it an important agenda.

With the rapid advancement of digital technology, we are experiencing many changes. Among these, new rules are forming within the financial industry that are determining the new growth conditions and success factors. The first change is the shift from a growth game to a survival game; the second is the emergence of non-face-to-face digital channels as an important primary channel; and the third is the competition among collaborative platforms rather than individual companies.

In particular, financial institutions, big tech companies, and fintech firms are actively entering the financial industry to innovate customer experiences for customer acquisition and retention. They are launching various digital financial and non-financial platforms to maximize network effects. For instance, various platforms such as O2O lifestyle finance platforms, comprehensive financial management platforms, integrated membership platforms, and digital payment platforms are being introduced to compete in the market.

In addition, under the leadership of financial authorities, digital innovation policies and data policies to strengthen the digital competitiveness of self-employed individuals and small businesses are being expanded. These include the Ministry of SMEs and Startups' digital transformation policy for small business owners, the Small and Medium Business Corporation's open big data platform for small businesses, and the Financial Services Commission's discussions on introducing My Data services for self-employed individuals.

So, who exactly are small business owners and self-employed individuals? According to the Small and Medium Enterprises Act, they are classified based on annual revenue, typically ranging from 1 billion to 2 billion Korean won. Specifically, manufacturing businesses are defined as those with annual revenues under 12 billion won, and other service industries are defined as businesses with annual revenues under 1 billion won. There are approximately

9 to 10 million self-employed individuals and small businesses, including both corporate and sole proprietorships. These businesses are spread across various industries such as retail, hospitality, food services, manufacturing, repair, education services, arts, sports, and leisure.

They face different needs and challenges depending on their industry and size, and they are greatly impacted by economic fluctuations, carrying significant uncertainty. Moreover, there is often a lack of reliable financial statements or information in the market, which often leads to these businesses not being served by financial institutions. When looking at some domestic banks serving small businesses, most small business owners using credit and deposit products are micro-sized enterprises with fewer than three employees and annual revenues under 200 million won, mainly in retail, manufacturing, hospitality, and restaurant industries.

These businesses are facing several operational challenges such as difficulties in managing business operations, responding to sales declines, rising rent and costs, increased competition, difficulties in hiring, funding challenges, and lack of technological and government support. They often struggle to obtain loans in a timely manner, face difficulties in accounting management, tax processing, marketing, and customer acquisition, and experience significant challenges in business management.

Therefore, financial institutions must provide dedicated services for self-employed individuals and small business owners. So, what services should a service platform for small business owners and self-employed individuals offer? The service should be designed to effectively manage the challenges these businesses face. Several considerations are required to design such a service. First, it is important to understand whether the target customers for the digital platform are existing small businesses or new customers. It is necessary to define whether the strategic goal is to acquire new customers or deepen relationships with existing customers.

Additionally, identifying the needs of customers, particularly unmet needs, is essential. So, what is the appropriate service model from the perspective of financial institutions? Rather than focusing on specific products or categories, a comprehensive solution platform model for self-employed individuals and small businesses that provides a broad range of products and services seems most appropriate.

Such a platform would not only provide traditional core banking services such as loans, credit evaluations, and foreign exchange services, but also offer a variety of value-added services. For example, it could include services such as commerce improvement, cash flow management, revenue and expenditure management, logistics management, and productivity improvement. However, in Korea today, the services provided by banks are mainly limited to financing and some revenue/expenditure management and payroll management.

The strongest need for small business owners and self-employed individuals is funding. According to a recent study by global consulting firm Oliver Wyman, as the revenue scale of small businesses increases, the demand for loans also increases. However, only 25% of small businesses receive loans through banks, with the rest sourcing funds outside of the formal financial system. Many small business owners prefer banks due to the ease and speed of loan applications.

Financial institutions are now recognizing self-employed individuals and small businesses as important customer segments and are providing not only banking services through traditional apps but also management support services. Additionally, telecommunications companies are offering integrated services combining communication and non-financial services for business management, and platform companies are providing operational management services. The government and financial authorities are discussing the introduction of a dedicated fourth internet bank for small business owners and self-employed individuals.

Globally, banks are offering services beyond core banking to self-employed individuals and small businesses, including community services, advisory services, marketplace services, and group purchasing services. For example, banks such as Barclays (UK), Santander (Spain), Deutsche Bank (Germany), DBS (Singapore), and TB Bank (Turkey) offer trade financing portals, fund management, operation tools, and business analytics services.

Recent analysis of the needs of self-employed individuals and small businesses in Korea has identified various customer groups with different challenges and needs. These include issues such as lack of working capital, insufficient funds for new investments, difficulties in hiring, and the need for market access. Financial institutions must analyze customer groups with similar needs and offer service models tailored to those needs.

This service model should consider whether it offers a competitive advantage, whether it is easy to develop, and whether services can be provided through third-party partnerships. Additionally, to ensure the success of the service model, increased traffic, strong rewards programs, and promotions will be necessary. Financial institutions and platform providers must work together to create win-win relationships that address customer challenges.

In conclusion, the survival and growth of nearly 10 million self-employed individuals and small business owners significantly impact the sustainable growth of the national economy. By offering service models that address their challenges, financial institutions can position these businesses as key customer segments. These businesses have great potential in untapped markets, and government policy support along with proactive service provision from financial institutions will be essential.

Finally, the three key success factors for a successful platform model for self-employed individuals and small business owners are establishing a differentiated identity, addressing customer pain points, and continuously increasing traffic and monetizing the revenue model. Through this approach, financial institutions and service providers can collaborate to achieve greater outcomes. Thank you.

## Hong Jong-ho

Yes, Vice President Koo, thank you for your passionate remarks and for raising such an interesting topic. The theme of today's second session is "Climate Finance and Inclusive Finance." Vice President Koo, you specifically spoke about financial services for small business owners and self-employed individuals, as well as their effectiveness.

I would like to connect this topic with climate change and pose a question. As Dr. Vinod Thomas mentioned earlier, the discussion on climate adaptation not only focused on reducing carbon emissions but also highlighted the importance of adaptation. In fact, in Korea, we are frequently witnessing flood damage to small factories and shops due to heavy rainfall.

Given this, I am curious about the potential for expanding the direction of inclusive finance to include climate-related areas, and what the stance of financial institutions is on this matter.

## Koo Bonjay

In fact, what I have mentioned is related to climate change. This is because I have discussed the role of financial institutions and service models for supporting small business owners and self-employed individuals in their coexistence. As we have experienced, a few years ago, many small business owners and self-employed individuals faced significant crises due to the COVID-19 pandemic. During that time, the government took proactive measures and provided emergency funds, with banks serving as the channel for this support. Looking ahead, it is highly likely that certain industries and segments will face substantial risks due to the anticipated rapid climate changes. In such a situation, the role of financial institutions in providing support for their survival will become crucial. If such support is provided, I believe it will ensure the sustainable, symbiotic growth of the national economy.

## Hong Jong-ho

Thank you. Now we'll invite panelists. First, I would like to invite President of the Communication Committee of SK SUPEX Council.

## Lee Hyung hee

Greetings. My name is Lee Hyung-hee. Currently, I am responsible for communications with the media and government policies at SK Group. However, before taking on this role, from six years ago to two years ago, I was in charge of ESG-related strategy and implementation within SK Group.

At that time, the EU Green Deal policy was announced, ESG funds by financial institutions were growing, and international organizations were increasingly focused on ESG issues. Our main concern at the time was that ESG, particularly the climate crisis, would continue to be a global agenda.

Therefore, we needed to think about how to play a leading role in this area. At that point, no South Korean company had made a commitment to RE100 or net-zero goals. As a result, the major companies within SK Group made commitments to RE100 and went through the process of applying to international organizations. Subsequently, we set net-zero targets, with each company aiming to achieve zero emissions by 2030 or 2050.

SK Group's main business sectors include energy, semiconductors, ICT, and bio. Within the energy sector, we were using petrochemical and carbon-based energy sources, leading to questions about whether we would be able to adapt to future global changes. To address this, we shifted our focus to renewable energy, energy efficiency, and recycling-based chemical industries. Additionally, we made significant investments in the battery sector.

The reason I am sharing this at length is not to boast, but because it raises an important question. We have been striving to lead change by pursuing post-move advantages, but recent events such as the war in Ukraine, conflicts in the Middle East, and the results of the US presidential election have all increased uncertainty. Financial institutions are now expressing different views compared to the past, and since companies are not rule-setters, the uncertainty in rule-setting has become a major issue.

In this context, companies are struggling with how to set their goals. The risks associated with being a post-mover have increased. Many companies are facing difficulties in developing technologies to address the climate crisis. These challenges are issues that global research institutions must also consider, and discussions are needed on how financial institutions should set future goals. Governments around the world must now carefully consider what goals to set for companies within the changed environment, ensuring these goals are practical and achievable. Thank you.

## Hong Jong-ho

Thank you very much. We need to continue growing and surviving in this changing environment. The Russia-Ukraine war, conflicts in the Middle East, and the challenges surrounding Trump's victory are all factors we must consider.

While these are completely different situations, they all involve complex issues that will take time to resolve. There may be cracks in systems that were once very aggressive and depraved, with longer processes and rising risks.

Companies are now in a position where they must respond and adapt. Whether it is international organizations or national governments, the rules they set will ultimately determine the overall direction for these companies. Thank you.

Now, we will move on to the policy segment. We have General Lee Jin from the Financial Supervisory Service of Korea.

## Lee Jin

Good afternoon, everyone. My name is Lee Jin, and I am the Director of the Financial Market Safety Bureau at the Financial Supervisory Service (FSS). Today, I would like to briefly share the efforts we are undertaking at the FSS to address the climate crisis.

First, I would like to provide a brief answer to the question of whether South Korea is responding to the climate crisis in a timely manner or not. In conclusion, I believe South Korea is responding to climate crisis regulations at an appropriate pace. This is because, first, the country declared its 2030 and 2050 net-zero targets in 2020 and enshrined them into law. This legal measure aligns with the global trends in addressing climate change.

Additionally, this April, the government decided to establish and execute a fund of approximately 300 trillion KRW through policy financial institutions to expand low-carbon investments. This demonstrates the active role South Korea is playing in providing financial support for the low-carbon transition. On the other hand, responses such as the carbon border tax or disclosure requirements are proceeding at an appropriate pace, considering South Korea's position as an exporter to the EU, in order to minimize the burden on companies.

Next, I will outline the role of the FSS in addressing the climate crisis. First, we have established and are implementing the "Climate Risk Management Guidelines." The purpose of these guidelines is to ensure that CEOs clearly set investment goals for carbon reduction when formulating corporate strategies, and that the board of directors supervises the implementation of these goals by the CEO and management team. In turn, business units are required to implement the goals set by the board and CEO, and disclose the results. We regularly assess whether financial institutions have incorporated these climate risk management guidelines into their strategies and whether they are being properly executed, thereby encouraging greater attention to climate risk management.

Secondly, the FSS is conducting joint climate stress tests with financial institutions. A climate stress test helps companies assess the potential losses related to climate-related disasters caused by global warming. Due to the financial burden of carbon trading, businesses may face deteriorating profitability, which could lead to an increased risk of bankruptcy. We are helping financial institutions measure these risks in their lending and investment portfolios, allowing them to quantify the financial risks they face. The purpose of these stress tests is twofold: first, to strengthen pricing capabilities for climate-related financial products, and second, to encourage financial institutions to transition to low-carbon portfolios.

Thirdly, the FSS's key initiative for this year and next is to develop "Green Lending Management Guidelines" to promote green lending. Currently, approximately 27 trillion KRW in green bonds have been issued in South Korea, in line with the Green Bond Guidelines of the Korea Securities Exchange. However, there have been no clear standards for green lending. To address this, we plan to establish green lending standards based on the green bond guidelines, and from next year, we will encourage financial institutions to increase their green lending activities based on these standards.

The difference between green lending and green bonds is that while green bonds are self-certified and disclosed by the issuer, green lending involves financial institutions assessing whether the borrower's loan qualifies as being aligned with green economic activities, offering interest rate benefits or certifications if it does. The Green Lending Management Guidelines will be integrated into the lending process of financial institutions. When a borrower applies for a loan, the bank's dedicated department will assess whether the loan qualifies as a green economic activity, and if it does, the borrower will be offered reduced interest rates or certifications. Additionally, the use of the funds for green activities will be monitored post-disbursement.

Lastly, I would like to highlight the challenges faced by small and medium-sized enterprises (SMEs) in responding to the climate crisis. While large corporations generally have the resources to manage these challenges, SMEs, especially those that supply products to large corporations, are struggling. To support these SMEs, the FSS is working with banks and large corporations to provide consulting services. For instance, in October of last year and again this year, in collaboration with Samsung Electronics, banks have established a 2 trillion KRW fund to support green and carbon reduction investments in SMEs.

In conclusion, I have shared with you the FSS's efforts and directions related to climate finance. I believe that responding to the climate crisis is an essential task for future generations, and I assure you that the FSS is fully committed to this mission and will continue to actively promote these initiatives. Thank you.

## Hong Jong-ho

Thank you, Mr. Lee. He talked about the efforts that are being made by the FSS of Korea in terms of climate change and climate finance.

To conclude this session, I would like to invite Dr. Vinod Thomas to share his final thoughts on climate finance and decarbonization, following the insightful comments made by our three discussants in the context of Korea. Please, Dr. Thomas.

## Vinod Thomas

Thank you. I find myself struggling between offering a succinct summary of what has been said and adding a few points that go beyond the discussions we've had. The speakers were extremely clear and provided some very critical insights into climate finance and the steps Korea is taking, along with the broader principles surrounding it, which should not be overlooked. I would like to pay tribute to this session; it's truly remarkable that this event is taking place at a time when COP 29 is ongoing, and I hope the findings from this discussion reach the people who matter in this regard.

If I may, I would like to take just three minutes to highlight two or three points that extend beyond what has already been discussed. First, we are witnessing an escalating climate risk for Korea, as well as for everyone else, and resilience must keep pace with this growing risk. It is no longer sufficient to simply rebuild after a flood; we need to build forward, as the next disaster could be even more severe. This is a key takeaway.

Second, in terms of financial architecture, the emphasis on green bonds is vital, and there is also a need to give more attention to guarantees, which have not been particularly emphasized. I would also suggest that Korea consider exploring a combination of emission trading systems, quantitative restrictions, and carbon taxes to optimize the outcomes. This approach could yield significant revenue with minimal drawbacks.

Third, the importance of stress testing, which was highlighted in the last discussion, cannot be overstated. I would urge the central banks around the world not to use the principle of independence as a reason to neglect climate issues, which will inevitably affect inflation, growth, and employment. If stress tests are conducted, a crucial question will arise: following climate-related disasters, there may be a tendency to increase interest rates due to economic strain. Conversely, there will also be a push to lower interest rates to facilitate long-term financing for renewable energy. Ultimately, the question arises whether a bifurcated interest rate structure is necessary. It's unorthodox and challenging, but given the externalities involved, it is worth considering. The central bank will have a role to play in this regard when conducting stress tests.

Next, I would pose a question for Korea in particular. We have discussed mitigation, prevention, adaptation, and living with the impacts of climate change—how do you prioritize them? What proportion of resources should be allocated to mitigation versus adaptation? I understand we don't have time to discuss this in detail, but is a 50-50 split the right approach for Korea? It's an important issue, as finance ministers need clarity on whether the resources are allocated for mitigation or adaptation.

In closing, I want to emphasize that Korea is punching above its weight on the global stage. The world looks up to Korea as a model, and this can ultimately be in Korea's own interest as the price of renewables continues to fall. The vision

I have is that Korea will not be struggling to create climate policy, but will instead be actively crafting it, because such policies are beneficial not only for the welfare of the people but also for the planet.

Thank you.

### Hong Jong-ho

Let's continue this discussion after the session concludes, particularly regarding adaptation versus mitigation, as I have some thoughts on the matter as well. With that, we will now conclude the second session.

This session on "Innovating Climate-Inclusive Finance for Sustainable Growth" has been insightful, highlighting the important balance between risk and return. I believe there have been many valuable takeaways from today's discussions. Thank you all for your participation.

# SESSION 3

# The Role of Finance in Mitigating and Overcoming the Demographic Crisis

**Moderator**

**Yi Insil** President, Korean Peninsula Population Institute for Future Fmr. Commissioner, Statistics Korea

**Keynote Speakers**

**Joan Wiliams** Sullivan Professor of Law and Founding Director of the Equality Action Center, UC San Francisco

**Charles Yuji Horioka** Prof., Kobe Univ., President, International Association for Research on Income and Wealth(IARIW)/Fmr. President, Japanese Economic Association

**Panelists**

**Suh Jeong Ho** Head of Demographic Change Research, Korea Institute of Finance(KIF)

**Kim Gyungrok** President & head of retirement research institute, Mirae Asset Global Investments

**Jeung Shin Dong** Head of KB Research, KB Financial Group

# Yi Insil

Hello, I am Yi Insil, the President, Korean Peninsula Population Institute for Future, and I will be moderating the final session today. I recently retired from my position at the university and established this research institute to address the serious population issues in Korea. The topic of today's session is "Strategies for Overcoming the Population Crisis and the Role of Finance." In this session, we have invited two distinguished international scholars: one is a legal scholar, and the other is an economist. Additionally, we have three panelists who will join us for the discussion. Allow me to briefly introduce our keynote speakers.

The first speaker is Professor Joan Williams, a professor at the University of California, Hastings College of the Law, in San Francisco. She is widely recognized for her provocative statement, "Korea is doomed," which she made publicly. When she visited Korea and we discussed that remark, she acknowledged that it was an extreme statement at the time, but she expressed her concerns about the current situation in Korea. Professor Williams is an expert on diversity and inclusion at the United Nations and has provided extensive consulting for companies. She is also well-known for her research on workplace bias, which she has published in the Harvard Business Review. Recently, she has published 11 papers and several books, solidifying her as an outstanding scholar.

The second speaker is Professor Charles Yuji Horioka, an economist and a distinguished professor at Kobe University. He is currently serving as the president of the International Association for Research on Income and Wealth (IARIW). Professor Horiooka has received the Nakara Award from the Japan Economic Association, which is given to young economists, and he has profound insights into issues related to population crises and finance.

Now, let me introduce our panelists. The first panelist is Dr. Suh Jeong Ho, the Head of Demographic Change Research, Korea Institute of Finance. Dr. Suh has extensive experience, having worked at the Bank of Korea, the Financial Supervisory Service, and Hana Bank. He has a deep understanding of the financial industry and digital finance, and we look forward to his valuable insights on the role of finance in addressing the population crisis.

The second panelist is Mr. Kim Gyungrok, Head of retirement research institute, Mirae Asset Global Investments. Mr. Kim has a distinguished career, having worked in bond and asset management at Mirae Asset and serving as the head of their Retirement Research Institute. He has conducted in-depth research on population issues, and we expect his perspectives on these matters to be particularly insightful.

The third panelist is Dr. Jeung Shin Dong, Head of KB Research, KB Financial Group. Dr. Jeung holds a Ph.D. in economics and has served as a financial policy advisor and director of research at the Financial Supervisory Service. Currently, he is leading the research on population crisis responses at KB Financial Group, and we look forward to hearing his expertise on this topic.

We will now begin by watching a pre-recorded presentation by Professor Joan Williams.

## Joan Wiliams

Hello, I'm Joan Williams. Let me begin by congratulating IGE and KB Financial Group on hosting the 2024 Sustainability Conference. I'm truly honored by your invitation, and I regret that I cannot join you in person this time—my travel schedule this month is particularly demanding.

By way of introduction, I am a professor at the University of California, San

Francisco, and an emerita professor of law. My work has long focused on issues of social inequality. Over the course of my career, I've authored a dozen books, more than a hundred scholarly articles, and, together with my team, nearly forty pieces in the Harvard Business Review. That's just a brief snapshot of my background.

Today, I'd like to turn to the central topic: Korea's declining birth rate—and why it matters profoundly for the future of finance.

Many people have seen the meme of me reacting to the OECD fertility graphs that show Korea absolutely at the bottom in terms of fertility rates. I was really, really shocked to see how low the fertility rate was, and I've been thinking a lot about it ever since. One conclusion I've reached is that there's a real irony: the same cultural values that produced the Korean economic miracle now threaten to produce no generation to enjoy it. Korea has also made some significant investments in trying to raise the fertility rate. It's among the top OECD countries in childcare and education funding, for example. And it has greatly expanded parental leave in recent years and now is actually paying women to have children.

But unfortunately, these investments—although expensive—just won't solve the problem. Too often, the fertility rate is thought of as a women's issue. But the problem goes much deeper. So let's start out by talking about the work system. It's really designed around a very specific ideal—the ideal of a worker as someone who works 50 or more hours a week, pretty much for 40 years straight, taking no time off for childbirth, childcare, eldercare, or really anything else. And if you compare Korea to the OECD average, Korean men are twice as likely, and women are actually two and a half times as likely, to work 50 or more hours a week.

Part of the work system also in Korea is discrimination against mothers. My institute has helped document this. In fact, this is called maternal role bias, and it's the most prevalent and the strongest discrimination against women. It really stems from assumptions that mothers are discriminated against and should be less committed and less competent than they were before they had children. Now that's very open discrimination based on motherhood.

Another part of the work system is the high cost of taking a career break. In Korea, my understanding is that it's very, very hard to get back into regular work if you take a break in your career. So I think many women get the message that if they go, if they have children and take even a short period off, that they will pay for that forever and not be able to really achieve anything like their full career potential. And I think that has a big influence on people.

And we also found that older women felt that they needed to prove themselves even more than younger women whereas older men felt they needed to prove themselves less. So again, I think this all goes into women's sense that perhaps the workplace is so heavily stacked against them that having children just is a bad idea. So all of those are characteristics of the work system.

Let's look now at the family system in Korea. One thing that really struck me as an outsider looking in was the intense pressure on mothers to quit. One study said that 87 of Koreans believe that mothers of preschool children should work at most part-time. But of course, part-time work is really rare in Korea. It's less than one-sixth as common as compared to Europe, for example. And so the result is really that only one third of Korean mothers stay in the same job after they have children. And it's one of the only OECD countries that still has what's called the M curve, where women, young women enter the workforce. But then when they have children, they tend to drop out and then reenter much later, but at jobs at home, usually quite a lower level. So that M curve has disappeared in most of the OECD countries, but not Korea.

Another part of the family system is the education system. Mothers are expected to manage tutoring, to manage cram schools, to manage homework. And the cram schools can be hard to afford, along with housing on one income. So I think families really feel pretty much caught. They know that if they have a child, the mother will be marginalized at work and she'll have to be doing things like managing tutoring cram schools. But it's going to be hard even to afford that on one income. And that's why families don't see a path forward. The good news in Korea is that the childcare system is excellent. I mean, from the point of view of an American, I'm green with envy. But child care and after-school care, it ends long before parents are home from work. And again, that's part of a work system that just assumes that the wife is at home full-time. That's hard to buck.

And Korea is very similar to other Asian countries, but quite different from the West in its attitudes and practices about elder care. 67% of Koreans rely on family members for elder care. And who are those family members? Typically, their daughters and daughters-in-law. And that, I think, makes some women reluctant to marry. So what's the path to material well-being that younger Koreans see? You know, far too often it's don't marry and don't have children. That's really the only path they see.

You know, there's a third element that we have to enter in here, and it has to do with masculinity and with marriage. There's a study by the Korean national budget office that found that 76 of the decline in births in Korea between 2019 and 2022 is attributable to the decrease in marriage. Women in Korea do eight times more housework and six times more child and elder care than men do. And men's household contributions are very low, in fact, the second lowest in the entire OECD.

And one of the ways to see this is that the divorce rate in Korea rises after the holidays. Why is that? Well, first of all, the children are home. There's a lot of cooking. There's a lot of family work that goes into the holidays, and typically the wife does most of it. In addition, my understanding is that there is sometimes conflict, since the tradition is to visit parents—about, you know, whether you visit the husband's parents first. So there are a lot of different expectations that tend to destabilize marriages that already exist and discourage people from getting married in the first place. And I think many people probably saw this reported in the Financial Times.

There was also a similar study in The Economist about the mismatch of expectations between young men and young women in Korea. Young women have gotten steadily more liberal, but young men have gotten very sharply more conservative. And What's going on there? This is actually something that also happened in the recent election in the United States. And so young men, they feel like they can't deliver many of them. They feel like they can't deliver on what's expected of them and what they expect of themselves, the apartment and the family wage. Many young men blame young women for the fact that they just can't get a full purchase in life and launch into adulthood with a good, stable job. Nearly 80% of Korean men in their 20s believe that discrimination against men is a serious problem.

You know, it's really striking. That is 50 points higher than for men over 65. Men over 65 are very like women over 65 in their assessments of the prevalence of discrimination against women. But younger men, there's this huge divergence. And the prevalence of the belief that discrimination against men is a problem, it's really astonishing because Korea still has one of the largest pay gaps of any developed country. But I think what has happened is that young men in the context of this growing inequality with access often only to irregular work or only to irregular work for quite a long period of time, they're very anxious. And their anger, some of it has been focused on young women. So what are the solutions to this? Well, I'll first tell you what unfortunately just is not going to work.

Paying women to have children, it just won't work. A 2021 study said that, that calculated that Korea would have to pay about 15 times more than the current rates. in order for this solution really to solve the problem. And one of the problems is that it's a very inefficient program because the research suggests that three-fourths of the births would have happened anyway. So you're paying a lot of money to a lot of people who would have had a baby anyway. The one anxiety I feel in Korea, again, with the very long work hours, is the sense that this is what has worked for us. This is what has been our economic engine. How on earth can we find a different path? Why would we want to?

I think it's important to recognize in that context that productivity in Korea is 48 lower than in the U.S., And there has been research going back to the 1940s that link very long work hours with low productivity. And I think it's really important to differentiate between enacting the work devotion norm and actually working efficiently. I don't think that controlling the work hours more is going to have the kind of economic effects that some fear that it will. So here are 10 steps I think that could help address the low fertility rate in an effective and efficient way. First, reward managers for productivity, not work devotion.

Second, create a 30-hour work week in regular jobs, not irregular work, but regular jobs with ordinary proportional career progression. And I know this is something that is not something that has been seen in Korea, but one of the things that has become clear in Europe is that what mothers very often want are high quality, long part-time jobs, not 15 hours a week or 20 hours a week, but 30 hour a week jobs that keep them on the career path. The third point is that some of the proposals that have been floated, for example, eliminating the 52-hour-a-week limit on the number of hours that can be worked, that was put in place by the prior administration, there's been a proposal to eliminate that.

And another proposal that's been floated is the so-called flexibility proposal that would allow employers to work, to require employees to work quite long hours in week one if they allowed the employees to work many fewer hours in week two so that the number of hours averaged out. The problem with that is that you can't put children on ice. If you have children at home, that's going to have an extremely punitive effect and send families into really a tailspin. So I think it's important to keep the 52-hour limit, and the flexibility proposal is unfortunately just not very practical. And then equally important, number four, is to make it easy to return to regular activities. employment after one to three years out. Now, if someone has been out of the workforce for 15 years, that's obviously a different situation.

But if someone is out only for a year or two or three, they should be able to return to the career track that they left. The fifth measure really is that employers need to replace employees who are on leave instead of overworking their colleagues. Remember the extraordinary Attorney Wu episode where the woman only took two weeks of leave because she didn't want to burden her colleagues? Well, the obvious solution is to hire a temporary worker. And since the government is covering much of the cost of the leave, there's no reason that the company should kind of pocket the difference. You have this huge irregular employment sector hire a temporary worker in order that the worker, when she comes back from leave, doesn't face a lot of angry colleagues because they've had to work even longer hours to make up for her leave.

It's also important, the research shows, to set the expectation that both parents will take the full amount of leave available to them because if men don't take leave, the research shows that women who do so will be very stigmatized. It's also important to recognize that leaves of longer than a year have been shown to discourage women's workforce participation. What doesn't discourage women from workforce participation and probably from having children is if the leave is split between the father and the mother. It's also important to enforce prohibitions against discrimination against mothers. There's a recent study, it's actually this year, 2024, that showed that women with access to leave are 3.6 times as likely to say they want children, but only if they don't report gender discrimination in their environment.

Because if they feel that they're going to be penalized for having children, they just don't want to go there. That's the hard fact. There's also, number eight, a very important recent Korean Supreme Court decision that held that employers have a duty of care to accommodate mothers. Now, this isn't absolute. It's a duty of care. It's not an absolute right. But it's important to recognize that the Supreme Court has said that where it's practical for an employer to accommodate a mother, the employer should be doing so. And then finally, and I know this is controversial, Korea really has to do something to provide a workforce to provide elder care. Expecting daughters and daughters-in-law to drop everything and take care of parents and parents-in-law is, it's actually a very, very, very costly policy.

It's costly because you encourage women who invested a lot in their careers and the state has invested in their careers as well. You encourage them to drop out and it's really costly because it is really fueling a birth rate that, as you know, is just unsustainable. So I offer these thoughts really in the spirit of humility. I'm not a Korean. I'm not even a Korean expert. But what I am is an American who knows that the U.S. has a really special relationship with Korea. Korea is very important. important to us. Its success is very important to us.

And it's in that spirit that I offer these thoughts. And again, thank you so much for the invitation. And I'm so very sorry I can't join you in person, but thank you for attention.

## Yi Insil

Thank you, Professor Williams, for your insightful presentation. You have shared valuable insights on Korea's low birth rate, the social issues stemming from it, and potential solutions, using a variety of data.

Now, let's move on to the next keynote speaker. Dr. Horioka, would you like to take the floor, please?

## Charles Yuji Horioka

Good afternoon. I'm Charles Horioka of Kobe University in Japan. It's my great honor and pleasure to be able to take part in this exciting event as a keynote speaker. I would like to thank the Institute for Global Economics and the KB Financial Group for organizing and sponsoring this event and for inviting me to take part. So the first speaker in this session, Professor Williams, she talked about the birth rate, fertility rate. And I'm glad that she focused on that topic because it's very complementary to my own talk. I'll be looking at the other end of the age distribution, namely the elderly population.

And in particular, the object of my talk is to document trends, well, has four objectives. The first objective is to document trends in population aging, defined as an increase in the proportion of people who are aged 65 or older. Second objective is to explore the challenges posed by population aging. The third objective is to explore solutions to these challenges. And the fourth objective of my talk is to explore the role that the financial sector can play to mitigate the demographic crisis. So, let me talk about each of these in turn.

And just for your information, my own research interests are as follows. I'm an economist, and in particular, my field of expertise is a field known as household economics.

I look at various aspects of the behavior of individuals and households. So, my remarks today will be based largely on my own field of expertise. So let me turn to the first topic that I want to talk about, trends in population aging. Population aging is occurring throughout the world, but its speed and timing varies greatly from country to country and region to region. So let me show you this table. I'm sorry that the type is very small. But this table shows the proportion of the population aged 65 or older at three points in time 2020, 2030, and 2050. So the figures for 2020 are actual figures. The figures for 2030 and 2050 are obviously projections made by the United Nations.

And the first thing to note is that in 2020, Japan was by far the most aged society in the world, if you exclude some very small countries. Japan, the share of the elderly was 28.4 in Japan, almost 30%, far higher than any other country. Most of the other top-ranking countries are from Europe, so you can see from this that population aging occurred earliest in Europe rather than in Asia or any other part of the world. And Korea was still in 42nd place. with an elderly share of only 16%. If we fast forward to 2030, Japan is still number one, and the share of the elderly has increased even further to close to 31%. But again, most of the other countries in the top 10 are from Europe, except for now Hong Kong is in the top 10, the only other Asian country.

And Korea is rising rapidly from 42nd to 15th place, but still not quite in the top 10. If we fast forward to 2050, Korea has now surpassed Japan, is number one in the world in terms of population aging, with an Asian elderly share of 38%. Japan is slightly behind at 37.7%. But another thing to note is that the European countries have been largely replaced by Asian countries in the top

10, in addition to Korea and Japan, Taiwan, Hong Kong, and Singapore have also joined the top 10, whereas many European countries have dropped out. So what I wanted to point out is that this timing and speed of population aging varies greatly from region to region. It happened first, earliest in Europe, but Asia is rapidly catching up or even surpassing Europe.

And in particular, Japan and Korea are very much at the top. So that concludes my discussion of the first topic. Now I want to turn to the second and third topics, the challenges posed by population aging and the solutions to these challenges. There are many, many challenges posed by population aging, but because I'm an economist, I want to focus on three challenges that are sort of economics related. The first is the possibility of a labor shortage. The second is the population of a deterioration of government finances. And the third is possible changes in consumption and saving. So let me talk about each of these in turn. So the first challenge I want to talk about is the labor shortage.

So it's true that population aging may lead to a labor shortage as the ratio of the working age population to the retirement age population declines. But there are at least three ways to avoid labor shortages. First, we can delay retirement and encourage the elderly to work longer. So as one of the speakers this morning was pointing out, people are not only living longer, but also remaining healthy for longer. And if they're healthy, of course, they're capable of continuing to work. And so it is quite possible for the elderly to work longer than they are now. And moreover, many elderly people want to continue working because it gives them gives more meaning to their lives and also perhaps for economic reasons.

A second possible solution to the problem is that In most, in many, if not most countries, females are not able to realize their full potential in the labor market for the reasons that the first speaker, Professor Williams, pointed out.

And enabling women to do so would also help to alleviate any potential labor shortages. And third, allowing more foreign workers into the country is yet another way of alleviating potential labor shortages. So there are a number of possible ways solutions to this first challenge, namely the possibility of a labor shortage. Let me turn now to the second possible challenge caused by population aging, that's the deterioration of government finances.

Since government Since expenditures on social safety nets, for example, public pensions, long-term care insurance, health insurance, and so on, are heavily biased toward the elderly, Population aging means that there will be an increase in expenditures on social safety nets, and there is a danger that this will lead to a deterioration of government finances. To put it another way, government finances will be strained because population aging will lead to an increase in the number of retired people that each worker needs to support. So the most obvious solution to this problem is to reduce benefits, increase contributions, and/or to delay the age at which people can start collecting public pensions, long-term care benefits, etc.

But this will, of course, is not a good thing in the sense that it will threaten the retirement security of the elderly. Other solutions, I won't talk about these in too much detail because of the lack of time, but one possibility is to shift from a pay-as-you-go system to a fully funded system, and the advantage of this change is that the system will no longer be affected by demographic trends such as population aging. Let me skip the other possible solutions and turn to what I think is the best solution to the problem. In my opinion, the best solution to the problem is extending the retirement age because this will increase the number of people paying contributions and reduce the number of people collecting benefits. So in other words, what I'm proposing is that we extend the retirement age and make it easier for the elderly to work longer.

This will not only solve the labor shortage problem, but also help to solve the problem of the deterioration of public, of government finances. So we can kill two birds with one stone. Turning to the third and final challenge that I wanted to talk about, that is possible changes that population aging will cause in saving and consumption behavior of households. And there are a number of possibilities, but first I wanted to talk a little bit about the theoretical considerations. The most commonly used model of household behavior in economics is the life cycle hypothesis or model.

In this model, this model is assumes that when individuals are young, they work, earn income, and save part of their income to prepare for their living expenses during retirement, and that when people are old, they retire, quit, stop working, and finance their living expenses using the wealth they accumulated during their working years. So if this model is correct, it predicts that the elderly, that into elderly individuals, at least those who are retired, should be dissaving or decumulating their previously accumulated saving and that the aggregate household saving rate will be lower, the higher is the ratio of the retirement age population to the working age population. So this implies that population aging will lead to a decline in the aggregate household saving rate. Well, is that a good thing or a bad thing?

Well, saving is important because it provides the funds needed to finance investment. And household saving plays the important role of providing the funds needed to finance household investment in housing, corporate investment in plant and equipment, government investment in social infrastructure, and saving shortages abroad. So there is a danger that if there's a decline in the aggregate household saving rate, this will lead to a saving shortage in the country, in the economy, or perhaps even in the world as a whole. However, this is not necessarily the case because many of the countries experiencing population aging will simultaneously show absolute declines in population, which will reduce the need to expand the productive capacity of the economy and therefore reduce the need to engage in corporate investment in plant and equipment.

Furthermore, there's always the option of borrowing from abroad, borrowing from countries with savings surpluses to meet domestic savings shortages. So the declines in aggregate household savings that may occur as a result of population aging will not necessarily cause any problems in the economy as a whole. But actually, I have been assuming until now that elderly individuals de-save, de-accumulate their wealth after they retire as predicted by the life cycle hypothesis.

But my own extensive research about the saving behavior of the elderly in Japan and Europe Unfortunately, I haven't done any work on Korea, has found that even the retired elderly in these countries are either continuing to accumulate wealth or that they are decumulating their wealth, but not only very slowly, and that they can be expected to leave large bequests when they pass away. In other words, the problem is not that the retired elderly are dissaving too much or saving too little, but that they are dissaving too little or saving too much. Since saving and consumption are two sides of the same coin, this implies that the retired elderly in these countries are not saving enough. And this will lower the quality of life of the retired elderly and prevent them from enjoying the fruits of their many years of hard work.

Moreover, it will also lower aggregate consumption in the household sector as a whole and may cause the economy as a whole to fall into recession. In other words, there's a real possibility that population aging will lead to too much saving and too little consumption, not only by the retired elderly, but also in the household sector as a whole. In fact, in the June 1st issue of The Economist earlier this year, there was this article, baby boomers are loaded why are they so stingy? in this article, they talk about the fact that baby boomers are entering their retirement years, but that they are not consuming very much and saving too much. And in fact, in this article, they refer to several of the papers that I have written on this subject. And in fact, the conclusion of this article is the same.

As my own conclusion, namely that the elderly in many countries are saving too much and not consuming enough. Well, I have looked in my own research about why it is that people are saving too much and consuming too little, and there are two possibilities. First, that they have bequest motives. People are not consuming more because they want to have some money left over at the end to leave as a bequest to their children. Second possibility is that people are worried about the future, about how long they will live or about uncertain medical and long-term care expenses in the future, and that they are engaged in precautionary saving in response to these uncertainties. And possible solutions to these problems are as follows. If it's bequest motives that are the problem, we can simply raise inheritance taxes and gift taxes to encourage people to spend more of the money on themselves and leave less as a bequest to their children.

If the problem is precautionary saving, the obvious solution is to maintain or expand public and private social safety nets so people will be less worried about the future and be more willing to consume more. And both of these policies that I am recommending would encourage the elderly to decumulate their considerable wealth holdings more rapidly and to use this wealth for consumption, which would be good for the elderly individuals themselves as well as for the country as a whole. Moreover, both of my proposals have the added advantage of discouraging bequests and inter-be-votes transfers, thereby alleviating the extent to which wealth disparities are passed on from generation to generation and leading to a more equitable society. So I'm sorry I'm out of time, but in the last minute or two, I just wanted to talk about the fourth and final topic, namely what role the financial sector can play.

In alleviating the problem of excess saving and inadequate consumption by the elderly. One thing the financial sector can do is to offer a variety of private pension health insurance and long-term care insurance policies that will help reduce the various risks faced by households and thereby reducing the amount of precautionary saving they do and increasing their consumption. And since public social safety nets will probably have to be scaled back because of the deterioration of government finances, there could be a larger role that needs to be played by private safety nets. And in particular, I would encourage the financial sector to offer innovative financial products such as reverse mortgages, which are essentially a lifetime annuity that uses one's own home as collateral.

Another thing that the financial sector can do is to help the elderly manage their assets wisely, whether or not they're planning to use them themselves or to leave them to their children. And the final thing the financial sector could do is to provide seminars, training, et cetera, to increase the financial literacy of the elderly, which is often not very high. So all of these policies would help the elderly to make more optimal consumption and bequest decisions and will, at the same time, help to increase consumption in the household sector as a whole, causing the elderly as well as society as a whole to be better off. So the financial sector can play an important role in meeting the challenges of population aging and the demographic crisis. Thank you very much for your kind attention, and I'm sorry I went over time. Thank you very much.

## Yi Insil

Thank you, Professor Horioka, for your in-depth presentation on the key issues related to Korea's aging population and the measures to address them.

Next, let's invite Dr. Suh Jeong Ho. We will connect with Dr. Suh via Zoom. Dr. Suh?

## Suh Jeong Ho

Hello, my name is Suh Jeong Ho, and I am the Head of Demographic Change Research, Korea Institute of Finance. I would like to sincerely thank the IGE and KB Financial Group for inviting me to the 2024 Sustainable Global Summit. The issues of low birthrates and aging populations have become critical national concerns. To address these, our institute has established the Population Change Response Research Center this year to conduct systematic research. I am grateful for the opportunity to speak at such a distinguished event today. However, I regret that I am unable to attend in person and ask for your understanding.

It is truly an honor to hear from two distinguished scholars today. Professor Williams has provided valuable insights on the issue of low birthrates, while Professor Horioka has shared Japan's aging experience, offering key insights into the challenges Korea faces. My presentation will focus primarily on Korea's situation, but it overlaps with and follows similar themes as those presented by the two professors, so I believe it will be interesting to compare and contrast the perspectives.

Today, I will address three main points. First, I will briefly review the population changes occurring in Korea. Second, I will consider the implications of these demographic changes on the financial sector in Korea. Finally, I will discuss what role the financial sector can play in addressing these issues.

Firstly, let's look at the population trends in Korea. In 2020, Korea's total population was around 52 million, but since then, the population has started to decline. Despite increased life expectancy, the low birthrate has led to a decrease in the population. Korea has recorded the lowest birthrate among OECD countries, and it is expected that by next year, the birthrate will fall to around 0.6. This level of fertility can be described as extremely low, even considered a "ultra-low birthrate" nation.

Next, the structure of Korea's population is undergoing significant and rapid changes. The population under 65 is decreasing sharply, while the population over 65 is increasing. As a result, Korea's population pyramid is shifting from an hourglass shape to a rapidly narrowing triangle. This change is occurring much faster than in Japan. It is expected that by 2045, Korea's elderly population will surpass that of Japan. This shift is particularly remarkable because Korea will transition from an aging society to a super-aged society in a much shorter time frame than Japan—about 8 years compared to Japan's 11 years. In fact, next year marks Korea's official entry into the super-aged society.

In addition, Korea faces a challenge in that it is experiencing aging not only domestically but also globally. Both developed and emerging countries are facing a declining share of the working-age population, which presents a further challenge for Korea, given its high degree of external dependency.

These demographic changes have direct implications for the financial sector. For example, aging could lower economic growth rates, reduce funding opportunities, and harm the profitability and soundness of financial institutions. Additionally, aging will affect economic agents' preferences for safer assets, which will, in turn, influence financial markets.

To address these challenges, the financial sector can take two main approaches.

First, it can focus on mitigating the issues related to low birthrates and aging. Second, it needs to adapt to these rapid demographic changes and find ways to maintain or improve its competitiveness. Financial institutions must also consider how to preserve the stability of the financial system in the face of these structural changes.

From a mitigation perspective, the government can play a significant role by offering strong incentives to promote stable wealth accumulation among younger generations. It is essential to alleviate the financial concerns around marriage and childbirth, which can be addressed through financial measures. Such proactive steps could help ease the future financial burden that the government will eventually bear.

As aging progresses, financial assets may increasingly flow into safe assets like cash, deposits, and bonds, which could reduce overall risk capital in the economy and decrease economic dynamism. Therefore, it is crucial to manage this shift away from excessively safe assets. Also, as low birthrates and aging inevitably lead to changes in household structures, the rise of single- and two-person households could negatively impact the real estate market, especially given Korea's heavy reliance on real estate in its financial sector. Therefore, managing exposure to real estate risks is important.

From the perspective of financial institutions, with such drastic changes in the demographic landscape, it is crucial to explore new revenue streams to replace the expected decline in demand for loans and investments due to aging. Furthermore, financial institutions should consider expanding into countries with a younger population, such as India, Vietnam, and Indonesia, to diversify risks and benefit from the growing working-age populations in these regions.

Moreover, given that more than 70% of Korean household wealth is tied up in real estate, there is a need to manage the potential impacts of a real estate sell-off. Financial products that help households gradually liquidate their real estate holdings, such as reverse mortgages, could play a key role in this. While Korea already has a public reverse mortgage program, there is a need to develop competitive private sector products to meet the needs of an aging population.

Lastly, financial institutions can develop products specifically targeting the elderly to seize growth opportunities in this demographic shift. Additionally, as Professor Williams mentioned regarding improving the work environment, the financial sector should take the lead in fostering a work environment that balances work and family, which will be crucial in managing the effects of demographic changes.

To conclude, many companies are increasingly focusing on ESG efforts, but in Korea, addressing the challenges of low birthrates and aging populations may be even more urgent than other issues like climate change. To ensure the sustainability of our society, it is critical to proactively address these demographic issues. That concludes my discussion. Thank you.

### Yi Insil

Thank you very much for your insightful message, Dr. Suh. Now, our next discussant. Mr. Kim, floor is yours.

### Kim Gyungrok

I would like to begin by expressing my appreciation for the insightful presentations by the two speakers. They discussed the issues of population aging and under-consumption, and I would like to focus my comments on how South Korea can address these challenges.

Japan, for example, has already experienced significant aging, and discussions around how to convert accumulated assets into consumption have become a crucial issue. However, South Korea has not yet reached that level of aging. For now, the priority in South Korea is to address the issue of asset accumulation. Alongside that, the task of stimulating consumption among the elderly in the future will be a key challenge. I will now elaborate on these points.

Firstly, it is important to recognize the differences between South Korea and other countries that have already experienced aging. Japan entered the super-aged society in 2007, 18 years ahead of South Korea, and Germany reached this milestone in 2010, 15 years before us. On the other hand, South Korea is expected to enter the super-aged society around next year. As the timing of entry into super-aged societies differs from that of other advanced countries, it is critical for South Korea to seek tailored solutions based on its own current stage.

Another significant difference lies in the definition of "youth" in different OECD countries. In South Korea, the youth age is considered to be 60, while in most OECD countries, it is 65 or above, or there is no retirement age at all. In addition, the actual retirement age in South Korea is typically around 55, which sets it apart from other advanced nations. This has led to the formation of a unique labor market for reemployment between the ages of 55 and 65. Addressing how to develop and manage this market will be an essential task specific to South Korea.

Moreover, the demographic structure in South Korea is highly distinctive, as the "baby boomer" generation, born between 1955 and 1995, constitutes a significant portion of the population. This has a profound economic impact, which is quite different from the experiences of other countries. These factors must be considered when formulating solutions.

Looking at the projected population structure for the next ten years, we can see that the population in their 50s and 60s will remain the central demographic group, and there is still a sizable population in their 30s and 40s. This is a key difference compared to other advanced nations. Therefore, in the next decade, the main focus for South Korea will be on how to manage the 50-60 age group and how to respond to the elderly population over 70.

In terms of addressing under-consumption and ensuring stable income for the elderly, I would like to propose four solutions. First, it is crucial to properly organize the reemployment market for people in their 50s and 60s. Currently, the employment rate for individuals aged 55 and above is high, but the proportion of non-regular workers is disproportionately high compared to other OECD countries. This leads to unstable incomes and, ultimately, under-consumption. Therefore, improving employment stability should be the top priority.

Second, housing plays a significant role in South Korea, so how to connect housing assets to income cash flow is an important issue. While reverse mortgages have been introduced, the uptake remains low. There is a need for discussions on how to activate these programs. In particular, exploring ways to link reverse mortgages with basic pensions to encourage consumption, especially for low-income groups, would be a key area to focus on.

Third, there is a need to establish reliable withdrawal products. South Korea lacks products such as longevity pensions or annuity bonds, which are essential for ensuring stable income in retirement. We need to develop such products to allow people to consume more securely.

Fourth, asset accumulation remains an issue. Many South Koreans are still in the stage of asset accumulation. The proportion of stocks in pension assets is very low, which is a crucial problem. To improve asset accumulation, it is necessary to increase the proportion of stock investments and activate various financial systems.

Finally, the issue of underutilized retirement systems, such as small business pension plans, also needs to be addressed. Specifically, the pension funds for small businesses with fewer than 30 employees play a crucial role in providing retirement income for low-income individuals. These systems should be enhanced to ensure secure retirement income.

With that, I will conclude my comments. Thank you.

**Yi Insil**

Thank you for excellent comments. Now we are going to hear from Mr. Chung of KB.

**Jeung Shin Dong**

Hello, I am very honored to join this panel today. I have listened to the presentations and discussions with great interest. I particularly resonated with Professor William's insightful remarks on the current situation in Korea. I also agreed with Professor Horioka's suggestions on responding to the aging population, which align with what we have been considering. Our research institute has also been closely monitoring and researching the population issue.

Today, I would like to share my thoughts on the role of finance in addressing this issue. First, since the population status has already been well covered by the previous speakers, I will not repeat that. Additionally, the impact of changes in population structure has been thoroughly discussed, so I will not delve into that either. However, I would like to briefly share some findings from a study presented by the Financial Association. It mentions that the stock market experiences a significant meltdown from the 1950s, and it also indicates that restructuring of financial institutions, including savings banks and the four major financial sectors, could occur.

Before discussing the role of finance in overcoming the low birthrate, I believe it is important to reflect on the fundamental causes of this issue. There are many factors, but a key reason is the shift in the awareness and rights of women, who are the primary bearers of childbirth. In the past, childbirth and childcare were seen as natural duties, but now they are viewed as personal decisions that women make. As a father of two daughters, I have experienced firsthand the challenges of balancing family life over the past 30 years. The root cause of these challenges often comes down to how society supports and accommodates women. In a patriarchal, male-centered society, women inevitably develop negative attitudes towards marriage and childbirth. This is reflected in the current divorce rate, which stands at 33%, contributing to the low birthrate.

To reverse this trend, we need to foster a societal environment that values and respects women and childcare, offering full support and care. One notable example is Hungary's approach, where financial support such as deferred loan repayment is provided based on the number of children a family has. This approach offers valuable lessons. Additionally, we can learn from the practices of advanced nations like the United States and France, which focus on balancing work and family life and providing high-quality post-birth care environments.

While Korea's work-family balance policies are comparable to those of advanced countries, there are still many gaps. Therefore, I believe one of the key roles of financial institutions is to build and disseminate models of organizational culture, especially to small and medium-sized enterprises (SMEs).

Regarding aging, I will keep my comments brief since it has already been extensively discussed. As the elderly population holds around 70-80% of real estate assets, how to convert these assets into cash flow is a critical role for the financial sector. In relation to reverse mortgages, which Professor Horioka mentioned, our research institute has looked into Japan's reverse mortgage market. While it is not as active as expected, Japan offers a variety of products, and it is worth learning from their experiences. I believe continued policy support and efforts from the private sector are necessary to make these financial tools more accessible in Korea.

Next, I would like to briefly discuss foreign workers. In April, Korea's foreign worker ratio exceeded 5%, marking our entry into a multicultural and multi-ethnic society. As we continue to expand our skilled workforce, the proportion of foreign workers is expected to grow. This calls for the inclusion of foreigners into the national fold and the provision of financial services tailored to them. Since the foreign-targeted financial market is still in its early stages, there is significant growth potential, and the financial sector should actively contribute to its development.

Finally, I would like to touch on the importance of education and talent development. I recall reading that the 21st century is not just a competition in education but a "war" over education. In today's aging society, securing national competitiveness through education is paramount. With the advent of artificial intelligence (AI), there is a growing trend that society will divide into those who can handle AI and those who cannot. In this context, some foreign media have argued that Korea's low birthrate could be a blessing, as fewer children could mean more concentrated investment in their education, producing globally competitive individuals.

However, there are growing concerns about the emigration of talented individuals from Korea. As seen in the graph, Korea's rate of population outflow per 100,000 people is much higher than that of countries like China and India. This is due to highly skilled professionals leaving for destinations such as Silicon Valley in the United States or China, which offers higher salaries and better working conditions. To overcome the population crisis, it is not enough to focus solely on increasing the birthrate; it is equally important to cultivate talented individuals and create environments where they can fully realize their potential.

Lastly, I would like to briefly mention KB's ongoing initiatives. We are actively working on building organizational culture and contributing to society through various programs such as childcare and education. Since 2018, we have collaborated with the Ministry of Education to invest 75 billion KRW to establish 2,265 elementary school after-school care centers nationwide. Additionally, starting in 2023, we have allocated another 50 billion KRW to establish larger centers in key locations. I hope that the discussions today will serve as a foundation for Korea to successfully address the population crisis and become a model for others to follow. Thank you.

## Yi Insil

Thank you for your excellent remarks. As we are running out of time, may I now ask Professor Horioka to deliver the closing remarks?

## Charles Yuji Horioka

Thank you very much for the opportunity to say a few more words. I had very little knowledge about Korea, so it was very beneficial for me to hear many excellent presentations about the case of Korea. Professor Williams' discussion about birth rate, fertility rate in Korea, and the other speakers' detailed discussions about various aspects of Korea. I learned a lot about similarities as well as differences between Japan and Korea, so I hope that the two countries can learn from each other to deal with the common challenges that we face, and I hope we can have similar meetings in the future as well. Thank you very much.

## Yi Insil

Thank you for your remarks. Due to time constraints, we will conclude the final session here. I hope that such diverse discussions on the sustainable development of the Korean economy will continue to expand more actively in the future. I truly believe that more meaningful and advanced discussions on today's conference topic will unfold moving forward. I sincerely thank everyone for staying with us until the end today.